trail thoughts

A DAILY COMPANION FOR YOUR JOURNEY OF FAITH

Eric Kampmann

BEAUFORT BOOKS
NEW YORK

Copyright © 2008 by Eric Kampmann

Library of Congress Cataloging-in-Publication Data

Kampmann, Eric M.
   Trail thoughts : a daily companion for your journey of faith / Eric Kampmann.
      p. cm.
   ISBN 978-0-8253-0580-1 (alk. paper)
   1. Bible--Meditations. 2. Devotional calendars. I. Title.
   BS483.5.K36 2008
   242'.2--dc22

                                                            2007046421

Cover painting by Prescott Gibbons

Scripture taken from the HOLY BIBLE: NEW INTERNATIONAL VERSION®. NIV®. Copyright © 1973, 1978, 1984 by the International Bible Society. Used by permission of Zondervan. The "NIV" and "New International Version" trademarks are registered in the United States Patent and Trademark Office by the International Bible Society.

Published in the United States of America by
Beaufort Books, Inc.
27 West 20th St.
New York, NY 10011
www.beaufortbooks.com

Distributed by Midpoint Trade Books, New York
www.midpointtradebooks.com

PRINTED IN THE UNITED STATES OF AMERICA

Dedicated to stargazers and trail-thinkers everywhere

PREFACE

As a young man, I was drawn to Manhattan because of its magnetic energy, its endless promise and its aura of mystery. To me, Manhattan was an imaginary city of glittering majesty, the city described by Fitzgerald as a place that has all the "…wild promise of all the mystery and the beauty in the world." I came to this city somewhat naïve to the ways of the world, but soon enough, I too was striving to climb to the highest floor of the best office with the best view.

The dream, if you can call it that, turned out to be little more than the commonplace pursuit of success, recognition and power. Little did I realize how ill equipped I was for this particular kind of race. One day, though, I awoke from this fantasy to find myself in a crisis that threatened the very foundations of the life I had attempted to create.

While the world barely noticed my plight, I was indeed in a struggle for survival. Worse, I was blindsided by this rising storm. After all, the times had been good and my goals had seemed attainable. Or so I thought. But then came the day of reckoning when the dream, built on a foundation of thin air, began to crumble of its own dead weight and I was left stripped of my steadfast belief in self-reliance and worldly achievement. Ironically, though, as this part of me was dying in a sea of troubles, something new was emerging within. I call this crisis and time of trouble my "Jonah Moment."

Jonah, in the Old Testament story, receives a call from God to go to Nineveh to proclaim God's judgment on that wayward city. Rather than acknowledge God by responding to his call, Jonah flees in the opposite direction, only to discover that his attempted escape has been in vain. Instead, he heads directly into a fierce storm which threatens to destroy him and everyone on board his ship. It appears that Jonah is finished.

Jonah's story of crisis and despair, however, does not end in his death. At his moment of greatest danger, when all seems to be lost, Jonah prays to the Lord and the Lord answers. Jonah's original decision to disregard God leads directly to the crisis that threatens his life. And it is when everything seems to be lost that Jonah turns to God for salvation and he receives it. The fact is that Jonah, the rebel, has died only to be reborn as a servant of the Lord. And then, for a second time, God instructs Jonah to go to Nineveh to save that city from certain destruction. This time he goes.

The biblical pattern of tacit or explicit rebellion followed by physical and spiritual crisis is a universal pattern that works itself out in thousands of ways in thousands of places, often leading to supplication, mercy and mission. In my own case, it would take years for this pattern to reveal itself to me. And it would take even more time to understand that God is always reaching out to all men and women who may be attempting to avoid his call by fleeing to places of their own desires. By pursuing my own path and seeking my own way, I too was avoiding the call. And in the turmoil of my own crisis I too cried out to God because by then all of my own self created gods had abandoned me. They proved to be utterly worthless. But discovering what was truly valuable would not come immediately. I had been stripped of my old pretensions. But I could still not bring myself to believe that God had actually bothered to intervene by answering my prayer.

Eventually, the free fall stopped and the pressure let up. I surveyed the wreckage and was amazed to find that little real harm had been done. My story moved from crisis management to second chances. Still, my mind remained clouded even though I had experienced a miracle of God. The fact is that I was not ready to bring God into my naturalistic way of thinking, and so, I ascribed natural causes to my survival story. Later though, when I was becoming familiar with the Bible and the amazing way it reflects everyday experience, I began to realize that a deeper reality lay behind my story of survival. The verse that crystallized how the natural and the supernatural intersected in my own life comes from one of David's psalms: "Call upon me in your day of trouble. I will deliver you and you will honor me" (Psalm 50:15). I had called out to God and I had been delivered against all odds. But what about the honor part? How would I respond to that? The answer came in an unexpected way in an unexpected place.

The day was Ash Wednesday, February 13, 1991. My family and I were on an island in the Caribbean which was not a well traveled place because the U.S. Navy had reserved large sections of the island for practice bombing runs. The bombs no longer were falling and the house we were renting was situated near the top of a hill. It was in that house on that day that I unexpectedly came across a two year lectionary hidden in the back of the Book of Common Prayer. When I discovered this lectionary, it was if I heard a voice telling me that this was the map I needed for the way ahead. So on that day many years ago, I quietly committed myself to following this biblical road map everyday of the year no matter where I was or what I was doing.

Thus began my response to God's call. I would honor God by coming to know his Word by setting aside time every morning of every day. This journey would be slow and it would require perseverance. But if I was going to truly honor God through my life, I would have to be equipped with a deeper understanding of God's Word. And through an everyday encounter with the Old and New Testaments, I began to understand what it meant to walk on God's ancient pathway.

In February of every year the light begins to change. Without much warning, the steel gray of deep winter gives way to intimations of a softer season ahead. Daylight lingers longer into the afternoon and the light reflecting off distant skyscrapers battles with the forbidding coldness of the moment. And when the sky is clear, the sunsets paint the western horizon in orange and reds suggestive that it is time to prepare to head out once again. This is the time when I yearn to return to the hills and mountains of the country beyond the shores of this water bound city. While I still trace a solitary path between the walls of the narrow glass and concrete canyons, I am no longer striving to climb to the highest floor of the best office building, for I have set my heart on an even better place. Herman Melville called us "Manhattoes," people of the island city who still have the capacity to wonder at the mystery of the world beyond. To Melville, they are "water-gazers…posted like silent sentinels all around the town, stand[ing] thousands upon thousands…fixed in ocean reveries." I am one of them now, though my mind and imagination take me beyond the rivers and oceans to the trails leading into the mountains and all the wonders of God's universe. So to all water-gazers, star-gazers and trail-thinkers, here's to your reverie. And here's to your quest to find and walk on the ancient and good paths. I am sure I will meet you there one day.

Eric Kampmann
January 2008

trail thoughts

BEGINNINGS

This is what the Lord says,

"Stand at the crossroads and look;
ask for the ancient paths, ask where the
good way is, and walk in it, and you
will find rest for your souls."

Jeremiah 6:16

Hear this, all you peoples; listen, all who live in this world, both low and high, rich and poor alike: My mouth will speak words of wisdom; the utterance from my heart will give understanding. I will turn my ear to a proverb; with the harp I will expound my riddle.

Psalm 49:1–4

LISTEN

At the center of our pilgrimage through this strange and mysterious world are a series of timeless questions: *How did we come to be? Were we born for a reason? Are we on the right path? What is the larger meaning of our lives?*

The Bible provides real answers, but not necessarily in a way we have been taught to expect. More than a book of ancient history or a book of rules and regulations, the Bible is a story that has a beginning but has not yet come to an end. It is a book filled with a vast array of people—some who are heroic, some who are scoundrels, and some who are quite ordinary—but all of whom represent the valleys and peaks of the human condition.

The Bible speaks of our beginnings—of the tragic choice that broke our relationship with the one who created us—and of the long and arduous journey toward the freedom that would release us from the consequences of that choice. And as we come to know the epic story that ties the depth and breadth of the entire Bible together, the more we realize that we need to listen closely to what it is telling us about ourselves.

Listen, therefore, as the Word fractures the preconceptions of worldly knowledge and wisdom. Listen as the Holy Spirit begins to speak to you through the Word of God. Listen as your heart and your mind open up to a world that includes God rather than excludes Him.

Be still and open and...*listen.*

For you created my inmost being; you knit me together in my mother's womb. I praise you because I am fearfully and wonderfully made; your works are wonderful, I know that full well. My frame was not hidden from you when I was made in the secret place. When I was woven together in the depths of the earth, your eyes saw my unformed body. All the days ordained for me were written in your book before one of them came to be.

Psalm 139:13–16

A MATTER OF FAITH

When David says, "I am fearfully and wonderfully made," (v14) he is not giving himself credit; rather he is marveling at the glory of God's creation as embodied in the form of the creature God made in his own image. (Genesis 1:27) David's wisdom grows out of knowing that without the creator, there would be no creature to praise. Man without God is little more than a sophisticated brute, capable of unlimited barbarity.

David has another view of man: "For you created my inmost being; you knit me together in my mother's womb." (v13) David is one the great men of the Bible; he was a warrior, a poet and a king, but despite all of this, he did not forget where his great gifts came from. Without God's blessings, he is nothing. He understands that at the heart of wisdom is mystery and at the center of mystery is God.

There are real limits to our ability to know, but no limit to our ability to believe: "Such knowledge is too wonderful for me, too lofty for me to attain." (Psalm 139:6) Though knowledge is important, salvation is not a function of knowledge. It is a function of faith.

One day the angels came to present themselves before the LORD, and Satan also came with them. The LORD said to Satan, "Where have you come from?" Satan answered the LORD, "From roaming through the earth and going back and forth in it." Then the LORD said to Satan, "Have you considered my servant Job? There is no one on earth like him; he is blameless and upright, a man who fears God and shuns evil."

—Job 1:6-8

WILL WE TURN AWAY?

Who, at some point in life, has not experienced a bad thing? And who, if you probe deep enough, does not think of himself as a genuinely good person? So why should it be surprising when an afflicted person cries out against the injustice of God?

At first glance, Job would seem to fit this description perfectly, but throughout the time of his suffering, he never claims to be a man without sin. In fact, it is God who claims that Job is "…blameless and upright, a man who fears God and shuns evil." (v8) While terrible things come to afflict Job, including the deaths of his children, the loss of his wealth and the pain of disease, the core question is whether or not Job will lose patience with God, blame Him and forsake Him.

Loss of faith and betrayal are central facts in the Old and New Testaments and understanding Job's crisis is crucial to understanding our own response to crisis. Will we remain faithful, no matter what? Will we humble ourselves before God no matter what the circumstance? Or will we turn our backs on God, rejecting Him in anger because we have come to believe that He has not been faithful to us?

Blessed is the man who does not walk in the counsel of the wicked or stand in the way of sinners or sit in the seat of mockers. But his delight is in the law of the Lord, and on his law he meditates day and night. He is like a tree planted by streams of water, which yields its fruit in season and whose leaf does not wither. Whatever he does prospers.

—Psalm 1:1–3

WALKING THE STRAIGHT PATH

Life has been compared to a journey with many paths. This sounds very inclusive, but it is not biblical. David tells us that it is just as easy to "walk in the counsel of the wicked..." (v1) as it is to walk in the way of the Lord. We set off on a journey armed with map, compass and book, only to become utterly lost by taking a wrong turn here or by not paying attention there. If we want to stay on the straight path, then we must delight..."in the law of the Lord and on his law meditate day and night." (v2)

The right way is not an easy path; we are called to exercise wakefulness and exert effort. The wisdom of the Lord requires that we seek the Lord in everything we do: "Seek the Lord while he may be found; call upon him while he is near." (Isaiah 55:6) Otherwise, we will wander alone on a trackless path with no hope of ever finding our way back to where the Lord always intended us to be. A journey may have many roads, but only one leads to the Lord, for "...narrow is the road that leads to life..." (Matthew 7:14)

We have heard with our ears, O God; our fathers have told us what you did in their days, in days long ago. With your hand you drove out the nations and planted our fathers; you crushed the peoples and made our fathers flourish. It was not by their sword that they won the land, nor did their arm bring them victory; it was your right hand, your arm, and the light of your face, for you loved them.

—Psalm 44:1–3

HISTORY

In most contemporary accounts of historical events, man plays the central role of hero or villain. In Winston Churchill's four volume History of the English Speaking Peoples, for example, the real hero is the genius of the peoples of the British nation. It is essentially a progressive view of history, and therefore, modern, because it tells a tale of greater and greater national triumphs. It is a wonderful story of kings and queens and leaders of all sorts carrying the growing empire forward to its ordained destiny of a saving civilization. Yet in a sense, Churchill's account is a very unsatisfying meal, because the hand of God is nowhere to be found.

Conversely, the Bible is also a work of history with its own kings and queens, battles won and lost, civilizations rising and falling, warriors and cowards, saints and villains. But while earthly events are important to the unfolding story, the supernatural hand of God is everywhere from the first page through the last. If we subscribe to the biblical account of history, then the importance of particular civilizations diminishes substantially, while the salvation of the individual soul becomes paramount. From the fall in the Garden of Eden to the resurrection of Jesus Christ and the bestowing of the Holy Spirit, it is a story that continues to unfold to this very minute through people just like you and me. This history becomes the revelation of the will of God, with each one of us participants in his great narrative: "It was not by their sword that they won the land...; it was your right hand, your arm, and the light of your face, for you loved them." (v3)

Have mercy on me, O God, according to your unfailing love; according to your great compassion blot out my transgressions. Wash away all my iniquity and cleanse me from my sin. For I know my transgressions, and my sin is always before me. Against you, you only, have I sinned and done what is evil in your sight, so that you are proved right when you speak and justified when you judge. Surely I was sinful at birth, sinful from the time my mother conceived me. Surely you desire truth in the inner parts; you teach me wisdom in the inmost place.

—Psalm 51:1–6

THE LIGHT OF THE WORLD

Today the Church celebrates Epiphany, the coming of "a light for revelation to the Gentiles and for glory to your people Israel." (Luke 2:32) David's song of confession is appropriate for this moment because he boldly reveals why all people need a savior: "Surely I was sinful from birth, sinful from the time my mother conceived me." (v5) David, Israel's most powerful king, understands the intractable nature of the inheritance of Adam that cannot be wished away. He calls out to God for Mercy.

If we want to understand the reason the coming of Christ was necessary, we can start with this Psalm. What David (and all men and women) so desperately needed was still to come. In time, the promise was fulfilled with the birth of the one who would "save his people from their sins." (Matthew 1:21) Jesus came to light the way to eternal life. And the way to eternal life is through him: "I am the light of the world." (John 8:12)

The LORD brought me forth as the first of his works, before his deeds of old;
I was appointed from eternity, from the beginning, before the world began.
When there were no oceans, I was given birth, when there were no springs
abounding with water; before the mountains were settled in place, before
the hills, I was given birth, before he made the earth or its fields or any of
the dust of the world. I was there when he set the heavens in place, when
he marked out the horizon on the face of the deep, when he established the
clouds above and fixed securely the fountains of the deep, when he gave the
sea its boundary so the waters would not overstep his command, and when
he marked out the foundations of the earth. Then I was the craftsman at
his side. I was filled with delight day after day, rejoicing always in his
presence, rejoicing in his whole world and delighting in mankind.

—Proverbs 8:22-31

BEFORE THE CREATION OF THE WORLD

Solomon tells us that God's wisdom was "appointed from eternity, from the beginning before the world began." (v22) This spiritual truth is echoed throughout the Bible. From David: "When I was woven together in the depths of the earth, you saw my unformed body." (Psalm 139:15) From Jeremiah: "Before I formed you in the womb, I knew you; before you were born I set you apart." (Jeremiah 1:5) From Isaiah: "Before I was born the Lord called me, from my birth he has made mention of my name." (Isaiah 49:1) From Paul: "For he chose us in him before the creation of the world." (Ephesians 1:4) And Jesus says this at the end of his prayer for all believers: "Father, I want those you have given me to be with me where I am, and to see my glory, the glory you have given me because you loved me before the creation of the world." (John 17:34)

Today many are taught that life begins at birth and ends with the finality of death; they are taught that there is no reality to either God or to eternal life. The Bible, however, tells another story. According to Scripture, you and I were created by God before we were born. And from the beginning, He had a purpose for us. In our blind foolishness, we can choose to disregard that purpose. We are free to choose to live without God, but like everything else, that choice has profound implications.

Do you rulers indeed speak justly? Do you judge uprightly among men? No, in your heart you devise injustice, and your hands mete out violence on the earth. Even from birth the wicked go astray; from the womb they are wayward and speak lies. Their venom is like the venom of a snake, like that of a cobra that has stopped its ears, that will not heed the tune of the charmer, however skillful the enchanter may be.

—*Psalm 58:1–5*

A RIGHTEOUS RULER

Anyone who has lived through the 20th century with its wars and cataclysmic violence knows that an unjust and violent ruler will bring misery to the people and the land. But at the end of his life, King David spoke of the blessings that come from a righteous ruler: "When one rules over men in righteousness, when he rules in the fear of God, he is like the light of morning at sunrise on a cloudless morning, like the brightness after rain that brings the grass from the earth." (2 Samuel 23:3-4)

The tyrant scorches the land and decimates the prosperity of the people. The righteous ruler is a servant of the people and acknowledges that all genuine blessings come from God.

Men cry out under a load of oppression; they plead for relief from the arm of the powerful. But no one says, "Where is God my Maker, who gives songs in the night, who teaches more to us than to the beasts of the earth and makes us wiser than the birds of the air?"

—Job 35:9-11

A HARD TEACHING

People often express disappointment with God because their plea for help seems to go unanswered. They say, "Well, if God is love, why won't He help me? Or, why did God let this happen to me?"

But God is not a marionette dancing at the other end of our wishes. When we pray, do we pray with humility and supplication or are we making demands? And do we approach God with a pure heart?

Job continues: "He does not answer when men cry out because of the arrogance of the wicked. Indeed, God does not listen to their empty plea, the Almighty pays no attention to it." (Job 35:12-13). And Psalm 66 says, "If I had cherished sin in my heart, the Lord would not have listened." (Psalm 66:18)

This is difficult to hear, but we really do need to examine the condition of our own hearts when we are entering the presence of God through prayer.

LORD, who may dwell in your sanctuary? Who may live on your holy hill? He whose walk is blameless and who does what is righteous, who speaks the truth from his heart and has no slander on his tongue, who does his neighbor no wrong and casts no slur on his fellowman, who despises a vile man but honors those who fear the Lord, who keeps his oath even when it hurts, who lends his money without usury and does not accept a bribe against the innocent.

—Psalm 15:1–5

THE ARDUOUS JOURNEY

We never start the journey at the summit of the holy hill, nor are we parachuted in. Arriving there is a life-long effort. How are we to get there?

Jeremiah says, "Stand at the crossroads and look; ask for the ancient paths, ask where the good way is, and walk in it, and you will find rest for your souls." (Jeremiah 6:16) Jesus tells his disciples to travel light: "Do not take along any gold or silver or copper in your belts; take no bag for the journey, or an extra tunic or sandals or a staff…" (Matthew 10:9-10) And Paul says to be careful in everything you do on the way: "… become blameless and pure, children of God without fault in a crooked and depraved generation, in which you shine like stars in the universe as you hold out the word of life…" (Philippians 2:15-16)

The journey is arduous; the reward eternal.

Then the LORD said to Satan, "Have you considered my servant Job? There is no one on earth like him; he is blameless and upright, a man who fears God and shuns evil. And he still maintains his integrity, though you incited me against him to ruin him without any reason."

—*Job 2:3*

ARMED FOR BATTLE

The conflict in heaven over the integrity of Job may seem to be a battle over the soul of one man, but as we will see later, this represents the struggle faced by all men and women. For the struggle of Job foreshadows the epic battle that will be engaged with the advent of the Messiah, Jesus Christ. When Satan tempts Jesus in the wilderness, he attacks his integrity. Satan offers Jesus the easy way out with promises of kingdoms, sustenance and earthly salvation.

Every man engages in an epic struggle within the heart over what that heart will believe and how the individual will act upon it. "For our struggle is not against flesh and blood, but against the rulers, against the authorities, against the powers of this dark world and against the spiritual forces of darkness in the heavenly realms." (Ephesians 6:12) When Job says, "...till I die, I will not deny my integrity. I will maintain my righteousness and never let it go," (Job 27:5-6) he is laying down the marker for each one of us. For the external battle has an internal antecedent within the heart of every man and woman.

We live on a battlefield. Have we armed ourselves for the inevitable conflict?

O LORD, do not rebuke me in your anger or discipline me in your wrath. For your arrows have pierced me, and your hand has come down upon me. Because of your wrath there is no health in my body; my bones have no soundness because of my sin. My guilt has overwhelmed me like a burden too heavy to bear.

—Psalm 38:1–4

A PAINFUL BURDEN

Superficially, King David's situation seems comparable to Job's. Both are suffering. But where the cause of Job's suffering is mysterious to him, the cause of David's heavy burden is clear to both him and to God. He also says in the same Psalm, "I confess my iniquity; I am troubled by my sin." (Psalm 38:18) Even though David has become the most powerful of men, and even though he was anointed by God, David, as a mere mortal, is capable of falling away from God through sin: "My guilt has overwhelmed me like a burden too heavy to bear." (v4)

If a man as great and blessed as David was felled by sin, why do we believe we can withstand the power of its attraction?

Man born of woman is of few days and full of trouble. He springs up like a flower and withers away; like a fleeting shadow, he does not endure. Do you fix your eye on such a one? Will you bring him before you for judgment? Who can bring what is pure from the impure? No one! Man's days are determined; you have decreed the number of his months and have set limits he cannot exceed. So look away from him and let him alone, till he has put in his time like a hired man.

—*Job 14:1-6*

WILL HE LIVE AGAIN?

Job has lost everything; he is suffering from unimaginable afflictions and in his misery he seems to despair of the human condition. But we should understand that while it is generally true that "Man born of woman is of few days and full of trouble," (v1) this is not the full story, nor does Job imply that it is. Job never says that God has caused this or any misery. In fact, the suffering is inflicted by the hand of Satan and not by God.

In order to understand Job better, we need to attend to everything he says, including this: "If a man dies, will he live again? All the days of my hard service I will wait for my renewal to come. You will call and I will answer you; you will long for the creature you have made." (Job 14:14-15)

So, the hardships of the present are mitigated by the knowledge of the mercy and love of God for each one of his children.

Every word of God is flawless; he is a shield to those who take refuge in him. Do not add to his words, or he will rebuke you and prove you a liar.

—*Proverbs 30:5–6*

DO NOT ADD...OR SUBTRACT

For those who consider God optional, the words of the Bible mean very little. There are others, however, who seem to take the word of God seriously, but want to add or subtract from it for their own purposes. For example, Thomas Jefferson excised the miracles because his 18th century sensibility was offended by the improbability of the supernatural.

At the other end of the spectrum are the high-octane embellishers who believe that the Bible needs to be added to in order to be relevant to modern followers.

Either way, the authority of the biblical witness of God's word is placed under attack. If the enemies of God can find a small thread to unravel, then they can proceed to cast doubt on the whole fabric of God's revelation. In speaking about God's law, Moses warned against altering any of it: "Do not add to what I command you and do not subtract from it, but keep the commands of the Lord your God that I give you."(Deuteronomy 4:2)

The truth is that we must approach the word of God with humility; we must have the attitude of a thirsty sojourner who wishes nothing more than to drink in every word that God has blessed us with through His Holy Scripture.

If clouds are full of water, they pour rain upon the earth. Whether a tree falls to the south or to the north, in the place where it falls, there will it lie. Whoever watches the wind will not plant; whoever looks at the clouds will not reap.

—Ecclesiastes 11:3-4

LITTLE DID SHE SUSPECT

The sluggard may dream of riches but if he never gets up and plants, he will never reap. God calls each one of us to purpose and to action no matter how insignificant that action may seem at the time. When Ruth went to the fields of Boaz to glean the grain behind the harvesters, little did she suspect that her seemingly insignificant work would lead to marriage and later to the birth of Obed the father of Jesse who was the father of David. (Ruth 2) And it is through David that we received the promise of God that would lead to Bethlehem and the birth of the savior for the whole world: "I will establish his line forever, his throne as long as the heavens endure." (Psalm 89:29)

Out of the gleaning of one woman would grow the vine of Jesus Christ.

The heavens praise your wonders, O LORD, your faithfulness too, in the assembly of the holy ones. For who in the skies above can compare with the LORD? Who is like the LORD among the heavenly beings? In the council of the holy ones God is greatly feared; he is more awesome than all who surround him. O LORD God Almighty, who is like you? You are mighty, O LORD, and your faithfulness surrounds you."

—Psalm 89:5–8

NOW CHOOSE LIFE

The hand of God in creation should be obvious to all, but since the 19th century, many leaders, under the influence of the philosophy of scientific progress, proclaimed God dead and therefore not a factor in the creation of the world.

Matthew Arnold, the poet, captures the desolate spirit of this "enlightened" new age in his poem "Dover Beach": *The Sea of Faith was once, too, at the full, and round earth's shore lay like the folds of a bright girdle furled. But now I only hear its melancholy, long, withdrawing roar, retreating, to the breath of the night-wind, down the vast edges drear and naked shingles of the world.*[1] But as we now know, the god of that age became the shipwreck of the next century with its sinister technologies resulting in world wars, mass murders and atomic weapons.

When we no longer see God's hand in the stars and the seas and splendors of the earth itself, we consign ourselves to the desolate and dark places of this world without the possibility of rescue. As Moses approaches the end of his long journey, he tells the people of Israel (and us) that we have a choice and that we should choose wisely: "See, I set before you today life and prosperity, death and destruction…Now choose life, so that you and your children may live and that you may love the Lord your God, listen to his voice and hold fast to him." (Deuteronomy 30:15, 19-20)

I have seen a grievous evil under the sun: wealth hoarded to the harm of its owner, or wealth lost through some misfortune, so that when he has a son there is nothing left for him. Naked a man comes from his mother's womb, and as he comes, so he departs. He takes nothing from his labor that he can carry in his hand.

—Ecclesiastes 5:13-15

MEANINGLESS?

When we spend the best days of our lives chasing after fame or wealth, then we are to be pitied, for in the end, nothing of lasting value will be ours. "Meaningless! Meaningless! Everything is meaningless." (Ecclesiastes 1:2)

But unlike many of the popular writers of the "lost generation" who reflected a world stripped of God, Solomon is not writing as a stoic or nihilist. He is simply describing a truth that has been lost in our time: The world is nothing more than a wasteland without God. "All things are wearisome, more than one can say. The eye never has enough of seeing, nor the ear its fill of hearing. What has been will be again, what has been done will be done again; there is nothing new under the sun." (Ecclesiastes 1:9)

Without God, man's existence is incomplete and desperate.

Why are you downcast, O my soul? Why so disturbed within me? Put your hope in God, for I will yet praise him, my Savior and my God. My soul is downcast within me; therefore I will remember you from the land of the Jordan, the heights of Hermon—from Mount Mizar. Deep calls to deep in the roar of your waterfalls; all your waves and breakers have swept over me.

—Psalm 42:5–7

SEEK THE LORD

Sometimes a dark mood comes upon us unexpectedly. Maybe it was hovering at the edge of our consciousness like a curtain of fog at the edge of a placid sea. The wind shifts and what was bright sunlight becomes a monotonous wall of gray. And so it happens that the sunshine disposition is enshrouded by feelings of longing, loneliness and anxiety.

We suffer through these moments, saying with the psalmist, "Why are you downcast, O my soul? Why so disturbed within me?" (v5) We long for the sunlit moments again, but no amount of distracting activity seems to work. Out of desperation we may seek relief through an addictive diversion or we may anesthetize our suffering through medication.

But none of it works for long, because we are seeking physical relief with merely physical implements. David seems to be saying that the cause of his despair has its roots in a fractured relationship with God. Healing begins when David says, "Put your hope in God…" (v5)

When we have departed from the company of God to pursue our own purposes, we allow ourselves to become vulnerable to all life's afflictions and we experience what it is like to be unarmed in the midst of battle. "The Lord is with you when you are with him. If you seek him, he will be found by you…." (2 Chronicles 15:2) Life presents may calamities, but comfort and safety comes when we walk with the Lord: "Seek the Lord, all you humble of the land, you who do what he commands." (Zephaniah 2:3)

Praise the LORD from the earth, you great sea creatures and all ocean depths, lightning and hail, snow and clouds, stormy winds that do his bidding, you mountains and all hills, fruit trees and all cedars, wild animals and all cattle, small creatures and flying birds, kings of the earth and all nations, you princes and all rulers on earth, young men and maidens, old men and children. Let them praise the name of the LORD, for his name alone is exalted; his splendor is above the earth and the heavens.

—*Psalm 148:7-13*

TEACH US TO PRAY

The Lord of the universe, whose "splendor is above the earth and the heavens," (v13) stooped to take us by the hand to teach us how to speak to him in prayer.

Jesus gave us the Lord's Prayer in his Sermon on the Mount, but he did not ask us to slavishly memorize it and repeat it by rote. He wanted it to come from a heart filled with love, devotion and gratitude. He gave us the form of prayer to pray and asked each of his followers to fill it in with the words that well up from within.

Paraphrasing Jesus, we might pray: *Father, holy is your name. I pray that you will bring revival to the land. I pray that you will provide your children with bread for this day. I pray that you will forgive us for our sins, conscious and unconscious. I pray that you will teach us compassion so that we will learn to forgive as you have forgiven us. I pray that your hand will guide us on right paths and away from temptations and you will strengthen us so that we will resist the evil one. I pray this because you are God. To you be glory and power forever and ever. Amen.*

Eat honey, my son, for it is good; honey from the comb is sweet to your taste. Know also that wisdom is sweet to your soul; if you find it, there is a future hope for you, and your hope will not be cut off.

— *Proverbs 24:13–14*

SWEET TO THE SOUL

In one of his Psalms, David says, "...taste and see that the Lord is good." (Psalm 34:8) Elsewhere, receiving the Holy Spirit is compared to partaking of a great feast: "It is impossible for those who have once been enlightened, who have tasted the heavenly gift, who have shared in the Holy Spirit, who have tasted the goodness of the word of God" (Hebrews 6:4-6) to ever again be content to taste the feasts of this life.

As honey is sweet to the senses, how much sweeter is the wisdom of God as given to us by the Holy Spirit? As honey may satisfy our physical hunger for a time, God promises to satisfy for all time the infinite hunger of our souls.

I, wisdom, dwell together with prudence; I possess knowledge and discretion. To fear the LORD is to hate evil; I hate pride and arrogance, evil behavior and perverse speech. Counsel and sound judgment are mine; I have understanding and power. By me kings reign and rulers make laws that are just; by me princes govern, and all nobles who rule on earth. I love those who love me, and those who seek me find me. With me are riches and honor, enduring wealth and prosperity. My fruit is better than fine gold; what I yield surpasses choice silver. I walk in the way of righteousness, along the paths of justice, bestowing wealth on those who love me and making their treasuries full.

—Proverbs 8:12-21

HIS HUMAN FACE

We often think of wisdom in the abstract—as if it represents a human philosophy constructed by the hands of men with no particular application to everyday life. But according to scripture, wisdom pre-existed the creation of the world and comes from the heart of God. (Jeremiah 10:12) For us, therefore, living wisely means that we are living in complete harmony with the character of God. And that character is perfectly reflected in the Son He loves, Jesus Christ.

As with Christ, the wise person embodies the values of prudence, knowledge and discretion. He is humble in all things and he chooses his words with care because he knows that words are powerful, and when used carelessly, can wound. The wise person is sought out by others because he exhibits sound and fair judgment. Most importantly, love is at the very center of who he is. He is patient and kind. He neither envies, nor boasts. He is not proud or rude. The wise person is not self-seeking, is not easily angered and does not keep a record of wrongs. He takes no delight in evil but rejoices with the truth. He always protects, always trusts, always hopes, always perseveres. (1 Corinthians 13:4-7)

When we live in harmony with God, as Christ did, we reflect all this wisdom of God that, from the beginning, He has always wanted to share with His children. The face of God is the face of love and it is the wise man who allows that love to wash over him and through him and from him to others who have not yet seen or fully experienced the beauty of that face., which is "the glory of God in the face of Christ." (2 Corinthians 4:6)

But to the wicked, God says: "What right have you to recite my laws or take my covenant on your lips? You hate my instruction and cast my words behind you. When you see a thief, you join with him; you throw in your lot with adulterers. You use your mouth for evil and harness your tongue to deceit. You speak continually against your brother and slander your own mother's son. These things you have done and I kept silent; you thought I was altogether like you. But I will rebuke you and accuse you to your face."

—*Psalm 50:16–21*

BY THEIR FRUIT

Only God can fully discern between the appearance of things and the reality behind them.

The reality here is one of wickedness, but the appearance is one of righteousness. While God can never be fooled, men can easily be blinded by the smooth words of charlatans and false purveyors of the Word. One of the most reprehensible examples of this is the deceitful and self-serving holy man who steals from God's vineyard and spreads corruption amongst the people.

Before the fall of Jerusalem, Jeremiah proclaimed that false priests would bring devastation to the land: "From the least to the greatest, all are greedy for gain; prophets and priests alike, all practice deceit. They dress the wound of my people as though it were not serious. 'Peace, peace,' they say, when there is no peace." (Jeremiah 6:13-14). And Jesus warned all disciples to be vigilant at all times: "Watch out for false prophets. They come to you in sheep's clothing, but inwardly they are ferocious wolves. By their fruit you will recognize them." (Matthew 7:15-16)

Why do the nations conspire and the peoples plot in vain? The kings of the earth take their stand and the rulers gather together against the LORD and against his Anointed One. "Let us break their chains," they say, "and throw off their fetters." The One enthroned in heaven laughs; the Lord scoffs at them.

—Psalm 2:1-4

THE WAR WITHIN

When we speak of war, we usually think of epic conflicts like the World Wars of the last century. But according to the 2nd Psalm, our earthly battles began as an act of war against God Himself. Our defiance began in the Garden of Eden when both the man and the woman allowed themselves to be deceived by listening to the intriguing lies of Satan while disregarding the warning of God Himself.

The choice of Adam and Eve had universal consequences. Every generation that followed seemed to inherit the same lethal virus. So each one of us is born with the contradictory impulse to worship and rebel, to serve God and to serve ourselves. Only through painful experience and God's grace do we come to understand what Jesus meant when he said: "…just as the Son of Man did not come to be served, but to serve, and to give his life as a ransom for many." (Matthew 20:28)

Thus, the peace spoken of in the Bible must begin within the heart of every man and woman. Until that happens we can know only conflict, division and discord and not the peace that passes all understanding. (Philippians 4:7)

The highest heavens belong to the LORD, but the earth he has given to man. It is not the dead who praise the LORD, those who go down to silence; it is we who extol the LORD, both now and forevermore. Praise the LORD.

—Psalm 115:16–18

RETURNING TO THE ORIGINAL STORY LINE

The biblical account of the first man begins in a garden: "Now the Lord God had planted a garden in the east, in Eden, and there he put the man he had formed."(Genesis 2:8) The garden was designed to be a pleasant place for the man, a place he could enjoy and cultivate: "The Lord God took the man and put him in the Garden of Eden to work and take care of it."(Genesis 2:15)

God planted all kinds of trees and brought beasts of the field for the man to name. And God created a companion for the man so that together the man and the woman would fulfill God's purposes for them. From the very beginning, God created the earth for man's dominion. It was only when the man and the woman defied God's one prohibition that a very different story began to unfold.

At the center of the new story is conflict, for where there was harmony, now we find rebellion; where there was a sweet home, now we find exile; and where there was abundance, now we find hard labor and travail.

The original story line was radically changed by one act of thoughtless defiance. The new story is the tale that culminated as a stupendous act of love on a cross on Calvary. At that moment, all men once again could enter the original story line that had its origin in Eden.

There are six things the LORD hates, seven that are detestable to him: haughty eyes, a lying tongue, hands that shed innocent blood, a heart that devises wicked schemes, feet that are quick to rush into evil, a false witness who pours out lies and a man who stirs up dissension among brothers.

—Proverbs 6:16–19

DETESTIBLE IN THE EYES OF GOD

How can God hate when everyone says that God is love? If God is love, then it would be illogical to assume that God can hate.

If you take the biblical perspective, however, then it becomes clear that while God loves us, he hates anything that separates us from him. The verse says that He hates haughty eyes, which I take to mean pride. And it was pride that brought Eve low when she was deceived into believing that by eating the forbidden fruit from the tree, she would "be like God, knowing good and evil." (Genesis 3:4)

But rather than bringing Adam and Eve closer to God, their act violated their relationship with Him. Oswald Chambers puts it this way: "God loves the world so much that He hates with a perfect hatred the thing that is twisting people away from Him."[2] Here we have seven things that twist us away and are therefore detestable in the eyes of God.

You turn men back to dust, saying, "Return to dust, O sons of men."
For a thousand years in your sight are like a day that has just gone by,
or like a watch in the night. You sweep men away in the sleep of death;
they are like the new grass of the morning— though in the morning it
springs up new, by evening it is dry and withered.

—Psalm 90:3–6

REALITY CHECK

As we grow older, time begins to play unexpected tricks on us.

What once took forever now passes by with lightning speed. Often, when we sense time accelerating, we default to crisis mode because we feel suddenly trapped by the constrictions of limited time. We are frustrated that we have accomplished so little with so little time left to do the things we always planned to do. We begin to feel a sense of panic and an air of regret forms within us.

It is at this moment, when we are experiencing one of life's reality checks, that either we run away or we embrace the moment, taking what we have left and building from it. For while "death is the destiny of every man," (Ecclesiastes 7:2) we are called to God's purposes now; the minute or the hour is not important, for the laborer will receive his wages and the wages for the faithful servant is life eternal.

The path of the righteous is like the first gleam of dawn, shining ever brighter till the full light of day. But the way of the wicked is like deep darkness; they do not know what makes them stumble.

—Proverbs 4:18-19

GOD IS LIGHT

Solomon compares "righteousness" to the first light of morning and, in contrast, he compares the deeds of the "wicked" to deep darkness. The light and dark imagery point to our relationship with God in a language that speaks to our spiritual longing for truth.

The language of Scripture has beauty and truth embedded in its very core and it is through the power of its language that it reveals the truth of the power of God. The Bible opens with God saying, "Let there be light." (Genesis 1:3) Before there was light the universe was void and without life and form.

And here is how John describes the second creation story, the birth of God's one and only son: "In him was life, and that life was the light of men. The light shines in the darkness, but the darkness has not understood it." (John 1:4-5)

And here is Jesus during his three year ministry: "I am the light of the world. Whoever follows me will never walk in darkness, but will have the light of life." (John 8:12)

And here is John in his first letter: "God is light; in him there is no darkness at all." (1 John 1:5)

When reading Scripture, look for patterns of imagery and language, for within these patterns is revelation.

The first to present his case seems right, till another comes forward and questions him.

—*Proverbs 18:17*

STANDING FIRM ON THE FIELD OF BATTLE

Many want to believe what they are told, but this passage suggests that buyer should always beware, because it is easy to be fooled, just as it is easy for some to fool. We hear a persuasive argument and we automatically say, "That's right!" when we should have said, "No, that can't be what he means."

Eventually though, experience and knowledge should alert us to the danger of listening to only one voice when we know that another side of the story might exist. In order to question a false argument, we must be armed with knowledge; in the case of Scripture, we are called to know it intimately.

Otherwise, when the worldly man makes his case, there will be no one to answer, leaving the field of battle open to those who represent, consciously or unconsciously, the interests of the "father of lies."

Show me your ways, O LORD, teach me your paths; guide me in your truth and teach me, for you are God my Savior, and my hope is in you all day long. Remember, O LORD, your great mercy and love, for they are from of old. Remember not the sins of my youth and my rebellious ways; according to your love remember me, for you are good, O LORD.

—Psalm 25:4-7

A GREAT TEACHER

How we long for a great teacher! All these years later, I still remember the teachers of my youth who had the skill, character and heart to reach me in all my reluctant and rebellious ignorance. What patience and forbearance they had!

Still vivid in my memory are Mr. Charles and Mr. Wales and Mr. Briggs and, most of all, Mr. Keller, a man with great musical talent and great compassion.

Yet none of these men, or any teacher for that matter, can compare to the profound wisdom God can convey, if only we will approach Him with an attitude of humility and prayer.

James says, "If any of you lacks wisdom, he should ask God, who gives generously to all without finding fault, and it will be given to him." (James 1:5) Remember to acknowledge all men and women who have helped lead you towards wisdom and knowledge, but understand that behind each one of them stands God who wants you to draw ever closer to the source of all wisdom and truth.

As the deer pants for streams of water, so my soul pants for you, O God. My soul thirsts for God, for the living God. When can I go and meet with God? My tears have been my food day and night, while men say to me all day long, "Where is your God?" These things I remember as I pour out my soul: how I used to go with the multitude, leading the procession to the house of God, with shouts of joy and thanksgiving among the festive throng.

—Psalm 42:1–4

GOD IS SPIRIT

As David uses figurative speech to awaken our hearts to spiritual reality, so Jesus uses spiritual language to distinguish between matters of God and matters of this world. Nowhere is it more evident than in John's Gospel.

While Jesus speaks in a rich and figurative language, his enemies (and sometimes even his disciples) speak in the language of reason, common sense and physical reality, which makes it difficult for them to understand the truth of Jesus' words.

When Jesus asks the Samaritan woman for a drink from a well, she responds literally and superficially, though she seems to want to understand more. The woman is puzzled because she thinks of water as merely water, whereas Jesus is speaking about water as a metaphor for the power of the indwelling Holy Spirit.

In another place, Jesus confronts his enemies by saying, "Why is my language not clear to you?" (John 8:43) Throughout the gospel of John, Jesus is only understood by those who have placed their faith and their life in his hands. Unrepentant sinners cannot possibly submit and, therefore, their understanding remains clouded and constricted. Pilate asks, "What is truth?" (John 18:38) when he has the truth of God standing right before him. Pilate sees only a man, whereas Peter at an earlier time has the revelation that Jesus is not just a man; he is the Christ. (Mark 8:29)

When Jesus is speaking, it is never just about thirst. It is about the power of God to transform each one of us through the Holy Spirit. "Yet the time is coming and has now come when the true worshipers will worship the Father in spirit and in truth...God is spirit, and his worshipers must worship in spirit and in truth." (John 4:23-24)

The proverbs of Solomon son of David, king of Israel: for attaining wisdom and discipline; for understanding words of insight; for acquiring a disciplined and prudent life, doing what is right and just and fair; for giving prudence to the simple, knowledge and discretion to the young— let the wise listen and add to their learning, and let the discerning get guidance—for understanding proverbs and parables, the sayings and riddles of the wise.

—Proverbs 1:1-6

A DISCERNING HEART

Solomon was not just a man of wisdom; he was one of the most powerful rulers on earth, the son of King David and a man of tremendous wealth.

And yet King Solomon prized wisdom above everything else, for when he became king upon his father's death, God favored him by granting him whatever he might ask for.

Here is how Solomon responded: "So give your servant a discerning heart to govern your people and to distinguish between right and wrong. For who is able to govern this great people of yours?" (1 Kings 3:9)

And here is how God replied: "Since you have asked for this and not for long life or wealth for yourself, nor have asked for the death of your enemies but for discernment in administering justice, I will do what you have asked." (1 Kings 3:11-12)

God is exalted in his power. Who is a teacher like him? Who has prescribed his ways for him, or said to him, 'You have done wrong?' Remember to extol his work, which men have praised in song. All mankind has seen it; men gaze on it from afar. How great is God—beyond our understanding! The number of his years is past finding out.

—*Job 36:22-26*

SING AND MAKE MUSIC

Music has always played a central role in worship. In trying to describe the power that Holy Scripture has on the hearts of men, one might think of it as the power of the language of the spirit of God. Poetry and music are both aspects of this language; both appeal to an appetite and intuition for God that is common to all men.

Music awakens in us a sense of the eternal; we forget the momentary troubles of our everyday life, singing joyfully to the Lord. Hence, Paul says of worship: "...be filled with the Spirit. Speak to one another with psalms, hymns and spiritual songs. Sing and make music in the heart to the Lord, always giving thanks to God the Father for everything, in the name of the Lord Jesus Christ." (Ephesians 5:18-20)

Men praise God in song because music has the capacity to awaken our slumbering spirit to the power and reality of the God of the universe.

How can a young man keep his way pure? By living according to your word. I seek you with all my heart; do not let me stray from your commands. I have hidden your word in my heart that I might not sin against you. Praise be to you, O LORD; teach me your decrees. With my lips I recount all the laws that come from your mouth. I rejoice in following your statutes as one rejoices in great riches. I meditate on your precepts and consider your ways. I delight in your decrees; I will not neglect your word. Do good to your servant, and I will live; I will obey your word. Open my eyes that I may see wonderful things in your law. I am a stranger on earth; do not hide your commands from me.

—*Psalm 119:9–19*

SPENDING THE GIFT

"I seek you with all my heart." (v9) It is one thing to say this, but it is another thing to live it. When the sun rises on a new day, we are given a choice of how we plan to dedicate our time. Time is a gift given freely by God, but it is a finite gift, and therefore precious.

God also gives us the gift of choice. We can choose to spend the gift of time on the giver or we can spend it on ourselves. "Open my eyes that I may see wonderful things in your law." (v19) Open my eyes so that my heart may discern how you would have me spend your precious gifts today.

How long, O men, will you turn my glory into shame? How long will you love delusions and seek false gods? Know that the LORD has set apart the godly for himself; the LORD will hear when I call to him.

—Psalm 4:2-3

DRIFTING AWAY

Perhaps one of the deadliest delusions is the desire of men to chase after false gods. We must be alert to this subtle desire of the heart because it inclines us to wander away from the faith and indulge in religious fantasies. "We must pay more careful attention, therefore, to what we have heard, so that we do not drift away." (Hebrews 2:1)

To drift away from the truth sends us into bizarre and uncharted territory where we become the center of our own alternative universe. God asks us to walk in faith because He wants us to avoid the pitfalls of a pitiless world that exists apart from Him. The only reality apart from God is death. God continuously calls us to live in the light of His love; therefore, He says, choose life.

Can anyone teach knowledge to God, since he judges even the highest? One man dies in full vigor, completely secure and at ease, his body well nourished, his bones rich with marrow. Another man dies in bitterness of soul, never having enjoyed anything good. Side by side they lie in the dust, and worms cover them both.

—Job 21:22–26

HIS LIFE BLESSED MANY

The Bible is full of difficult passages that may not conform to our own idea of justice or rightness. When something bad happens, we immediately look to God and say "How can this be! If God is love and if God is good, He would never let this happen."

When I was nineteen, I was faced with the sudden death of my father. Just as in this passage, "he was full of vigor, completely secure and at ease," but then one May morning in 1963, he was wrenched from his family. Years have not erased the pain and shock that we experienced that morning.

I remember my mother, only forty-two years old, crying out in pain, "Why did God let this happen?" I couldn't answer her question then, and I can't answer it today for "Can anyone teach knowledge to God...?" A friend of mine said that we should focus on the blessings that my father brought to so many people, blessings so strong that they live on to this very day.

When you consider every life as a gift from God, then the mystery of an early death is mitigated by the blessings of the life. No one can remove the pain of death with easy words of solace, but our suffering should be seasoned with humility and gratitude for every blessing that is given by the creator of all things. I wish my father were alive and with me today, but at the same time I thank God for the gift of his life in the first place.

Do not put your trust in princes, in mortal men, who cannot save. When their spirit departs, they return to the ground; on that very day their plans come to nothing.

—Psalm 146:3-4

A PARABLE

Where do we place our faith? Below the seemingly solid structures of this world is the dust of millions of shattered dreams, for "on that very day their plans come to nothing." (v4)

Jesus uses a parable to make the same point: "Then he said to them, 'Watch out! Be on your guard against all kinds of greed; a man's life does not consist in the abundance of his possessions.' And he told them this parable: 'The ground of a certain rich man produced a good crop. He thought to himself, What shall I do? I have no place to store my crops. Then he said, 'This is what I'll do. I will tear down my barns and build bigger ones, and there I will store all my grain and my goods. And I'll say to myself, You have plenty of good things laid up for many years. Take life easy; eat, drink and be merry.' But God said to him, 'You fool! This very night your life will be demanded from you. Then who will get what you have prepared for yourself?' This is how it will be with anyone who stores up things for himself but is not rich toward God." (Luke 12:15-21)

What is man, that he could be pure, or one born of woman, that he could be righteous? If God places no trust in his holy ones, if even the heavens are not pure in his eyes, how much less man, who is vile and corrupt, who drinks up evil like water!

—Job 15:14–16

SUBSTITUTING TRUTH FOR A LIE

The voices from the chorus of the popular culture swell in unison against the wisdom of Job. Popular culture is built on a fantasy that we can explore the outer reaches of personal freedom without considering the consequences. But this is nothing more than the ancient hoax repeating itself in modern dress backed up with the same old false promise:

"...and you will be like God, knowing good and evil." (Genesis 3:5) We are blinded by the glare of our over-abundant culture and have laid aside the truth of Christ for nothing more than baubles.

If we were to look at ourselves from God's point of view, we would recoil in shame and revulsion and would rebel against what is invading our homes every hour of every day. But we do not rebel; instead we "drink up evil like water" (v16) and thereby lose the will to resist a power that is eating away at our souls. We disregard the words of the prophet Isaiah at our own peril: "Woe to those who call evil good and good evil, who put darkness for light and light for darkness and who put bitter for sweet and sweet for bitter." (Isaiah 5:20)

Now then, my sons, listen to me; blessed are those who keep my ways. Listen to my instruction and be wise; do not ignore it. Blessed is the man who listens to me, watching daily at my doors, waiting at my doorway. For whoever finds me finds life and receives favor from the LORD. But whoever fails to find me harms himself; all who hate me love death.

—Proverbs 8:32–36

THROUGH ALL AND IN ALL

Scripture tells us that the Wisdom of God, the Word of God and the Holy Spirit are different aspects of the same God.

In Proverbs 8, Wisdom, speaking through the words of Solomon says, "I was there when he set the heavens in place, when he marked out the horizon on the face of the deep, when he established the clouds above and fixed securely the fountains of the deep...and when he marked out the foundations of the earth." (Proverbs 8:27-29)

The Gospel of John begins with the Word: "In the beginning was the Word, and the Word was with God, and the Word was God. He was with God in the beginning." (John 1:1-2)

And the second verse of Genesis introduces the Holy Spirit as the central agent in the creation of the world: "Now the earth was formless and empty, darkness was over the surface of the deep, and the Spirit of God was hovering over the waters." (Genesis 1:2)

All three, the Wisdom of God, the Word of God and the Spirit of God, come together in the person of Jesus Christ. We are told that the young Jesus "grew in wisdom and stature and in favor with God and men." (Luke 2:52) The Gospel of John opens by stating "the Word became flesh and made his dwelling among us." (John 1:14) And Mark tells us the Spirit of God descended on him like a dove. (Mark 1:10). We are told that when we proclaim the Lordship of Jesus, we affirm the oneness of God: "There is one body and one Spirit-just as you were called to one hope when you were called-one Lord, one faith, one baptism; one God and Father of all, who is over all and through all and in all." (Ephesians 4:4)

By the rivers of Babylon we sat and wept when we remembered Zion. There on the poplars we hung our harps, for there our captors asked us for songs, our tormentors demanded songs of joy; they said, "Sing us one of the songs of Zion!" How can we sing the songs of the LORD while in a foreign land? If I forget you, O Jerusalem, may my right hand forget its skill.

—Psalm 137:1–5

THE WARNINGS WERE UNHEEDED

How beautiful and how melancholy! Jerusalem has been invaded and sacked and its people have been led as captives into exile. Jeremiah, the prophet, warned the people of Jerusalem of the impending doom, but his cries were unheeded. Instead, death and destruction descend on David's city and now it lies deserted. The entire book of Lamentations, written by Jeremiah, focuses on the downfall of Jerusalem: "How deserted lies the city, so full of people! How like a widow is she, who once was great among the nations! She who was queen among the provinces has now become a slave." (Lamentations 1:1)

His wife said to him, "Are you still holding on to your integrity? Curse God and die!" He replied, "You are talking like a foolish woman. Shall we accept good from God, and not trouble?"

—*Job 2:9-10*

PERSEVERING IN THE FACE OF SUFFERING

The question every person must face at some critical time in his or her life is this: Will I maintain my integrity in the face of suffering? What did Abraham do when he was called to sacrifice his one and only son? What did Elijah do when confronted by Ahab and the 450 false prophets? And what did Jesus do when faced with betrayal and the agony of the cross?

Persevering in the face of suffering is at the heart of integrity for the man who loves God. Job's wife is foolish because she is making Satan's argument: "Curse God (for causing your suffering) and die!" (v10) Satan says, "A man will give all he has for his own life. But stretch out your hand and strike his flesh and bones, and he will surely curse you to your face." (Job 2:4-5)

When we face trouble, real trouble, do we turn on God and curse Him to his face? Or do we say with Job, "Shall we accept good from God, and not trouble?" (v10)

Hear my prayer, O LORD; let my cry for help come to you. Do not hide your face from me when I am in distress. Turn your ear to me; when I call, answer me quickly. For my days vanish like smoke; my bones burn like glowing embers. My heart is blighted and withered like grass; I forget to eat my food. Because of my loud groaning I am reduced to skin and bones. I am like a desert owl, like an owl among the ruins. I lie awake; I have become like a bird alone on a roof.

—Psalm 102:1–7

ON THE EDGE OF A PRECIPICE

David is at the edge of the abyss with nowhere to go or turn. He is in distress; his days vanish like smoke; his heart is blighted and withered like grass; He is "like a desert owl, like an owl among the ruins." (v6) The vivid imagery communicates utter hopelessness.

This is the language of the wasteland, a place of violence and death. It is a place where we have run out of second chances and where we scrape together a bare existence among the ruins of our life. It is in such a place that we call out to God to save us, for all the other options have vanished. Either we call out to God or we plummet off the edge with no one to catch or rescue us before we fall.

Can you raise your voice to the clouds and cover yourself with a flood of water? Do you send the lightning bolts on their way? Do they report to you, "Here we are?" Who endowed the heart with wisdom or gave understanding to the mind? Who has the wisdom to count the clouds? Who can tip over the water jars of the heavens when the dust becomes hard and the clods of earth stick together?

—Job 38:34–38

WHO, INDEED?

In order to avoid hard questions about the bigger issues of life, we construct our own intellectual and emotional cocoons. We build ourselves up by miniaturizing the world around us, reducing it to bite-sized pieces that are easy to digest.

People do this with the Bible all the time. They reduce it to a few sound bites in order to make it fit into their own preconceptions of God and reality. They reduce the beauty, majesty and complexity of the Old Testament to the story of an angry God and of His wandering and wayward people. The New Testament is marginalized by defining Jesus to fit the latest scholarly fad. And none of this addresses the question of God to Job: "Who endowed the heart with wisdom or gave understanding to the mind?" Who, indeed?

You rule over the surging sea; when its waves mount up, you still them. You crushed Rahab like one of the slain; with your strong arm you scattered your enemies. The heavens are yours, and yours also the earth; you founded the world and all that is in it. You created the north and the south; Tabor and Hermon sing for joy at your name. Your arm is endued with power; your hand is strong, your right hand exalted. Righteousness and justice are the foundation of your throne; love and faithfulness go before you. Blessed are those who have learned to acclaim you, who walk in the light of your presence, O LORD. They rejoice in your name all day long; they exult in your righteousness. For you are their glory and strength, and by your favor you exalt our horn. Indeed, our shield belongs to the LORD, our king to the Holy One of Israel.

—Psalm 89:9–18

A FURIOUS STORM

Jesus had been performing miracles throughout the day, healing the demon possessed and the sick. Matthew writes that, "This was to fulfill what was spoken through the prophet Isaiah: 'He took up our infirmities and carried our diseases.'" (Matthew 8:17) But apparently his own disciples did not understand who this healer was.

Then Jesus bid his followers to join him in a boat to cross the Sea of Galilee. Suddenly, as they were crossing "a furious storm came up on the lake, so that the waves swept over the boat." (Matthew 8:24) The disciples were overcome with fear and they cried out to Jesus: "Lord, save us! We're going to drown." (v25)

Jesus rebuked the winds and the waves and the sea became calm. The disciples are bewildered and ask, "What kind of man is this? Even the winds and the waves obey him." (v27) What kind of man, indeed? David, speaking of God, says, "You rule over the surging sea; when its waves mount up, you still them." (Psalm 89:9) When the disciples ask what kind of man is this, David provides the answer: *He is the holy one of God, the Messiah, the one who has been sent to crush sin, fear and death.*

Then I realized that it is good and proper for a man to eat and drink, and to find satisfaction in his toilsome labor under the sun during the few days of life God has given him—for this is his lot. Moreover, when God gives any man wealth and possessions, and enables him to enjoy them, to accept his lot and be happy in his work—this is a gift of God. He seldom reflects on the days of his life, because God keeps him occupied with gladness of heart.

—Ecclesiastes 5:18-20

A CHANGE OF DIRECTION

On this day in 1991, I received "a gift from God" that has given me "gladness of heart" ever since. It was on this day on the remote island of Vieques, off the east coast of Puerto Rico, that I discovered a daily Bible reading program that I have since followed every day.

The occasion was Ash Wednesday; it was also my son Alex's birthday, and I was looking for a way to have a small family service at home in recognition of the first day of Lent. I decided to look through the Book of Common Prayer and there I found the two-year daily reading guide more or less hidden at the very end of the book. It was on that day that I received the inspiration to follow the lectionary every day; and I have.

It took several years before I began to see that the Scriptures were more real than reality itself and slowly I began to see all experience from a biblical perspective. God blessed me unexpectedly that day and that blessing has been renewed every morning when I open my Bible as each new day begins to break.

To you, O LORD, I called; to the Lord I cried for mercy: "What gain is there in my destruction, in my going down into the pit? Will the dust praise you? Will it proclaim your faithfulness? Hear, O LORD, and be merciful to me; O LORD, be my help." You turned my wailing into dancing; you removed my sackcloth and clothed me with joy, that my heart may sing to you and not be silent. O LORD my God, I will give you thanks forever.

—*Psalm 30:8–12*

ALWAYS THERE

Joy is what we experience when we are connected to God. God created us to worship Him, but we cannot worship God if we choose to live apart from Him. God desires that we turn away from danger; He wants us back and will search us out to the farthest ends of the earth to show His mercy and lead us away from self-destruction.

But we must turn to embrace Him, to thank Him and to worship Him. He is always there sorrowing at our wailing, but delighting in our dancing.

Two things I ask of you, O LORD; do not refuse me before I die: Keep falsehood and lies far from me; give me neither poverty nor riches, but give me only my daily bread. Otherwise, I may have too much and disown you and say, "Who is the LORD?" Or I may become poor and steal, and so dishonor the name of my God.

—Proverbs 30:7-9

APPETITES

We live in a time of unusual plenty and many Americans have forgotten what it means to pray for your daily bread. Abundance can be a good thing, but when we forget the source, we are tempted to satisfy our appetites by wanting more and more of whatever it is we desire. Here the prayer recognizes the temptation to attribute our abundance to our own success, which inevitably causes us to begin to drift away from God. Our appetite for things begins to drive out our appetite for God.

To be human is to have appetites; the question is: will we fill our hearts, minds and bodies with an unquenchable appetite for God? "But if we have food and clothing, we will be content with that. People who want to get rich fall into temptation and a trap and into many foolish and harmful desires that plunge men into ruin and destruction. For the love of money is the root of all kinds of evil. Some people, eager for money, have wandered from the faith and pierced themselves with many griefs." (1 Timothy 6:8-10)

There is great danger in indulging our appetites with material objects or money, for then we cannot help but fall away from the only genuine appetite—for the health of our souls.

By day the LORD directs his love, at night his song is with me— a prayer to the God of my life. I say to God my Rock, "Why have you forgotten me? Why must I go about mourning, oppressed by the enemy?" My bones suffer mortal agony as my foes taunt me, saying to me all day long, "Where is your God?" Why are you downcast, O my soul? Why so disturbed within me? Put your hope in God, for I will yet praise him, my Savior and my God.

—Psalm 42:8–11

A SINNER LIKE YOU AND ME

When we think of King David, we often think of the great warrior king who dispatched enemies near and far and who united two kingdoms and succeeded beyond measure.

But David was more than a powerful political figure; he was the poet king, a composer of songs who could search the deepest depths of the human heart. It is through his songs that we discover the man behind the crown. And to our surprise we find a man with the same fears, guilt, doubts and anxiety of ordinary men. This is not what we might have expected.

He says, "Why are you downcast, O my soul? Why so disturbed within me?" (v11) David, the king, the anointed one of God, the slayer of giants and the builder of cities and kingdoms, has a heart very much like yours and mine. For David is a sinner who turns away from God at the very height of his earthly powers; he forsakes God for a momentary pleasure; but God does not forsake him. He receives forgiveness from the Lord and he is restored to a new life by the grace of God. He is then freed to "teach transgressors your ways" (Psalm 51:13) and help sinners turn back to the Lord. "Put your hope in God...," he says, "for I will yet praise him, my savior and my God." (v11)

There is no wisdom, no insight, no plan that can succeed against the LORD. The horse is made ready for the day of battle, but victory rests with the LORD.

—Proverbs 21:30-31

THE SOURCE OF WISDOM

There was a time when I believed, truly believed, that wisdom, insight and success came from...me. And so, it is not surprising that eventually I would run off the road and end up in a ditch.

When you are blinded by self-regard, it is hard to steer a straight course. The really sad thing is that I was a typical example of my generation. We were swerving all over the place when we thought we were plowing straight ahead.

Ironically, the experience of disaster eventually restored my sight and my sanity. And with the restoration came the realization that victory of any kind can never rest with the singular possessive. "This is what the Lord says: 'Let not the wise man boast of his wisdom or the strong man boast of his strength or the rich man boast of his riches, but let him who boasts boast about this: that he understands and knows me, that I am the Lord, who exercises kindness, justice and righteousness on earth for in these I delight,' declares the Lord." (Jeremiah 9:23-24)

The proverbs of Solomon: A wise son brings joy to his father, but a foolish son grief to his mother. Ill-gotten treasures are of no value, but righteousness delivers from death. The LORD does not let the righteous go hungry but he thwarts the craving of the wicked. Lazy hands make a man poor, but diligent hands bring wealth. He who gathers crops in summer is a wise son, but he who sleeps during harvest is a disgraceful son.

—Proverbs 10:1–5

FATHERS AND SONS

While we may be alternately proud and troubled by the behavior of our own children, there is a biblical example of the perfect father-son relationship. We know that the father loves the son because he says, "You are my Son, whom I love; with you I am well pleased." (Mark 1:11) Later, the same father says: "This is my Son, whom I love. Listen to him!" (Mark 9:7)

As a student is not above his teacher, so the son never strives to be greater than the father. Instead, he does what the good father asks of him. In his moment of greatest crisis, the son prayerfully humbles himself and submits to the will of his father: "Father, if you are willing, take this cup from me; yet not my will, but yours be done." (Luke 22:42)

This is the picture of perfect love between a loving and worthy father and his loving and obedient son. Of course, it is the picture of God, the Father and his Son, Jesus Christ, but what applies to God and His own Son also applies to each one of us as fathers and sons. This is the new standard, replacing the old norm that had been riddled with sin, conflict and discord: "Hear, O heavens! Listen, O earth! For the Lord has spoken: 'I reared children and brought them up, but they have rebelled against me.'" (Isaiah 1:2)

Your righteousness reaches to the skies, O God, you who have done great things. Who, O God, is like you? Though you have made me see troubles, many and bitter, you will restore my life again; from the depths of the earth you will again bring me up. You will increase my honor and comfort me once again.

—*Psalm 71:19-21*

THE POWER TO RESTORE

There is more than a hint of the resurrection in this verse: "...you will restore my life again; from the depths of the earth you will again bring me up." (v20)

References to the resurrection are not unique in the Old Testament. Job says in a famous passage, "I know that my Redeemer lives, and that in the end he will stand upon the earth. And after my skin has been destroyed, yet in my flesh, I will see God." (Job 19:25-26) Jonah is buried in the sea for three days, but returns and Hosea, the prophet, says, "After two days he will revive us, on the third day he will restore us, that we may live in his presence." (Hosea 6:2).

So Jesus is standing on the solid foundation of Holy Scripture when he says: "...the Son of Man must suffer many things and be rejected by the elders, chief priests and teachers of the law, and that he must be killed and after three days rise again." (Mark 8:31)

It is clear from all of Scripture that God not only has the power to create life; He also has the power to *restore* it.

He who robs his father and drives out his mother is a son who brings shame and disgrace. Stop listening to instruction, my son, and you will stray from the words of knowledge.

—Proverbs 19:26–27

HONOR YOUR FATHER AND MOTHER

Parents know that obedience is a choice that a child may or may not exercise. Also, most of us realize that disobedience is characteristic of behavior that many carry well into adult life.

The command to honor your father and your mother was given to Moses by God, but even while Moses was receiving the Ten Commandments, disobedience reigned among the Jewish people at the base of Mount Sinai. And as the people of Israel would soon learn, choosing to break God's natural law is an invitation to chaos, not peace.

When we disobey, whether as children or as adults, we disrupt the natural order and harmony that flows from it. Hatred and discord replace love and trust and the most intimate familial relationships are torn asunder. When a son dishonors his father and mother, that son is establishing shame and disgrace as the central condition of the relationship with only sorrow and suffering binding together parent and child. We see it everywhere, but the great commandment of love reminds us that disobedience is not from God, but from us.

Do not lie in wait like an outlaw against a righteous man's house, do not raid his dwelling place; for though a righteous man falls seven times, he rises again, but the wicked are brought down by calamity. Do not gloat when your enemy falls; when he stumbles, do not let your heart rejoice, or the LORD will see and disapprove and turn his wrath away from him. Do not fret because of evil men or be envious of the wicked, for the evil man has no future hope, and the lamp of the wicked will be snuffed out.

—Proverbs 24:15-20

THE HOPE OF THE CROSS

Do you believe that "the evil man has no future hope?" (v20) Don't we complain that evil seems to be an overwhelming force in the world and nothing good seems to be found anywhere. This seems to be true not only of our time but of all time. "...for I see violence and strife in the city. Day and night they prowl about on its walls; malice and abuse are within it." (Psalm 55:9-10) "Everyone has turned away, they have become corrupt; there is no one who does good, not even one." (Psalm 53:3) Jesus says to the rich, young ruler, "Why do you call me good?....No one is good-except God alone." (Mark 10:18)

It would seem to be a hopeless situation for evil is pervasive. But wait! Paul tells us that there is hope, real hope, in the person of Jesus Christ "who gave himself for our sins to rescue us from the present evil age, according to the will of our God and Father..." (Galatians 1:3-5) The hope is not in us, for left to our own devices, we cannot help but sin. Our hope lies with the Cross and Jesus Christ who stepped in the path of that which would destroy; he died that we might live.

*To you I call, O LORD my rock; do not turn a deaf ear to me. For if
you remain silent, I will be like those who have gone down to the pit.
Hear my cry for mercy as I call to you for help, as I lift up
my hands toward your Most Holy Place.*

—Psalm 28:1-2

THE RIGHT WORD

A missionary friend from Ukraine told a story that painted a picture
of what the world might look like if God were permanently silent. The
story begins with his encounter with a young woman who was showing
him around the city of Odessa. As they walked from place to place, she
began to open up, and at some point, she told him how ridiculous it
was to believe in God. She said that there was no point to believing in
anything and that she was doing fine without God in her life.

As they were talking, they came to a blighted intersection that was
a ruin left over from the devastation of World War II. The remnant
buildings were fragmented shells. Rubble rather than trees created an
impression of an arid wasteland.

The missionary turned to the woman and gently observed: "Look
around. If you want to know what the world looks like without God,
here it is." She gazed at the wretched scene and pondered silently in her
heart whether her belief in a world without God was sustainable. My
missionary friend believes he touched her with that image of despair. He
did not make his point with words alone. Sometimes, the right word is
an image rather than an argument.

Who knows the power of your anger? For your wrath is as great as the fear that is due you. Teach us to number our days aright, that we may gain a heart of wisdom.

—Psalm 90:11-12

FOLLOW ME

What is "a heart of wisdom?" (v12) It would be impossible to know based solely on these short lines. The link to the rest of the Psalm may be found in the beginning of the sentence: "Teach us to number our days aright…" We are asked to consider our short lives of "seventy years or eighty, if we have the strength" (Psalm 90:10) in the context of eternity. The second verse says this: "Before the mountains were born or you brought forth the earth and the world, from everlasting to everlasting you are God." (Psalm 90:2)

During the short span of our own lives, we might ask the question asked of Jesus: "Good teacher…what must I do to inherit eternal life?" (Mark 10:17) Elsewhere, the Bible tells us that God "set eternity in the hearts of men…" (Ecclesiastes 3:11), so in the face of our obvious mortality, we have a longing for the eternal. Jesus is the bridge between the temporal and the eternal. The heart of wisdom has only one reasonable response when face to face with Jesus. It says, "I will follow you."

When you sit to dine with a ruler, note well what is before you, and put a knife to your throat if you are given to gluttony. Do not crave his delicacies, for that food is deceptive.

—Proverbs 23:1–3

THE COST IS GREATER

Why are the delicacies of the ruler deceptive? This passage does not elaborate on the exact nature of the danger, though common sense might lead us to an appropriate interpretation. Rather another passage in Psalms helps to pinpoint the meaning with great clarity: "Let not my heart be drawn to what is evil, to take part in wicked deeds with men who are evildoers; let me not eat of their delicacies." (Psalm 141:4)

The warning in Proverbs relates to rulers who are evildoers. For we may be tempted to eat at their table because of their position and power, even though there is great danger to anyone who might fall under their control. We all are warned: the temptation to eat the delicacies at such a table are great, but the cost could be much greater.

With persuasive words she led him astray; she seduced him with her smooth talk. All at once he followed her like an ox going to the slaughter, like a deer stepping into a noose till an arrow pierces his liver, like a bird darting into a snare, little knowing it will cost him his life.

—Proverbs 7:21-23

FORBIDDEN FRUIT

The forbidden seems to have a gravitational pull on our hearts and minds. It is as if we find that when we thirst, we choose the polluted rather than the pure well to satisfy that thirst. We try the patience of a loving God in our foolish pursuit of self–indulgence and lawlessness: "'Why should I forgive you? Your children have forsaken me and sworn by gods that are not gods. I supplied all their needs, yet they committed adultery and thronged to the house of prostitutes. They are well-fed, lusty stallions, each neighing for another man's wife. Should I not punish them for this?' declares the Lord." (Jeremiah 5:7-9)

Hear, O LORD, my righteous plea; listen to my cry. Give ear to my prayer— it does not rise from deceitful lips. May my vindication come from you; may your eyes see what is right. Though you probe my heart and examine me at night, though you test me, you will find nothing; I have resolved that my mouth will not sin.

—Psalm 17:1–3

POWERFUL AND EFFECTIVE

This prayer is not a plea, but a "righteous" plea. His lips are not "deceitful;" if the Lord probes to the very depths of his heart, he will find nothing detestable there.

This is the point: when we pray, we must come to God with a sincere heart; to be half-hearted or detached means that we are truly not willing to reach out to God. James says, "Therefore confess your sins to each other and pray to each other so that you may be healed. The prayer of a righteous man is powerful and effective." (James 5:16)

The fruit of the righteous is a tree of life, and he who wins souls is wise. If the righteous receive their due on earth, how much more the ungodly and the sinner!

—Proverbs 11:30-31

RESTORATION

The tree of life appears in several places in the Book of Proverbs, but it did not originate there. It can be found at the very beginning of the Bible in Genesis and at the very end in Revelation.

In Genesis, almost everyone remembers the tree of knowledge of good and evil. God commanded Adam not to eat of its fruit, "for when you eat of it you will surely die." (Genesis 2:17) And we remember what happens. Adam and Eve are deceived into tasting the forbidden fruit of that tree which leads to the penalty of death. But what of that other tree, the tree of life? If Adam and Eve must suffer death, then they cannot have access to the tree of life. "'The man has now become like one of us, knowing good and evil. He must not be allowed to reach out his hand and take also from the tree of life and eat, and live forever.' So God banished them from the Garden of Eden...." (Genesis 3:22-23)

The sin of pride leads to rebellion, which leads to separation from eternal life. One could sum up the rest of the story of mankind by saying it is a story of finding our way back to the tree of life with God's help. "Therefore, just as sin entered the world through one man, and death through sin, and in this way death came to all men, because all sinned... But the gift is not like the trespass. For if the many died by the trespass of the one man, how much more did God's grace and the gift that came by the grace of the one man, Jesus Christ, overflow to the many!" (Romans 5:12-15)

If you make the Most High your dwelling — even the LORD, who is my refuge — then no harm will befall you, no disaster will come near your tent. For he will command his angels concerning you to guard you in all your ways; they will lift you up in their hands, so that you will not strike your foot against a stone. You will tread upon the lion and the cobra; you will trample the great lion and the serpent.

—Psalm 91:9–13

THE FULL ARMOR OF GOD

Satan is a liar by nature, but often he wraps a lie in a package that resembles the truth. In the 4th chapter of the Gospel of Luke, Satan tempts Jesus with a variation from Psalm 91. In the Psalm it says, "If you make the Most High your dwelling," but Satan says, "If you are the Son of God...throw yourself down from here." In other words, Satan says, if you do as I ask, not as God asks, then angels will guard you in all your ways.

But this is not true. And Jesus simply replies, as we should, "Do not put the Lord your God to the test." Jesus quotes Scripture in reply to the challenge, but he quotes Scripture as God intended it to be used. Satan on the other hand uses Scripture to confuse and deceive, thereby keeping us enslaved in his web of lies. One defense against Satan's offensive use of Scripture is to know the Bible well. That is what Paul means when he advises Christians to put on "the full armor of God." (Ephesians 6:10)

What does man gain from all his labor at which he toils under the sun? Generations come and generations go, but the earth remains forever. The sun rises and the sun sets, and hurries back to where it rises. The wind blows to the south and turns to the north; round and round it goes, ever returning on its course. All streams flow into the sea, yet the sea is never full. To the place the streams come from, there they return again. All things are wearisome, more than one can say. The eye never has enough of seeing, nor the ear its fill of hearing. What has been will be again, what has been done will be done again; there is nothing new under the sun. Is there anything of which one can say, "Look! This is something new"? It was here already, long ago; it was here before our time. There is no remembrance of men of old, and even those who are yet to come will not be remembered by those who follow.

—Ecclesiastes 1:3–11

A HANDFUL OF DUST

It is a truism that "Generations come and generations go." (v4) And all can see that "The sun rises and the sun sets, and hurries back to where it rises."

Solomon provides a vision devoid of hope and passion. He seems to be saying that life is purposeless and futile and in the end, everything we strive to create will disintegrate into a handful of dust. But is Solomon expressing a universal truth or is he merely voicing the sad reality of his own excesses? "The eye never has enough of seeing, nor the ear its fill of hearing," (v8) he says.

In old age, Solomon's life had declined into sinful indulgence; the futility he expresses reveals that it is nearly impossible ever to quench the lusts of the sinful nature once it has gained a foothold. When men live under the burden of sin, nothing good seems possible. When that heavy load is lifted, (and it *can* be lifted) then what once seemed impossible becomes probable.

"It's no good, it's no good!" says the buyer; then off he goes and boasts about his purchase.

— Proverbs 20:14

GOD'S UNDIVIDED ATTENTION

The mundane matters of daily life would appear to be beneath the Bible; after all, isn't the Bible about God and higher spiritual concerns?

Of course it is, but it is also about you and me; it is about our generation and all the countless generations that have come before us. It is about our highest aspirations and our lowest desires; it is about feeding and being fed; it is about wanderers and wayfarers; and it is about those who seek God in the city and those who seek to flee from Him at any cost. The study of man cannot be man alone; it must encompass man in all his complexity in relationship to the One who created him. No aspect of man is beneath God's notice, not even getting and spending. "What is man that you make so much of him, that you give him so much attention, that you examine him every morning and test him every moment?" (Job 7:17-18) Even lowly buyers and sellers have God's undivided attention.

Do not fret because of evil men or be envious of those who do wrong; for like the grass they will soon wither, like green plants they will soon die away. Trust in the LORD and do good; dwell in the land and enjoy safe pasture. Delight yourself in the LORD and he will give you the desires of your heart.

—Psalm 37:1–4

SEEK FIRST HIS RIGHTEOUSNESS

Can you hear the voice of Jesus in this Psalm of David's? Both David and Jesus speak of our inclination to worry about things we cannot control, as well as things that are insignificant: "And why do you worry about clothes? See how the lilies of the field grow. They do not labor or spin. Yet I tell you that not even Solomon in all his splendor was dressed like one of these. If that is how God clothes the grass of the field, which is here today and tomorrow is thrown into the fire, will he not much more clothe you, O you of little faith? So do not worry, saying, 'What shall we eat?' or 'What shall we drink?' or 'What shall we wear?' ...But seek first his kingdom and his righteousness, and all these things will be given to you as well." (Matthew 6:18-33)

Save me, O God, for the waters have come up to my neck. I sink in the miry depths, where there is no foothold. I have come into the deep waters; the floods engulf me. I am worn out calling for help; my throat is parched. My eyes fail, looking for my God. Those who hate me without reason outnumber the hairs of my head; many are my enemies without cause, those who seek to destroy me. I am forced to restore what I did not steal. You know my folly, O God; my guilt is not hidden from you.

—*Psalm 69:1–5*

NO GREATER LOVE

The movie *The Passion of the Christ* opens in the depth of night. A full moon hangs ominously in the sky, creating a supernatural light of dark blue streaked with silver. The place is the garden of Gethsemane and Jesus is the man fervently praying. Quietly, a shadowy figure emerges from the background looking on with a cool curiosity. Jesus has already begun to suffer and some of his words are preserved in the four gospels, but many words are not recorded and so we can only imagine what Jesus was saying.

The words of this Psalm, beginning with "Save me, O God," could easily reflect the words that Jesus uttered alone in that garden: "I am worn out calling for help…Those who hate me without reason outnumber the hairs of my head…My eyes fail."

Jesus knows what is in store for him; he knows why he came to earth and he knows that the shadowy figure wants him to give in to temptation by escaping from what is about to happen. Satan would appeal to Jesus' human nature, but as the gospels show, Jesus' God nature prevails out of love. Before he is betrayed into the hands of the religious leaders, Jesus says "As the Father had loved me, so have I loved you…My command is this; Love each other as I have loved you. Greater love has no one than this, that he lay down his life for his friends. You are my friends." (John 15:9-14)

Let us examine our ways and test them, and let us return to the LORD. Let us lift up our hearts and our hands to God in heaven, and say: "We have sinned and rebelled and you have not forgiven. "You have covered yourself with anger and pursued us; you have slain without pity. You have covered yourself with a cloud so that no prayer can get through. You have made us scum and refuse among the nations.

—Lamentations 3:40–45

AFTER THE REBELLION

Lamentations was written by the prophet Jeremiah. It is not considered a wisdom book, but it is important because it expresses sadness and horror at the consequences that befall those who have abandoned God for idols and other forms of false worship.

By the time Jeremiah wrote Lamentations, Jerusalem had been attacked, the temple had been destroyed and the people had been taken captive and led into exile. Before any of this had happened, Jeremiah warned the people of Jerusalem of the pending disaster brought on by their own drift into sinfulness, but the people turned against him; he was attacked and almost killed. He had become salt in the wound of the people by predicting the coming invasion, war, exile and death: "The Lord said to me, 'from the north disaster will be poured out on all who live in the land....I will pronounce my judgments on my people because of their wickedness in forsaking me, in burning incense to other gods and in worshiping what their hands have made.'" (Jeremiah 1:14, 16)

In the course of my life he broke my strength; he cut short my days. So I said: "Do not take me away, O my God, in the midst of my days; your years go on through all generations. In the beginning you laid the foundations of the earth, and the heavens are the work of your hands. They will perish, but you remain; they will all wear out like a garment. Like clothing you will change them and they will be discarded. But you remain the same, and your years will never end. The children of your servants will live in your presence; their descendants will be established before you.

—*Psalm 102:23–28*

HE WILL REMAIN

In the middle of our busy lives, with little irritations commanding our complete attention, it is hard to imagine that one day it will all be gone; no worries, no problems and little or no evidence of all the sound and fury that once was center stage. The whole world will perish; the earth, the moon, the stars, everything we consider permanent—all will vanish except God; He will remain, for "... your years will never end."

The Lord says this: "Lift up your eyes to the heavens, look at the earth beneath; the heavens will vanish like smoke, the earth will wear out like a garment and its inhabitants die like flies. But my salvation will last forever, and my righteousness will never fail." (Isaiah 51:6)

Blessed is he whose transgressions are forgiven, whose sins are covered. Blessed is the man whose sin the LORD does not count against him and in whose spirit is no deceit. When I kept silent, my bones wasted away through my groaning all day long. For day and night your hand was heavy upon me; my strength was sapped as in the heat of summer. Then I acknowledged my sin to you and did not cover up my iniquity. I said, "I will confess my transgressions to the LORD"— and you forgave the guilt of my sin.

—Psalm 32:1–5

A HEAVY BURDEN

Sin is a spiritual affliction that is powerful enough to bring on physical pain and suffering. "When I kept silent, my bones wasted away...."

When a paralytic is lowered on a mat through a roof, Jesus does not play the ordinary doctor by checking the physical source of the disease; rather he simply says, "Son, your sin is forgiven." (Mark 2:5) We know little more about this man than that Jesus' diagnosis was right on target, for the man got up and walked.

Are we like a paralyzed man on a mat, debilitated by unconfessed sin? Are we carrying around a burden that we cannot possibly bear alone? The psalmist tells us exactly what we must do to become well: "Then I acknowledged my sin to you and did not cover up my iniquity...and you forgave the guilt of my sin."

The truth is "all have sinned and fallen short of the glory of God" (Romans 3:23), but it is just as true that many of us deceive ourselves by claiming we have *not* sinned and, consequently, the symptoms of our afflictions cannot be treated. We do not overcome the paralysis; we cannot pick up our mats and walk.

He makes springs pour water into the ravines; it flows between the mountains. They give water to all the beasts of the field; the wild donkeys quench their thirst. The birds of the air nest by the waters; they sing among the branches. He waters the mountains from his upper chambers; the earth is satisfied by the fruit of his work.

—Psalm 104:10-13

THE PRIZE

In the spring of every year, hundreds, if not thousands, of enthusiastic hikers take their first steps on a 2,185 mile journey on the Appalachian Trail. Months of preparation have led to this moment. They have read books, bought equipment, packed food and talked to others who have come before them. They have diligently studied every aspect of the journey to come, and now they stand under the stone portal as they prepare to ascend Springer Mountain, the true starting point of the trail.

Yet no amount of study can prepare them for what lies ahead. Nature is beautiful and alluring and very hard. There will be sore knees, turned ankles, persistent thirst, lonely nights and lingering doubt. They will become exhausted from the searing summer heat in Pennsylvania, sudden lightning strikes in Virginia, downpours in New Hampshire, snow in the Smokey Mountains, or mud in Maine, and from unexpected obstacles of all kinds everywhere.

But, as they walk the trail and become hardened by its challenges, hikers will experience a change of heart and mind. With time and miles, a veteran slowly emerges; the novice at Springer becomes the confident and knowledgeable Thru-Hiker who will keep on striving to achieve victory over every large and small adversity. The postcard landscape of the armchair hiker has given way to a more profound understanding. What began as toil and trouble has become something akin to joy.

The seasoned hiker overcomes through endurance and perseverance. In this respect, he is like the faithful pilgrim. Both are on a long journey; both must endure hardships; both are tested at every turn. And both keep pushing on to the goal, knowing that there is a prize to be won: "Forgetting what is behind and straining toward what is ahead, I press on toward the goal to win the prize for which God has called me heavenward in Christ Jesus." (Philippians 3:13-14)

He reached down from on high and took hold of me; he drew me out of deep waters. He rescued me from my powerful enemy, from my foes, who were too strong for me. They confronted me in the day of my disaster, but the LORD was my support. He brought me out into a spacious place; he rescued me because he delighted in me.

—*Psalm 18:16–19*

SALVATION COMES FROM THE LORD

David, the anointed one of God, is under enormous pressure. He is being hunted down by King Saul, who is consumed by jealous rage at David's growing success and fame. David cries out, "The cords of death entangled me; the torrents of destruction overwhelmed me." (Psalm 18: 4)

In his desperation, he turns to the Lord: "In my distress I called to the Lord; I cried out to my God for help." And the Lord heard and delivered him: "From his temple he heard my voice; my cry came before him into his ears." (v6) Jonah, who flees from the call of the Lord and goes down to the depth of the sea before he is restored, utters a spiritual truth that should resonate in every man's heart: "Salvation comes from the Lord." (Jonah 2:9)

Without the Lord, there is no salvation, and no hope. Salvation, indeed, does come from the Lord.

I will exalt you, O LORD, for you lifted me out of the depths and did not let my enemies gloat over me. O LORD my God, I called to you for help and you healed me. O LORD, you brought me up from the grave; you spared me from going down into the pit.

—*Psalm 30:1–3*

A DANGEROUS FANTASY

David was blessed with many gifts, but he still faced countless trials throughout his long life. Yet, while his circumstances may have varied wildly, David seldom wavered in his absolute allegiance to his Lord and his Creator. At various times in his Psalms, David calls the Lord his rock, his strong tower, his fortress, his refuge and his salvation. No wonder David begins this Psalm with "I will exalt you, O Lord." David knows that God is his strength and the protector of his soul.

By contrast, today it seems normal to heap praise on our own strengths and talents. Or we seek the praise from others as if our good moments deserve praise comparable to the self-adulation lavished on our cultural icons. But from David's point of view, self-praise is nothing more than seeing things through the wrong end of the lens. God is great, strong and powerful. We are not; our only strength can come through acknowledging God in every aspect of our lives. To see it otherwise, according to Scripture, is to indulge in a fearful and dangerous fantasy.

They return at evening, snarling like dogs, and prowl about the city. They wander about for food and howl if not satisfied. But I will sing of your strength, in the morning I will sing of your love; for you are my fortress, my refuge in times of trouble. O my Strength, I sing praise to you; you, O God, are my fortress, my loving God.

—Psalm 59:14–17

THE ENEMY IS AT THE GATES

The city is under attack. The enemy is swarming at the gates and all may be lost. This passage can certainly be read as historical fact, but with David there is often a spiritual analogy to be gleaned. For every one of us, both then and now, is under assault with the enemy trying with all of his power and craftiness to gain a foothold in the citadel of the human heart.

God warns us of the threat, but just as often as we hear it, we turn away, letting our guard down. He tells Cain, for example, that "sin is crouching at the door; it desires to have you...." (Genesis 4:7) Peter says the same thing: "Your enemy the devil prowls around like a roaring lion looking for someone to devour." (1 Peter 5:8) The wars and battles of the Old Testament are historical, but we should also see the spiritual back story behind the experiences in this life. "For our struggle is not against flesh and blood, but against the rulers, against the authorities, against the powers of this dark world and against the spiritual forces of evil in the heavenly realms." (Ephesians 6:12) To disregard the reality of spiritual warfare is to open the gates of our heart to the enemy who desires to destroy us.

There are those who rebel against the light, who do not know its ways or stay in its paths. When daylight is gone, the murderer rises up and kills the poor and needy; in the night he steals forth like a thief. The eye of the adulterer watches for dusk; he thinks, 'No eye will see me,' and he keeps his face concealed. In the dark, men break into houses, but by day they shut themselves in; they want nothing to do with the light. For all of them, deep darkness is their morning; they make friends with the terrors of darkness.

—Job 24:13–17

IN THE SHADOWS

We seem to have a perverse compulsion to dwell in darkness even when we could just as easily move into the light. Why is this?

Here is the biblical diagnosis: "This is the verdict. Light has come into the world, but men loved darkness instead of light because their deeds were evil." (John 3:19-20) It began in the original garden when the man and woman disobeyed God's simple command: "But you must not eat from the tree of the knowledge of good and evil, for when you eat of it you will surely die." (Genesis 2:17)

From there the infection of knowledge of evil spread like a plague corrupting mankind almost beyond recognition, casting us in the role of "rebel(s) against the light." (v13) As a result, "All have turned aside, they have together become corrupt; there is no one who does good, not even one." (Psalm 14:3) Jesus, who tells us that he has come to heal sinners, says, "For from within, out of men's hearts, come evil thoughts..." (Mark 7:21) and so, "in the night (we) steal forth like a thief...and (we) make friends with the terrors of darkness."(v17)

If we choose to live without God, then we have chosen to live under the tyranny of our sinful nature.

Blessed are all who fear the LORD, who walk in his ways. You will eat the fruit of your labor; blessings and prosperity will be yours. Your wife will be like a fruitful vine within your house; your sons will be like olive shoots around your table. Thus is the man blessed who fears the LORD.

—Psalm 128:1–4

ETERNAL VALUE

Some believe they are blessed when they are prosperous; others believe that their prosperity is an outward sign of their inward goodness. But the Bible links blessings and prosperity only incidentally. The opening line of this verse has it just right: "Blessed are all those who fear the Lord." In other words, you are blessed by your right relationship to the Lord; little counts beside that because God's blessings confer life with him, even when the whole world is lined up against you.

Jesus says in the Sermon on the Mount: "Blessed are those who are persecuted because of righteousness for theirs is the kingdom of heaven," and "Blessed are you when people insult you, persecute you and falsely say all kinds of evil against you because of me." (Matthew 5:10-11) God's blessings can come at a great cost, but they are always of eternal value.

The sayings of King Lemuel— an oracle his mother taught him: "O my son, O son of my womb, O son of my vows, do not spend your strength on women, your vigor on those who ruin kings. It is not for kings, O Lemuel— not for kings to drink wine, not for rulers to crave beer, lest they drink and forget what the law decrees, and deprive all the oppressed of their rights. Give beer to those who are perishing, wine to those who are in anguish; let them drink and forget their poverty and remember their misery no more."

—Proverbs 31:1–7

SAMSON

Samson is an Old Testament superhero apparently brought low by a fatal flaw. He is mighty in power, vanquishing entire armies, terrifying the enemies of Israel, but his weakness for women saps him of his supernatural strength and he is led away in defeat and humiliation. Or so goes the conventional reading of the story.

On another level, we might reduce the tale of Samson to a morality play where the son, gifted with great strength, fails to cleave to the admonition not to "spend your strength on women, your vigor on those who ruin kings." (v3)

But this version neglects the role that God plays in the story, for the actual account of Samson begins with the visitation of an angel to his barren and aging mother before he is born. The angel tells her that she will give birth to a son who will "be a Nazirite, set apart to God from birth, and he will begin the deliverance of Israel from the hands of the Philistines." (Judges 13:5) The story progresses along expected lines until an act of folly delivers Samson into the hands of his enemies. He is bound, blinded, tortured and humiliated, but then, unexpectedly, he returns and triumphs through a redeeming act that brings about his own death.

The annunciation, the miraculous birth, the great triumphs, the capture, torture, death and final victory foreshadow a pattern God will use at a later time. But whereas Samson's mission is to "begin" to deliver Israel, Jesus will complete God's purpose by liberating not only Israel, but *all* peoples from their bondage of sin. The story of Samson is wonderful, but it is more wonderful when read in light of the birth, life, death and resurrection of Jesus Christ.

There are those who curse their fathers and do not bless their mothers;
those who are pure in their own eyes and yet are not cleansed of
their filth; those whose eyes are ever so haughty, whose glances are so
disdainful; those whose teeth are swords and whose jaws are set with
knives to devour the poor from the earth, the needy from among
mankind.

—Proverbs 30:11–14

SOMETHING OUT THERE

The modern thinker likes to think of evil as something beyond oneself or one's immediate circle of friends. Instead of looking inward, we are more likely to identify some distant group or nation as embodying everything that is evil in this world. And we are just as likely to ascribe naturalistic causes or reasons for the existence of evil.

It is uncomfortable to think of evil as so close that it could be inside rather than outside of oneself. Who wants to think of themselves as being capable of being evil or doing wrong? Even the symbol of all evil in the modern world, Adolph Hitler, undoubtedly believed that he himself was right in his quest to conquer his enemies. He would never have admitted that he was the instrument of unthinkable evil. After all, who willingly recognizes that they are susceptible to inclinations of the heart that can lead them to terrible places?

Here Solomon says that people can curse their fathers and do not bless their mothers and still they remain pure in their own eyes; yet he also says they are "not cleansed of their filth." (v11) When it comes to determining our own purity, are we to be trusted? Or are we blind to the nature of what might lurk within our own hearts? And how do we think God is judging us? Would God agree that we are "really good people"?

We need to be wise in our humility when it comes to pointing our fingers at others.

I denied myself nothing my eyes desired; I refused my heart no pleasure. My heart took delight in all my work, and this was the reward for all my labor. Yet when I surveyed all that my hands had done and what I had toiled to achieve, everything was meaningless, a chasing after the wind; nothing was gained under the sun.

—*Ecclesiastes 2:10–11*

HOW SHOULD WE LIVE?

Solomon, who wrote Ecclesiastes, had access to every material advantage known to man. He ruled over a powerful kingdom and he denied himself nothing his eyes desired; however, even with everything in the world in his possession, it added up to nothing in the end. He felt a hunger for something more, something greater, and nothing in this world, absolutely nothing, could satisfy that persistent and lingering hunger and thirst.

What was true for Solomon is true for every one of us. Instead of being surprised by Solomon's conclusion that "everything was meaningless," we need to step back and see what it is we are actually doing. Do we have eternity in mind as we maneuver through our daily lives or are we allowing "the worries of this life, the deceitfulness of wealth and the desires for other things" (Mark 4:19) to deflect us from God's purposes? It is worth thinking about.

Blessed is he who has regard for the weak; the LORD delivers him in times of trouble. The LORD will protect him and preserve his life; he will bless him in the land and not surrender him to the desire of his foes. The LORD will sustain him on his sickbed and restore him from his bed of illness.

—Psalm 41:1–3

THE REWARD IN HEAVEN IS GREAT

In his teaching, Jesus expands on David's description of the blessed among us. The poor in spirit are blessed, as are those who mourn. The meek are blessed and so are those who hunger and thirst for righteousness. The merciful, the pure in heart, the peacemakers, all are blessed. Then Jesus tells us that being blessed also means we may be opposed by established forces in this world who may persecute us because of righteousness. More specifically, they may persecute us because we have given our lives over to Jesus Christ. So "rejoice and be glad because great is your reward in heaven...." (Matthew 5:12)

The reward for righteousness may not what we anticipated for this life, but great is the reward in heaven for those who love and follow the Lord.

An oracle is within my heart concerning the sinfulness of the wicked: There is no fear of God before his eyes. For in his own eyes he flatters himself too much to detect or hate his sin.

—*Psalm 36:1–2*

FROM HEAVENLY TO HELLISH

When evil impulses are incubating deep within the heart, it is often hard for us, as well as others, to detect it. The psalmist says we flatter ourselves and become experts at self-justification. And as we become consumed by the evil desires within, outwardly we engage in lies and deceit. The progress of wickedness is often slow and plodding at first, but with time, it consumes the whole person, toppling the entire edifice.

C.S. Lewis said, "...every time you make a choice you are turning the central part of you, the part that chooses, into something a little different from what it was before. And taking your life as a whole, with all your innumerable choices, all your life long you are slowly turning this central thing either into a heavenly creature or into a hellish creature...."[3]

Why is life given to a man whose way is hidden, whom God has hedged in? For sighing comes to me instead of food; my groans pour out like water. What I feared has come upon me; what I dreaded has happened to me.

—*Job 3:23–25*

A TREASURED COMPANION

When Job says, "What I feared has come upon me," he is speaking to each one of us.

How common it is to grow up with all sorts of fears, some of which dissipate with time, while others carry on into adult life. It was only after my own fear of failure actually became reality that I was able to break down the paralyzing barrier of fear-driven inertia and take action against the forces that were crushing me. And by acting, I was able to begin to rebuild a life that had come to the edge of hopelessness.

It was in the middle of this crisis that a Bible came into my possession. From that time on, it has become a treasured daily companion. It has been the guiding light that has enabled me to walk in faith rather than fear.

Starting a quarrel is like breaching a dam; so drop the matter before a dispute breaks out. He who loves a quarrel loves sin; he who builds a high gate invites destruction.

—Proverbs 17:14

GENTLY INSTRUCT

We are not called by God to enter into endless controversies and arguments; rather, we are called to demonstrate the power of the Holy Spirit, not through words alone, but through our lives.

Here is Paul speaking to the young church in Corinth: "I came to you in weakness and fear, and with much trembling. My message and my preaching were not with wise and persuasive words, but with a demonstration of the Spirit's power, so that your faith might not rest on men's wisdom, but on God's power." (1 Corinthians 2:3-5)

If we believe that religion is an institution founded by men for men, then our preaching can be nothing more than quarrels dressed up as high-sounding truth. We lose the power to change lives and only serve the purpose of preserving particular traditions. It is good to remember that God is not impressed with our intelligence, knowledge or earthly accomplishments.

Rather, He wants us to open our hearts to His Holy Spirit so that we can share it with those who have not heard the truth. Paul instructs Timothy in the way of God's servant: "Don't have anything to do with foolish and stupid arguments, because you know they produce quarrels. And the Lord's servant must not quarrel; instead, he must be kind to everyone, able to teach, not resentful. Those who oppose him he must gently instruct, in the hope that God will grant them repentance leading them to knowledge of the truth, and that they will come to their senses and escape from the trap of the devil, who has taken them captive to do his will." (2 Timothy 2:23-26)

Do not eat the food of a stingy man, do not crave his delicacies; for he is the kind of man who is always thinking about the cost. "Eat and drink," he says to you, but his heart is not with you. You will vomit up the little you have eaten and will have wasted your compliments.

—Proverbs 23:6–8

CONSIDER THE SOURCE

People often offer us things; they may seem to be very generous and helpful and they may seem to care about our every need, but can we discern what is motivating them?

Here the act of generosity and hospitality is contradicted by a stingy and possessive heart. The man gives reluctantly and bitterly and will later demand a very high price for what he originally gave. Consider the source; know whom it is that gives, because if you receive a gift that is given for reasons other than love, you may learn to your surprise and regret that the cost is extremely dear.

I remember my affliction and my wandering, the bitterness and the gall. I well remember them, and my soul is downcast within me. Yet this I call to mind and therefore I have hope: Because of the LORD'S great love we are not consumed, for his compassions never fail. They are new every morning; great is your faithfulness. I say to myself, "The LORD is my portion; therefore I will wait for him."

—Lamentations 3:19–24

HIS COMPASSIONS NEVER FAIL

Pity anyone who experiences affliction and bitterness but chooses not to call on God. What hope do they have? What would be the reason for wanting to live another day?

We have learned from Job that even the righteous suffer and we know that Jesus was the suffering servant who was the object of hatred without reason. (John 15:25) But God suffers along with us when we suffer on behalf of Him. He will lift up the downcast soul and give comfort to those in need. Indeed, His compassions never fail those who believe: "...through glory and dishonor, bad report and good report; genuine yet regarded as impostors; known, yet regarded as unknown; dying yet we live on; beaten, and yet not killed; sorrowful, yet making many rich; having nothing, and yet possessing everything." (2 Corinthians 6:8-10)

Indeed, these are the words of the man of faith. Nothing in this world can turn the righteous man away from God.

Your throne, O God, will last for ever and ever; a scepter of justice will be the scepter of your kingdom. You love righteousness and hate wickedness; therefore God, your God, has set you above your companions by anointing you with the oil of joy.

—Psalm 45:6–7

A PROMISE KEPT

The promise began with Abraham: "...through your offspring all nations on earth will be blessed, because you have obeyed me." (Genesis 22:18) It carries through his son Isaac and to Isaac's son, Jacob, to whom God repeats the promise: "Your descendants will be like the dust of the earth, and you will spread out to the west and to the east, to the north and to the south. All peoples on the earth will be blessed through you and your offspring." (Genesis 28:14) To Moses God promises: "...you will be for me a kingdom of priests and a holy nation." (Exodus 19:6)

Finally, God says to David, "When your days are over and you rest with your fathers, I will raise up your offspring to succeed you, who will come from your own body, and I will establish his kingdom...and I will establish the throne of his kingdom forever." (2 Samuel 7:12-13) All of these promises culminate in the person of Jesus Christ, KING OF KINGS AND LORD OF LORDS (Revelation 19:16) of "the house and line of David." (Luke 2:4)

You are God my stronghold. Why have you rejected me? Why must I go about mourning, oppressed by the enemy? Send forth your light and your truth, let them guide me; let them bring me to your holy mountain, to the place where you dwell. Then will I go to the altar of God, to God, my joy and my delight. I will praise you with the harp, O God, my God. Why are you downcast, O my soul? Why so disturbed within me? Put your hope in God, for I will yet praise him, my Savior and my God.

—*Psalm 43:2–5*

I WILL NEVER DISOWN YOU

It is tempting in times of trouble to cry out against God, saying "Why have you abandoned me?" Sometimes the circumstances seem so dire and frightening that it appears as if we have been cast away.

But David is a model of how we should handle adversity because he remains faithful to God under the worst conditions. He does not turn against God; quite the contrary, he calls out for help and guidance: "Send forth your light and your truth, let them guide me...." (v3)

David's distress is not caused by God but by "deceitful and wicked men." (v1) David's faithfulness might be contrasted to the more common response to adversity seen in Peter and the disciples when Jesus is betrayed and arrested in the Garden of Gethsemane. Right before that hour, Peter said, "Even if I have to die with you, I will never disown you." (Mark 14:31) Shortly after saying this, "everyone deserted him and fled." (Mark 14:50)

When we feel most abandoned and in great peril, we must remain steadfast, putting our hope in God, saying "...I will yet praise him, my Savior and my God." (v5)

My son, do not forget my teaching, but keep my commands in your heart, for they will prolong your life many years and bring you prosperity. Let love and faithfulness never leave you; bind them around your neck, write them on the tablet of your heart. Then you will win favor and a good name in the sight of God and man.

—Proverbs 3:1–4

A MASQUERADE

When the father says to his son to "bind love and faithfulness around your neck," he is making a reference that lends power to his words. This reference was known by every child of Israel because he was required to memorize the most important commandment found in Scripture: "Hear, O Israel: The Lord our God, the Lord is one. Love the Lord your God with all your heart and with all your soul and with all your strength." Then the boy would be told to "tie them as symbols on your hands and bind them on your foreheads." (Deuteronomy 6:4, 8)

The love and faithfulness referred to by the father is not some vague generalization; it is the love of the commandment. Our love must be for the Lord before anything else. Love that exists apart from a love of God is a mere shadow of authentic love, a masquerade. Authentic love begins with our relationship with God and then filters through our relationship with family, friends and neighbors. When love focuses only on self, it is but a counterfeit of the original thing.

Listen to this, Job; stop and consider God's wonders. Tell us what we should say to him; we cannot draw up our case because of our darkness. Should he be told that I want to speak? Would any man ask to be swallowed up? Now no one can look at the sun, bright as it is in the skies after the wind has swept them clean. Out of the north he comes in golden splendor; God comes in awesome majesty. The Almighty is beyond our reach and exalted in power; in his justice and great righteousness, he does not oppress. Therefore, men revere him, for does he not have regard for all the wise in heart?

—Job 37:14,19-24

BARRIER BUILDERS

Even though God comes in "awesome majesty" and "golden splendor," He still has regard for all of us and especially the wise in heart. God seeks us out one by one, but we often respond by putting up our own barriers in order to hide behind them. We often hear how men long for a relationship with God, but the opposite is just as true; we are barrier builders. We either magnify ourselves through pride or we miniaturize ourselves by saying that God is way too big and important to care about us. Either way, God is saying, "Tear down that wall; tear down the barrier you have built between us." God is calling out to each one of us. Are we listening? Can we hear?

But I am a worm and not a man, scorned by men and despised by the people. All who see me mock me; they hurl insults, shaking their heads: "He trusts in the LORD; let the LORD rescue him. Let him deliver him, since he delights in him."

—Psalm 22:6–8

ONE FOR ALL

How one responds to the crucifixion of Jesus depends very much on how the gospels are read. If Jesus is looked at as only a mere man caught up in the religious and political turmoil of the time, then it will be hard to fathom the purpose behind the terrible suffering.

To many, the punishment of Christ is R-rated violence, which appears to be gratuitous and meaningless. However, if one believes that Jesus is the Son of God, who came to take away the sin of the world, then the punishment exacted on him shows how grave one's situation really is.

The passion of Christ is not a story of mortals; this is the story of spiritual warfare at its highest pitch. The suffering of Jesus was not only foreshadowed by the description of crucifixion in Psalm 22, but also by Isaiah who spoke of the suffering servant who was "pierced for our transgressions…crushed for our iniquities…." (Isaiah 53:5) He died so that we might live. He died a perfect sacrifice, one for all that all might once again experience a relationship of love with God.

We are consumed by your anger and terrified by your indignation. You have set our iniquities before you, our secret sins in the light of your presence. All our days pass away under your wrath; we finish our years with a moan. The length of our days is seventy years— or eighty, if we have the strength; yet their span is but trouble and sorrow, for they quickly pass, and we fly away.

—Psalm 90:7–10

THE GOSSAMER MOMENT

It is startling to read that "the length of our days is seventy years or eighty if we have the strength," because it is humbling to realize how little life's basic facts have changed over the course of time. This verse was written one thousand years before Christ and yet the average life span is the same today.

Every day, we are propelled forward with greater momentum and we say with the psalmist that our years "pass quickly away." We are no longer impatient schoolchildren looking at the slow-paced clock ticking away each minute. Now we do everything in our power to slow it down, digging in our heels, trying in vain to capture and hold the gossamer moment. Time does fly away, but we often come to realize this when we can only regret the loss.

Does not wisdom call out? Does not understanding raise her voice? On the heights along the way, where the paths meet, she takes her stand; beside the gates leading into the city, at the entrances, she cries aloud: "To you, O men, I call out; I raise my voice to all mankind. You who are simple, gain prudence; you who are foolish, gain understanding. Listen, for I have worthy things to say; I open my lips to speak what is right. My mouth speaks what is true, for my lips detest wickedness. All the words of my mouth are just; none of them is crooked or perverse. To the discerning all of them are right; they are faultless to those who have knowledge. Choose my instruction instead of silver, knowledge rather than choice gold, for wisdom is more precious than rubies, and nothing you desire can compare with her. "I, wisdom, dwell together with prudence; I possess knowledge and discretion. To fear the LORD is to hate evil; I hate pride and arrogance, evil behavior and perverse speech."

—Proverbs 8:1–13

GOD NEVER FAILS

According to Scripture, wisdom and love come from the same source. Love "does not envy, it does not boast, it is not proud. It is not rude, it is not self-seeking, it is not easily angered, it keeps no record of wrongs. Love does not delight in evil, but rejoices with the truth." (1 Corinthians 13:4-6)

Likewise, wisdom declares that "to fear the Lord is to hate evil; I (wisdom) hate pride and arrogance, evil behavior and perverse speech." Genuine wisdom for man is to love God and hate everything that stands in the way of our relationship with Him. Wisdom calls us to see with the eyes of our heart that God and love for his children are one and the same: God is patient, God is kind...He always protects, always trusts, always hopes, always perseveres. God never fails.

To believe this makes all the difference. To believe this is the beginning of wisdom.

Let the assembled peoples gather around you. Rule over them from on high; let the LORD judge the peoples. Judge me, O LORD, according to my righteousness, according to my integrity, O Most High. O righteous God, who searches minds and hearts, bring to an end the violence of the wicked and make the righteous secure.

—Psalm 7:7–9

WHEN THE UNGODLY ARE IN COMMAND

This prayer ends with a plea to God to "bring an end to the violence of the wicked and make the righteous secure." But what would the world look like if the righteousness of God were absent altogether?

Thomas à Kempis, writing on the passion of the Christ, paints a bleak picture: "To what lengths is justice eviscerated when the ungodly are in command! Behold how the Just One perishes and there is none to free him. The One who is true is given over to the fraudulent, and the Holy One is scourged by the unholy. The Innocent is handed over rather than the guilty; a thief is chosen over Christ, and Barabbas is released from his bonds in place of Jesus of Nazareth. The Lamb is exchanged for a wolf, a saint for a criminal, the best for the worst, a desperado acquitted rather than true God. Darkness is preferred to light, vice to virtue, death to life, scum for gold, shell to pearl, and he who is infamous is favored over him who is noble."[4]

If you say, "But we knew nothing about this," does not he who weighs the heart perceive it? Does not he who guards your life know it? Will he not repay each person according to what he has done?

—Proverbs 24:12

MOTIVES OF THE HEART

Motives of the heart often contradict explanations of the head. We speak with confidence about the reason why someone acted in a certain way, but are we as confident when we examine our own behavior?

We usually are reduced to self-justification and rationalization because we cannot plumb any deeper than the reasoning provided by the latest psychological or medical fad. The prophet Jeremiah warns each one of us that "The heart is deceitful above all things and beyond cure. Who can understand it?" (Jeremiah 17:9)

The answer to the question is given through Solomon's own question: "Does not he who weighs the heart perceive it?" No motive of the heart can be hidden from God and no explanation of the head can mask the truth buried deep within.

Jerusalem has sinned greatly and so has become unclean. All who honored her despise her, for they have seen her nakedness; she herself groans and turns away. Her filthiness clung to her skirts; she did not consider her future. Her fall was astounding; there was none to comfort her. "Look, O LORD, on my affliction, for the enemy has triumphed." The enemy laid hands on all her treasures; she saw pagan nations enter her sanctuary— those you had forbidden to enter your assembly.

—Lamentations 1:8 –10

JERUSALEM

As Jesus approaches Jerusalem for the last time, he looks out upon what was once the Holy City of God, and says, "O Jerusalem, Jerusalem, you who kill the prophets and stone those sent to you, how often have I longed to gather your children, as a hen gathers her chicks under her wings, but you were not willing!" (Luke 13:34)

Jesus looks at the sacred place where Abraham had taken his son Isaac in obedience to God's command. He looks at the city of David and the city of Solomon who built the first temple. But now it is an occupied city, a place where "all the splendor has departed…" (Lamentations 1:6) and where "the faithful city has become a harlot…." It has become a place where "…your rulers are rebels, companions of thieves; they all love bribes and chase after gifts." (Isaiah 1:21-23) The once holy city of Jerusalem has come to represent the tragic condition of the city of man where all have turned away from God.

But Jesus does not turn back—for his purpose is one of restoration, not of a city or of a people or race, but of all mankind from the tragedy of sin. As God provided Abraham a substitute for his son Isaac, so God provided His one and only son as a substitute for all mankind. And through that act of absolute love, God provides each one of us a way back to Him. "But be glad and rejoice forever in what I create, for I will create Jerusalem to be a delight and its people a joy. I will rejoice over Jerusalem and take delight in my people; the sound of weeping and of crying will be heard in it no more." (Isaiah 65:18-19)

My lover spoke and said to me, "Arise, my darling, my beautiful one, and come with me. See! The winter is past; the rains are over and gone. Flowers appear on the earth; the season of singing has come, the cooing of doves is heard in our land. The fig tree forms its early fruit; the blossoming vines spread their fragrance. Arise, come, my darling; my beautiful one, come with me."

— *Song of Songs 2:10–13*

THE WORLD IS AWAKENING!

At long last, the hard ground has softened; shoots are pushing through the soil toward warmth and light; buds are emerging on the branches of bushes and trees and the robins are on the new green grass hunting for food. "The winter is past; the rains are over and gone" and love is in the air!

T.S. Eliot said that April is the cruelest month, which is true for the godless, but elsewhere, all the world is awakening to new life and hints of eternity. The land is beckoning us out of hibernation. Come out of the darkness into the warm and brilliant light. Come!

Others went out on the sea in ships; they were merchants on the mighty waters. They saw the works of the LORD, his wonderful deeds in the deep. For he spoke and stirred up a tempest that lifted high the waves. They mounted up to the heavens and went down to the depths; in their peril their courage melted away. They reeled and staggered like drunken men; they were at their wits' end. Then they cried out to the LORD in their trouble, and he brought them out of their distress. He stilled the storm to a whisper; the waves of the sea were hushed. They were glad when it grew calm, and he guided them to their desired haven. Let them give thanks to the LORD for his unfailing love and his wonderful deeds for men.

—Psalm 107:23–31

I WAS LIFTED OUT OF MY DISTRESS

When we face serious trouble, we often lose heart and sink into despair over the hopelessness of our situation. We cannot escape the grip of whatever it is that is overwhelming us. Whatever it was that originally caused the problem has become more and more irrelevant because nothing seems to heal us or make us whole. Doubt and fear turn into despair and hopelessness, but as this Psalm shows, there is a way to change all of this: "They reeled and staggered like drunken men; they were at their wits' end. Then they cried out to the Lord in their trouble, and he brought them out of their distress." (v27-28)

Are you at your wits' end? Have you run out of the common answers? Call out to God with all of your heart and He will answer you. "To the Lord I cry aloud, and he answers me from his holy hill. I lie down and sleep; I wake again, because the Lord sustains me. I will not fear the tens of thousands drawn up against me on every side." (Psalm 3:4-5)

Then the LORD answered Job out of the storm. He said: "Who is this that darkens my counsel with words without knowledge? Brace yourself like a man; I will question you, and you shall answer me. Where were you when I laid the earth's foundation? Tell me, if you understand. Who marked off its dimensions? Surely you know! Who stretched a measuring line across it? On what were its footings set, or who laid its cornerstone—while the morning stars sang together and all the angels shouted for joy?"

—Job 38:1–7

EXPLAINING CREATION

God makes it clear to Job that it is not possible for man to understand the full mystery of creation: "'Where were you when I laid the earth's foundations...? On what were its footings set, or who laid its cornerstone- while the morning stars sang together and all the angels shouted for joy?"(v3-7)

The power of God's questions stand in poetic contrast to the self-assured claims of the disciples of the natural sciences to answer every question that touches on the mystery of creation. Whereas Job is taught to abide in great humility in the questions at the center of the mystery of creation, many modernists slavishly adhere to a new naturalistic literalism that can be reductive and constrained.

Exploring the universe is one thing; explaining it, absent of God, is quite another.

Anger is cruel and fury overwhelming, but who can stand before jealousy?

—Proverbs 27:4

PLAGUED BY JEALOUSY

Jealousy is the stepchild of anger. They are related through the passion of hatred, but whereas anger often has a specific object as the focal point, jealousy is built on doubt, suspicion and fear. The fury generated by jealousy is often the product of inference, suggestion or doubt, such as the suspicion of betrayal by a loved one. With jealousy, the hurt often begins not with a specific action but within the mind of a person plagued by an imagined offense.

When the seed of doubt is planted, then it is watered and nurtured by an overheated imagination and soon what was merely the appearance of a wrong becomes a whole cause for war. Many marriages have shattered because of jealousy; much suffering has resulted from imagined slights and betrayals fed not by knowledge, but rather by the mere suspicion of a wrong.

Teach me your way, O LORD, and I will walk in your truth; give me an undivided heart, that I may fear your name. I will praise you, O Lord my God, with all my heart; I will glorify your name forever. For great is your love toward me; you have delivered me from the depths of the grave.

—Psalm 86:11–13

A HEART OF FLESH

When David prays for an undivided heart, he is speaking of the central conflict in every man's life: I want to do the right thing, but as a moth to a candle, I am drawn to the very thing that will hurt me and hurt the people I love.

If we have no understanding of the motives of the divided heart, we will never understand the attraction of so many harmful and destructive tendencies within us. It is only when we put God first that we begin to heal from so much of what afflicts us. It is then that we experience the promise of new life found in the Book of Ezekiel: "I will give you a new heart and put a new spirit in you; I will remove from you your heart of stone and will give you a heart of flesh." (Ezekiel 36:26)

This is the prophecy fulfilled in Jesus Christ. It is the reality of miraculous healing available to every divided heart, if we will only accept it by praying for the Holy Spirit to dwell within.

As surely as God lives, who has denied me justice, the Almighty, who has made me taste bitterness of soul, as long as I have life within me, the breath of God in my nostrils, my lips will not speak wickedness, and my tongue will utter no deceit. I will never admit you are in the right; till I die, I will not deny my integrity. I will maintain my righteousness and never let go of it; my conscience will not reproach me as long as I live.

—Job 27:2–6

FEARFUL TO BEHOLD

Job is answering the accusations of his three friends who are "comforting" him with superficial explanations for the terrible suffering he is experiencing. Job does not say that he is without sin; he knows that all men sin, but he is saying that an injustice has been done him, because he has lived a righteous life. He has not lived as a hypocrite, covering up secret wrongdoing. He knows his own heart and, even though the Almighty appears to have denied him justice and made him taste bitterness of soul, his lips will not speak wickedness by cursing God. Job's suffering is fearful to behold, but he maintains his integrity by not turning against God in his misery.

Commit your way to the LORD; trust in him and he will do this: He will make your righteousness shine like the dawn, the justice of your cause like the noonday sun. Be still before the LORD and wait patiently for him; do not fret when men succeed in their ways, when they carry out their wicked schemes.

—Psalm 37:5–7

BE STILL

"Be still before the Lord and wait patiently for him...." (v6) These are words to live by, yet we find them almost impossible to put into practice. Instead of stillness, we run around in a state of high distraction, rarely pausing to listen to anyone or anything. We never walk; we run. If we are involved in business, we go to our office with the intention of accomplishing specific tasks, but often end up diverted in a hundred ways.

How can we build a relationship with God if we always keep Him out in the waiting room while we busily go bouncing around from one distraction to the next? "Be still," says the psalmist.

When God appears before Elijah on Mount Horeb, God comes as a "gentle whisper." (1 Kings 19:12) Have we built so many noisy distractions into our lives that we cannot hear the "gentle whisper?" Be still. Wait patiently. Do not fret. God is calling you. Be still so that his word may be heard. "Be still and know that I am God." (Psalm 46:10)

My son, if you have put up security for your neighbor, if you have struck hands in pledge for another, if you have been trapped by what you said, ensnared by the words of your mouth, then do this, my son, to free yourself, since you have fallen into your neighbor's hands: Go and humble yourself; press your plea with your neighbor! Allow no sleep to your eyes, no slumber to your eyelids. Free yourself, like a gazelle from the hand of the hunter, like a bird from the snare of the fowler.

—Proverbs 6:1–5

BE FREE

The father is admonishing his son to do everything in his power to stay free, but what does he mean by freedom?

Today, freedom is a very loosely used word that has come to mean many different things. Politicians behave as though freedom means license to do whatever it takes to augment their own power. Business people promote the idea that freedom is all about choosing consumer products, particularly their own. Others push sexual freedom or the freedom to use illegal drugs. And there are those who push the idea that we should be free of all societal constraints.

But none of this is consistent with the biblical idea of freedom. Peter says, "Live as free men, but do not use your freedom as a cover-up for evil." (1 Peter 2:16) And Jesus, quoting Isaiah, says "He has sent me to proclaim freedom for the prisoners...." (Luke 4:18) by which he means prisoners to the sinful nature.

When man first used his freedom to rebel against the strictures of God, he did not become truly free; he became enslaved by sin and guilt. The freedom of Christ is the freedom to be free of the burdens of sin that separate us from God. This is the freedom that opens the door to eternal life.

The stone the builders rejected has become the capstone; the LORD has done this, and it is marvelous in our eyes. This is the day the LORD has made; let us rejoice and be glad in it.

—Psalm 118:22–24

BE GLAD NOW

When we wake in the morning, do we respond to the new day with a joyful heart? Or do we dread what lies ahead? I would imagine that many people have fallen into such a tight routine that they can hardly distinguish what day of the week it is, let alone consider who might have made it.

For many, the morning is anything but time chosen to spend with God. The psalmist, however, says we should rejoice every morning, thanking God for the day He has made. The new day is a time for rejoicing and gladness because it is a gift, and we should experience the feeling of gratitude because that gift has been given to each one of us. It is there to use in a thousand different ways, all to the glory of God.

This is the day the Lord has made. Feel joy *now*. Rejoice *now*. Be glad *now*!

Oh, that my words were recorded, that they were written on a scroll, that they were inscribed with an iron tool on lead, or engraved in rock forever! I know that my Redeemer lives, and that in the end he will stand upon the earth. And after my skin has been destroyed, yet in my flesh I will see God; I myself will see him with my own eyes—I, and not another. How my heart yearns within me!

—Job 19:23–27

WILL WE HAVE A DEFENDER?

Imagine what it would be like to be hauled into a court of law to stand before a judge without understanding the charges being lodged against you. A gentleman, full of confidence, sits to your right and is thumbing through a huge file of papers. Obviously, he is the Prosecutor. He is your Accuser, and while you want to declare your innocence, you know better. He has the dossier and in it is everything you have ever done from the time you were born. You don't stand a chance unless…unless you can find a Defender who will take on your case.

When Job says, "I know my Redeemer lives," he is saying that he has such a Defender and when he stands before the Ultimate Judge, he will receive justice. But in order to destroy the Accuser's case against you, you must have someone who will represent you. Without his help, your case is hopeless. Job's statement of faith resonates with Christians because it is foundational to our belief that one day all of us will stand before the Judge of the universe and that we will have a Defender at our side.

Set a guard over my mouth, O LORD; keep watch over the door of my lips. Let not my heart be drawn to what is evil, to take part in wicked deeds with men who are evildoers; let me not eat of their delicacies.

—Psalm 141:3–4

A SMALL SPARK—A BIG FIRE

The psalmist prays to the Lord to "keep watch over the door of my lips" because He knows that words that issue forth from our mouths can kill. James warns that the "tongue" is a small but exceedingly powerful instrument, and, therefore, must be controlled. He says, "Likewise the tongue is a small part of the body, but it makes great boasts. Consider what a great forest is set on fire by a small spark. The tongue also is a fire, a world of evil among the parts of the body. It corrupts the whole person, sets the whole course of his life on fire, and is itself set on fire by hell." (James 3:5-6)

What comes out of our mouths reflects the condition of our hearts. James concludes, "With our tongue we praise our Lord and Father, and with it we curse men, who have been made in God's likeness. Out of the same mouth come praise and cursing." (v9, 10) We need to remember that we were made to praise and not to curse. We should pray for self-control.

My son, keep your father's commands and do not forsake your mother's teaching. Bind them upon your heart forever; fasten them around your neck. When you walk, they will guide you; when you sleep, they will watch over you; when you awake, they will speak to you.

—*Proverbs 6:20–22*

THE GREATEST COMMANDMENT

Jesus was asked, "Teacher, which is the greatest commandment in the law?" (Matthew 22:36) He simply replies that love is the greatest commandment: Love God above all things and love your neighbor. This is the same supreme law of God given to Moses to pass on to the people of Israel: "Hear, O Israel: The Lord our God, the Lord is one. Love the Lord your God with all your heart and with all your soul and with all your mind." (Deuteronomy 6:4-5)

Moses told the people to impress this commandment on their hearts and teach it to their children so they could pass it on to *their* children: "Impress [these commandments] on your children. Talk about them when you sit at home and when you walk along the road, when you lie down and when you get up. Tie them as symbols on your hands and bind them on your foreheads. Write them on the doorframes of your houses and on your gates." (Deuteronomy 6:7-9)

The commandment the father gave his son is the same commandment God gave Moses to give to Israel and the same commandment Jesus gave the teachers of the law and to the entire world. It is the commandment that found its fullest and most profound expression on a cross on Calvary.

He determines the number of the stars and calls them each by name. Great is our Lord and mighty in power; his understanding has no limit.

—Psalm 147:4–5

THE EMPTY TOMB

No story better illustrates the power and purpose of God than the story of the resurrection of Jesus Christ. The story of the crucifixion would have been lost in the mists of time if the followers of Jesus had not found the tomb empty and witnessed the presence of the living Lord for many days after his death. This story was so powerful to first century Christians that many would die rather than deny the truth of the living Lord.

Today, many skeptics consider the resurrection to be pure fiction and they never tire of providing reasons to explain why Christ could never have risen from the dead. But others, including millions of people in our own time, have staked everything on the truth of the Gospel and on the power and might and love of God.

Paul summarized the good news of the resurrection in his first letter to the Corinthians. "For what I received I passed on to you as of first importance: that Christ died for our sins according to the Scriptures, that he was buried, that he was raised on the third day according to the Scriptures, and that he appeared to Peter, and then to the Twelve. After that, he appeared to more than five hundred of the brothers at the same time, most of whom are still living, though some have fallen asleep. Then he appeared to James, then to all the Apostles, and last of all he appeared to me also...." (1 Corinthians 15:3-8)

A word was secretly brought to me, my ears caught a whisper of it. Amid disquieting dreams in the night, when deep sleep falls on men, fear and trembling seized me and made all my bones shake. A spirit glided past my face, and the hair on my body stood on end. It stopped, but I could not tell what it was. A form stood before my eyes, and I heard a hushed voice: "Can a mortal be more righteous than God? Can a man be more pure than his Maker?"

—Job 4:12–17

A DESCENT INTO HELL

Listen to what Eliphaz, friend of Job, is saying: "Amid disquieting dreams in the night…a spirit glided past my face…A form stood before my eyes and I heard a hushed voice." He is filled with fear, making his bones shake. Eliphaz came face to face with spiritual reality, which reminded me of Howard Storm and his story as it is recounted in his bestselling book, *My Descent into Death: A Second Chance at Life*.

One summer day in Paris in the mid 1980's, Howard Storm became violently ill and was taken to a hospital where he appeared to die. He tells of rising from his own body and looking around the room and hearing voices beckoning him to follow. He is enticed to leave the hospital room, but begins to feel a desire to turn back. However, the voices become insistent, then vicious and finally cannibalistic. They start devouring him, but deep within he has enough strength to call out in desperation to Jesus with a prayer, begging for help. Suddenly, light appears and Howard returns to his bed and life.

Howard began that hot summer day as an atheist; he emerged shaken and changed forever. The modern mind refuses to consider the reality of both heaven and hell, but Howard's story should prompt those skeptics to think again.

Wisdom, like an inheritance, is a good thing and benefits those who see the sun. Wisdom is a shelter as money is a shelter, but the advantage of knowledge is this: that wisdom preserves the life of its possessor.

—Ecclesiastes 7:11–12

IT DIDN'T NEED TO END THIS WAY

Cain lacks wisdom when he disregards God's warning that he should not submit to his envious heart. God says, "Sin is crouching at the door; it desires to have you." (Genesis 4:7)

Instead, he foolishly submits to his sinful nature by turning against his brother to kill him, and as a result of his choice, Cain is condemned to be "a restless wanderer of the earth." (Genesis 4:12) Cain's sinful desire separates him (as it separates every man) from God and the wisdom that comes from God. He is condemned to wander in a barren landscape, but it did not need to end this way.

In the parable of the lost son, the younger son goes off to foolishly waste his inheritance. After he squanders everything, he repents and returns home to be embraced by his father. The father says, "Let's have a feast and celebrate. For this son of mine was dead and is alive again; he was lost and is found." (Luke 15:23-24)

Seek the wisdom of God and you will find your way to the right path; seek God with all your heart and He will take you by the hand to lead you where you need to go. Above all, cleave to God's warning: do not submit to the urgings of the sinful nature. Turn around and return to the path that leads to the loving arms of God.

I call to the LORD, who is worthy of praise, and I am saved from my enemies. The cords of death entangled me; the torrents of destruction overwhelmed me. The cords of the grave coiled around me; the snares of death confronted me. In my distress I called to the LORD; I cried to my God for help.

—*Psalm 18:3–6*

WAR

When we read about the early battles of David, beginning with his victory over the giant Goliath and the Philistines, we are reminded that war is the rule and peace the exception: "Here they come swift and speedily!...Their arrows are sharp, all their bows are strung, their horses hoofs seem like flint, their chariot wheels like a whirlwind. Their roar is like that of a lion, they roar like young lions; they growl as they seize their prey and carry it off with no one to rescue. In that day they will roar over it like the roaring of the sea. And if one looks at the land, he will see darkness and distress; even the light will be darkened by the clouds." (Isaiah 5:26-30)

War has always been part of the human experience, but over the years, many Americans have come to believe that they are exempt from the awful forces of history so evident in other parts of the world. That is, until September 11, 2001, when we were awakened from our slumber and reintroduced to the mainstream of history.

Whether we experience war as Isaiah or Tolkien or Tolstoy describe it, or we experience a battle of a more private sort, David's call to God for help in a time of trouble tells us exactly what we should always do. For when all else fails, David has a "rock, a fortress and a deliverer" who will never fail him.

A man can do nothing better than to eat and drink and find satisfaction in his work. This too, I see, is from the hand of God, for without him, who can eat or find enjoyment? To the man who pleases him, God gives wisdom, knowledge and happiness, but to the sinner he gives the task of gathering and storing up wealth to hand it over to the one who pleases God. This too is meaningless, a chasing after the wind.

—Ecclesiastes 2:24–26

HOW SHOULD WE EDUCATE OUR CHILDREN?

Who are we bringing our children up to be? It seems most schooling aims at educating children not so much for life but for work. After all, both parents often work to earn enough in hopes that their children may be accepted at a better college, which will provide a means to enter the workforce at a higher level, whereupon the cycle begins all over again.

If the purpose of life is to get a job and earn more and more money, then all we will be doing is "gathering and storing up wealth to hand it over…" (v26) If we do not consider ourselves children of God, made in God's own image, then work will simply be its own reward and we will live day to day saying, "Let us eat and drink, for tomorrow we die." (1 Corinthians 15:32)

In essence, this is the philosophy behind the communist experiment—feed the body and you feed the whole man. What a diminished world this venture turned out to be! The word of God speaks to the *whole* man and that makes all the difference. "Man does not live on bread alone but on every word that comes from the mouth of the Lord." (Deuteronomy 8:3)

He who is pregnant with evil and conceives trouble gives birth to disillusionment. He who digs a hole and scoops it out falls into the pit he has made. The trouble he causes recoils on himself; his violence comes down on his own head.

—Psalm 7:14–16

THE NATURE OF EVIL

If you believe in the perfectibility of man, then the idea that we can give birth to evil is an unsettling contradiction. This is why the world objects to the truth of the existence of sin as crucial to understanding the mystery of our human nature. David says, "Surely I was sinful at birth, sinful from the time my mother conceived me." (Psalm 51:5) And Paul says, "for all have sinned and fallen short of the glory of God." (Romans 3:23)

What this means is that we should never delude ourselves into underestimating the capacity for evil in any man who has not been saved. "For the sinful nature desires what is contrary to the Spirit....The acts of the sinful nature are obvious: sexual immorality, impurity and debauchery; idolatry and witchcraft; hatred, discord, jealousy, fits of rage, selfish ambition, dissensions, factions and envy; drunkenness and orgies, and the like." (Galatians 5:19-21)

Accepting the idea that sin flows out from within is hard for the world to accept. The world would prefer to believe that sin is imposed on us from the outside and therefore is not indigenous to our nature. If the world is right, then the truth of the power of the cross is wrong.

Shout with joy to God, all the earth! Sing the glory of his name; make his praise glorious! Say to God, "How awesome are your deeds! So great is your power that your enemies cringe before you. All the earth bows down to you; they sing praise to you, they sing praise to your name."

—Psalm 66:1–4

PRAISE GOD'S HOLY NAME

In another Psalm, David tells us why we should praise God's holy name continually: He "forgives all your sins…heals all your diseases…redeems your life from the pit…crowns you with love and compassion." He "satisfies your desires with good things so that your youth is renewed like the eagle's." (Psalm 103:3-5)

I went past the field of the sluggard, past the vineyard of the man who lacks judgment; thorns had come up everywhere, the ground was covered with weeds, and the stone wall was in ruins. I applied my heart to what I observed and learned a lesson from what I saw: A little sleep, a little slumber, a little folding of the hands to rest— and poverty will come on you like a bandit and scarcity like an armed man.

—Proverbs 24:30–34

INACTION BREEDS POVERTY

The sluggard is plagued by inaction; he is pathologically passive. He lets life happen to him; he waits for his chances; he puts off until tomorrow what could be done today. The problem for anyone afflicted by laziness is that life is cumulative; what began as something small becomes large and overwhelming, if action is not taken.

As an example, much of business life is processing information efficiently and effectively. If systems break down, then information mounts up and soon crushes all who stand in the way.

Life, therefore, has to be rigorously taken care of each and every day without fail. If we put off our responsibilities for another day, then poverty is likely to come on us like a bandit and scarcity like an armed man.

Let those who love the LORD hate evil, for he guards the lives of his faithful ones and delivers them from the hand of the wicked. Light is shed upon the righteous and joy on the upright in heart. Rejoice in the LORD, you who are righteous, and praise his holy name.

—*Psalm 97:10–12*

A PASSION FOR THE LIGHT

In the prologue to his gospel, John explains that being a child of God is very different than being a child of the world: "Yet to all who received him, to those who believed in his name, he gave the right to become children of God—children born not of natural descent, nor of human decision, or a husband's will, but born of God."(John 1:12-13)

According to John, this is the testimony of God: "God has given us eternal life, and this life is in his Son. He who has the Son has life; he who does not have the Son of God does not have life."(1 John 5:11-12) He who does not have the Son of God lives in darkness; Jesus, the Son of God, says: "This is the verdict: Light has come into the world, but men loved darkness instead of light because their deeds were evil. Everyone who does evil hates the light and will not come into the light for fear that his deeds will be exposed."(John 3:19-20)

As a child of God, born again of the Spirit, your greatest desire will be to love and serve the Lord your God with all your heart, mind, soul and strength. Your next greatest desire will be to love and serve your neighbor. It is when your heart is transformed by the Holy Spirit that the inclination of the heart shifts from a desire to live in darkness to a passion for the light.

By wisdom a house is built, and through understanding it is established; through knowledge its rooms are filled with rare and beautiful treasures.

—Proverbs 24:3–4

LIKE LIVING STONES

The house built on a rock is more than a metaphor. Jesus constructs an edifice of hope built on the most solid foundation possible: "But everyone who hears these words of mine and puts them into practice is like a wise man who built his house upon a rock..." (Matthew 7:24) Paul elaborates by showing us how this house or temple is furnished: "Do you not know that your body is a temple of the Holy Spirit, who is in you, whom you have received from God?" (1 Corinthians 6:19)

Peter builds even further on the same rock, the church: "As you come to him, the living stone-rejected by men but chosen by God and precious to him—you also, like living stones are being built into a spiritual house to be a holy priesthood, offering spiritual sacrifices acceptable to God through Jesus Christ." (1 Peter 2:4-5)

So what is this house built by the wisdom of God? It is the body of Christ, a temple of the Holy Spirit built with living stones offering spiritual sacrifices acceptable to God. This is the church, the temple built on the living stones of the children of God.

Do not move an ancient boundary stone or encroach on the fields of the fatherless, for their Defender is strong; he will take up their case against you.

—Proverbs 23:10–11

A PERVERSE IMPULSE

Even though we hear the warning, we often feel strangely compelled to ignore the danger in defiance of the obvious consequence. It happens all the time. When we hear someone say, "Don't touch the hot plate!" we touch the plate anyway.

Why does a warning cause us to want to defy the rules? Why do we irrationally embrace risk when we know better? Edgar Allen Poe called this dark impulse "the imp of the perverse." Dostoyevsky says that we have within our makeup an "underground man" who acts as a double, nudging us away from the good and beneficial life to ruin and despair. The Bible calls this subterranean tendency sin which is a corrosive desire to do the wrong thing when we know it is wrong.

The ancient boundary stone is the signpost that keeps us out of harm's way. Jesus invites us to follow him on this path, but we often demure by inventing excuses for wandering off into the thorns and brambles because we have allowed that other voice within to control our every step.

He who conceals his sins does not prosper, but whoever confesses and renounces them finds mercy. A man tormented by the guilt of murder will be a fugitive till death; let no one support him. He whose walk is blameless is kept safe, but he whose ways are perverse will suddenly fall.

—*Proverbs 28:13, 17-18*

MY BURDEN IS HEAVY— HIS BURDEN IS LIGHT

In case we have any doubt about what sin looks like, Paul gives a definitive description in his letter to the Galatians: "The acts of the sinful nature are obvious..." (Galatians 5:19) and then he delves into a catalog of horrors that should appall the sensibilities of all right thinking people.

The problem is that no one is exempt from the temptation to indulge in sinful acts. And what is worse, we often move from temptation to action through a momentary compulsion, as if we were not in our right minds. The inevitable consequence is a burden of guilt that cannot easily be unloaded. We try to bury our sin or transfer it, or we flee from it as if it were a demon pursuing us.

Here is the difficulty. Sin will not let go unless we call out to the Lord in our misery for His mercy. Covering up our sins will not work, nor will we benefit by unloading our burdens on a friend.

The only answer that universally works to obliterate the burden of past sins is the crucified Christ. Jesus asks us to consider turning our life over to him: "Come to me, all you who are weary and burdened, and I will give you rest. Take my yoke upon you and learn from me, for I am gentle and humble in heart, and you will find rest for your souls. For my yoke is easy and my burden is light." (Matthew 11:28-30)

The leech has two daughters. "Give! Give!" they cry. There are three things that are never satisfied, four that never say, "Enough!": the grave, the barren womb, land, which is never satisfied with water, and fire, which never says, "Enough!"

—*Proverbs 30:15–16*

NEVER ENOUGH

When the purpose of life is reduced to satisfying the appetites of the body, we ultimately discover that the appetites are insatiable and, like a fire out of control, they never have enough. Solomon explains how futile it is to only strive after things of this world: "I denied myself nothing my eyes desired; I refused my heart no pleasure. My heart took delight in all my work, and this was the reward for all my labor. Yet when I surveyed all that my hands had done and what I toiled to achieve, everything was meaningless, a chasing after the wind; nothing was gained under the sun." (Ecclesiastes 2:10-11)

Looking back over the course of his long life, Solomon realized that he had lost his way when he turned to pursue pleasure as the primary purpose of life. For no matter how much wealth he accumulated, no matter how much he built or possessed, the thirst could never be quenched, nor the appetite ever satisfied. The leech does have two daughters and they do cry, "Give, Give!" and the fire within will never say, "Enough!"

O God, you are my God, earnestly I seek you; my soul thirsts for you, my body longs for you, in a dry and weary land where there is no water.

—Psalm 63:1

WORDS TAUGHT BY THE SPIRIT

Every man who finds himself lost in a "dry and weary land" will experience physical thirst. But what about the soul? Is the Psalmist speaking about our physical need for water only?

When Jesus was passing through the parched land of Samaria, he came upon a woman at a well near the town of Sychar. While resting there, he asked her for water. When she questioned him, he began to speak figuratively about a different kind of "living water" that "will become...a spring of water welling up to eternal life." (John 4:14)

At first, the woman is confused but soon she realizes whom she is speaking with and goes to tell her townspeople to "Come, see a man who told me everything I ever did. Could this be the Christ?" (John 4:29)

Jesus uses figurative language to reveal a spiritual truth that remains the same in all places and times: We need to satisfy the thirst of the heart with the living water of the Spirit that is freely offered by God to all who will ask to drink it. The language of this world cannot adequately express the spiritual truth behind his words, which is why Jesus uses figurative speech when revealing a spiritual truth.

Paul, speaking about the power of the Holy Spirit, says," (T)he Spirit searches all things, even the deep things of God....This is what we speak, not in words taught us by human wisdom but in words taught by the Spirit, expressing spiritual truths in spiritual words. The man without the Spirit does not accept the things that come from the Spirit of God, for they are foolishness to him, and he cannot understand them, because they are spiritually discerned." (1 Corinthians 2:10-14)

But I pray to you, O LORD, in the time of your favor; in your great love, O God, answer me with your sure salvation. Rescue me from the mire, do not let me sink; deliver me from those who hate me, from the deep waters. Do not let the floodwaters engulf me or the depths swallow me up or the pit close its mouth over me. Answer me, O LORD, out of the goodness of your love; in your great mercy turn to me. Do not hide your face from your servant; answer me quickly, for I am in trouble. Come near and rescue me; redeem me because of my foes.

—Psalm 69:13–18

AMAZING GRACE

To be human is to know trouble.

Many years ago, I found myself facing bankruptcy, threats of lawsuits and financial devastation. With blinding speed, my self-confidence was blown away and I was rendered defenseless. Fear filled every corner of my life. But when the chips were down and there was absolutely nowhere to turn, I cried out to God in my distress...and He answered.

Trouble is the common denominator in everyone's life. Sometimes it is subtle and sometimes dramatic, but it always seems to be lurking on the fringe ready to pounce. In my case, when I found that I could not save myself, I called out to God, not knowing what to expect. What I received was undeserved beyond measure, and ultimately, the experience drew me back to Jesus Christ.

It was truly a life saving event; I was saved through my failure. I now look upon that period in my life as the time when I experienced God's amazing grace.

Great is the LORD, and most worthy of praise, in the city of our God,
his holy mountain. It is beautiful in its loftiness, the joy of the whole
earth. Like the utmost heights of Zaphon is Mount Zion, the city of
the Great King. God is in her citadels; he has shown himself to be her
fortress.

—Psalm 48:1–3

CITY OF GOD, CITY OF MAN

The city of God should never be confused with the city of man. The city of God is not of this earth; rather it is a promised home for those who believe. "Then I saw a new heaven and a new earth, for the first heaven and the first earth had passed away, and there was no longer any sea. I saw the Holy City, the new Jerusalem, coming down out of heaven, from God...." (Revelation 21:1-2)

Contrast this to the other Jerusalem described by Jeremiah in Lamentations: "How deserted lies the city, once so full of people!...All her gateways are desolate, her priests groan, her maidens grieve and she is in bitter anguish." (Lamentations 1:1, 3)

The city of man had turned against God: "The visions of your prophets were false and worthless; they did not expose your sin to ward off your captivity." (Lamentations 2:14)

As he approaches Jerusalem, Jesus sees that the favored city of God, the city of David and the Holy Temple, has become a city of man and he feels great sorrow and compassion. (Luke 13:34) God calls us to a New Jerusalem, but often we refuse and turn back to the old city, the city of man.

Keep silent and let me speak; then let come to me what may. Why do I put myself in jeopardy and take my life in my hands? Though he slay me, yet will I hope in him; I will surely defend my ways to his face. Indeed, this will turn out for my deliverance, for no godless man would dare come before him! Listen carefully to my words; let your ears take in what I say. Now that I have prepared my case, I know I will be vindicated. Can anyone bring charges against me? If so, I will be silent and die.

—*Job 13:13–19*

DIVINE JUSTICE

Job's friends have been inquiring into why Job might be experiencing such terrible suffering. Just as we can never know any story completely, Job's friends have assumed that he must have done something to offend God, and that he is now paying the price for his sins. They claim to have knowledge where they, in fact, have none. Job will have none of it: "Though he slay me, yet will I hope in him; I will surely defend my ways to his face." (v15)

Job claims a great injustice has been done him and yet "I know I will be vindicated." (v18) He has faith that in the end divine justice will prevail and that God will vindicate him.

But the friends have a very different view. They claim to know the reasons for Job's suffering; they believe that human reason is sufficient to understand the causes behind what has happened. But their vision is too earthbound, and while Job cannot fully understand the ways of God, he is completely confident that God is just and will restore him in the end.

Job is right, but the truth behind his claim for divine justice is based on revelation and not on the insufficiency of human reason.

Why, O LORD, do you reject me and hide your face from me? From my youth I have been afflicted and close to death; I have suffered your terrors and am in despair. Your wrath has swept over me; your terrors have destroyed me. All day long they surround me like a flood; they have completely engulfed me. You have taken my companions and loved ones from me; the darkness is my closest friend.

—Psalm 88:14–18

HIDING FROM GOD

Is God hiding from you…or are you hiding from God? The common complaint is that God has left us alone like homeless children and while we search everywhere, tragically, God cannot be found.

But the Bible would suggest a very different pattern. *We* are the ones who refuse to be found. God searches high and low for his lost sheep, but we will not come home when called. "We all, like lost sheep, have gone astray, each of us has turned to his own way…." (Isaiah 53:6)

The first thing that happens after Adam and Eve eat of the tree of knowledge of good and evil is that their eyes are opened to their own nakedness and they feel shame. Then, when God comes into the Garden, they both hide.

It is not our knowledge of good that causes us to experience shame and fear; it is the knowledge of evil that causes us to seek shelter in dark and hidden places away from the searching light of God.

If you are hiding from God rather than searching for Him, look to your own heart to seek the reason.

Come, my lover, let us go to the countryside, let us spend the night in the villages. Let us go early to the vineyards to see if the vines have budded, if their blossoms have opened, and if the pomegranates are in bloom— there I will give you my love. The mandrakes send out their fragrance, and at our door is every delicacy, both new and old, that I have stored up for you, my lover.

—Song of Songs 7:11–13

SOUNDS OF MUSIC AND LAUGHTER

It's May and evidence of spring is everywhere. The gentle breeze summons up summer memories of green pastures, rolling hills, the songs of birds heralding the newborn day and the sound of gentle waves lapping against a lake's rocky shore. The new season has banished the grays and whites of winter and the world has risen anew with songs and joy and love.

Time stands still and the sounds of laughter and music and dancing fill the soft evening air. The people have come out, joy is everywhere and music rises gladly up to the starry floor of heaven. So, "Sing to the LORD with thanksgiving…He covers the sky with clouds; he supplies the earth with rain and makes grass grow on the hills." (Psalm 147:7, 8)

To the faithful you show yourself faithful, to the blameless you show yourself blameless, to the pure you show yourself pure, but to the crooked you show yourself shrewd.

— Psalm 18:25–26

THE EYES OF THE LORD

We often hear that God is faithful and pure, but do we ever think of God as shrewd? To many of us this comes as a surprise because it is so unexpected and uncharacteristic.

But should it be? The reference here is to those who have departed from the way to pursue a fraudulent and dishonest living; God is shrewd with them because He cannot be fooled. They attempt to shield themselves by working under cover of darkness and secrecy, but God can penetrate any darkness and sees everything: "The eyes of the Lord are everywhere, keeping watch on the wicked and the good." (Proverbs 15:3)

To try to deceive God is vain and foolish because it is an impossibility; every attempt to deceive God will only be an exercise in self-deception.

O LORD, you will keep us safe and protect us from such people forever. The wicked freely strut about when what is vile is honored among men.

— Psalm 12:7–8

PANDEMONIUM

Pandemonium is the region ruled by Satan. It is a corrupted replica of heaven, built on discord and disorder, war and suffering, horror and despair. It is where everything that is vile is honored and where Satan rules over those condemned to serve him as prisoners of sin and despair. And it is Satan's chief desire to establish this counterfeit of God's kingdom here on earth.

No one would doubt, given the state of the world at any given moment that he has made serious inroads. It was into such a place that God sent "the Lord Jesus Christ, who gave himself for our sins to rescue us from the present evil age...." (Galatians 1:3-4)

When we pray the Lord's Prayer, saying "your kingdom come, your will be done on earth as it is in heaven," we are asking God to rescue us from a place that looks very much like Pandemonium, where what is vile is honored, and what is pure, righteous and godly, is hated. When we become Kingdom builders, we sign on to build a world that seeks to follow "whatever is true, whatever is noble, whatever is right, whatever is pure, whatever is lovely, whatever is admirable." (Philippians 4:8)

Shout for joy to the LORD, all the earth. Worship the LORD with gladness; come before him with joyful songs. Know that the LORD is God. It is he who made us, and we are his; we are his people, the sheep of his pasture. Enter his gates with thanksgiving and his courts with praise; give thanks to him and praise his name. For the LORD is good and his love endures forever; his faithfulness continues through all generations.

—Psalm 100:1–5

FOR THE LORD IS GOOD

I was nineteen and within a week of completing my freshman year in college. It was 1963 and only a promising future seemed to lie before me. I remember sitting outside the school dining hall with a group of friends planning the weekend and discussing course work and exams. I was oblivious to what was about to explode like a land mine only a few hours hence. For that night in a place far away, my father's life came to a sudden end on the road home.

Early that morning the police arrived at our home with the shattering news that my father was dead. From that moment on, my mother and her children began to live in the aftermath of unfathomable loss. When I got the phone call, I went to a nearby church and I prayed. I don't remember the prayers, but I prayed. It was the only thing I thought of doing.

I hope my prayer was one of thanksgiving for the extraordinary life of my father. I hope that I praised God, asking that His will be done, whatever that meant for my family and me. "For the Lord is good and his love endures forever; his faithfulness continues through all generations." (v5)

Remember your Creator in the days of your youth, before the days of trouble come and the years approach when you will say, "I find no pleasure in them"— before the sun and the light and the moon and the stars grow dark, and the clouds return after the rain; when the keepers of the house tremble, and the strong men stoop, when the grinders cease because they are few, and those looking through the windows grow dim; when the doors to the street are closed and the sound of grinding fades; when men rise up at the sound of birds, but all their songs grow faint; when men are afraid of heights and of dangers in the streets; when the almond tree blossoms and the grasshopper drags himself along and desire no longer is stirred. Then man goes to his eternal home and mourners go about the streets.

—Ecclesiastes 12:1–5

THE OLD MAN AT THE WINDOW

Thousands of years have passed since Solomon wrote this description of old age, but there is nothing old about it. It is immediate and contemporary and we can see and feel the dusty street "where the grasshopper drags himself along." (v5) Even if we are young, we can imagine, through this verse, what old age feels like.

The poet transports us back in time into the person of the old man and there we are, sitting in the shaded room by that same window, unable to hear the sounds of children playing in the street or the music of the organ grinder. At one time, that same old man was like one of the little children playing in the same street. And one day that same child outside the window will grow into the old man who looks out at a world where "songs grow faint." (v4)

Come and listen, all you who fear God; let me tell you what he has done for me. I cried out to him with my mouth; his praise was on my tongue. If I had cherished sin in my heart, the Lord would not have listened; but God has surely listened and heard my voice in prayer. Praise be to God, who has not rejected my prayer or withheld his love from me!

—*Psalm 66:16–20*

WHAT PASSION WILL RULE?

The human heart is a big place, but not so big that sin and the Holy Spirit can exist in it together. Jesus deals with this figuratively in the Sermon on the Mount: "No one can serve two masters. Either he will hate the one and love the other, or he will be devoted to the one and despise the other." (Matthew 6:24)

We are born into conflict and we thirst for resolution, but the greatest struggle most of us will ever experience is the struggle over what passion will rule in our hearts. Will it be a passion for sin or will it be a passion for Christ? If we cherish sin in our hearts, if we love darkness instead of light, then we cannot have fellowship with God through Christ: "God is light; in him there is no darkness at all. If we claim to have fellowship with him yet walk in the darkness, we lie and do not live by the truth." (1 John 1:5-6)

A genuine love of Christ opens the door for the Holy Spirit, but opening that door will be the cause of great struggle and pain as we shed the old and grow in the new.

Drink water from your own cistern, running water from your own well. Should your springs overflow in the streets, your streams of water in the public squares? Let them be yours alone, never to be shared with strangers. May your fountain be blessed, and may you rejoice in the wife of your youth. A loving doe, a graceful deer— may her breasts satisfy you always, may you ever be captivated by her love. Why be captivated, my son, by an adulteress? Why embrace the bosom of another man's wife?

—Proverbs 5:15–20

MEN AND MARRIAGE

Many years ago, George Gilder wrote a provocative book called *Men and Marriage*. In it, he argued that without marriage there can be no civilization and, furthermore, that without marriage men would essentially remain uncivilized. Gilder argued that women civilize men and that marriage is the essential structure through which this happens.

Before they marry, men are dreamers, warriors and adventurers. Without the self-limiting relationship fostered by marriage, men would be content to do whatever they wanted, whenever they wanted. Though this has changed over the past fifty years, marriage still defines the role of men as provider and protector built on the foundation of love. This creates the context for commitment that is the essential building block of any civilization.

And while marriage serves to reel in the dreamer, men benefit by growing into the adult that is necessary for that commitment to another. Men's instinct for adventure becomes circumscribed by the reality of a relationship that transcends self. The role of men and women in marriage has changed over the years, but this change has not diminished the importance of marriage to a coherent and vital civilization.

Where then does wisdom come from? Where does understanding dwell? It is hidden from the eyes of every living thing, concealed even from the birds of the air. Destruction and Death say, "Only a rumor of it has reached our ears." God understands the way to it and he alone knows where it dwells, for he views the ends of the earth and sees everything under the heavens. When he established the force of the wind and measured out the waters, when he made a decree for the rain and a path for the thunderstorm, then he looked at wisdom and appraised it; he confirmed it and tested it. And he said to man, "The fear of the Lord—that is wisdom, and to shun evil is understanding."

—Job 28:20–28

ETERNAL WISDOM

Biblical wisdom is not the wisdom of the earth or of man; rather it is the eternal wisdom that comes from God. It is the power of the wisdom of God as revealed in His Word. "In the beginning was the Word, and the Word was with God, and the Word was God. He was with God in the beginning." (John 1:1)

The message of the Bible is not about human power or wisdom; it is about God's eternal power that runs through everyone and everything. It is a gift that we can accept or reject, but whatever our choice, we have to realize that all our actions, both good and bad, will be measured against God's justice, tempered by His mercy.

He draws up the drops of water, which distill as rain to the streams; the clouds pour down their moisture and abundant showers fall on mankind. Who can understand how he spreads out the clouds, how he thunders from his pavilion? See how he scatters his lightning about him, bathing the depths of the sea. This is the way he governs the nations and provides food in abundance. He fills his hands with lightning and commands it to strike its mark. His thunder announces the coming storm; even the cattle make known its approach.

—Job 36:27–33

THE JOURNEY

Many years ago, during my first long hike on the Appalachian Trail in New Hampshire, I experienced a fleeting reflection of God's presence in this world.

Late one day, after an easy ten miles, I began to search for a place for the night. About a mile or so beyond a small town, I found an open cabin slightly off the trail. It was dark and empty inside; reluctantly, I resigned myself to another night in the woods alone. After a light dinner, I felt a strong desire to get out of the cold gloom of the shelter, so I left that place to take a walk toward an open field on a hillside surrounded by thick woods. The colors had turned to the deep contrasts and long shadows of a late summer day; stillness permeated the scene.

It was as if I had walked into a beautifully painted landscape. In the middle of this picture stood three deer grazing on the hillside. They didn't notice me, and so I gazed in wonder on this scene of magical beauty and perfection—no noise, no breeze, just an intuited sense that God was there and that I was witnessing the magnificent splendor of his creation. Then a sound intruded and the deer lifted their heads, sensing danger. Without further warning, they vanished and once again, I was alone.

Now, years later, I remember that momentary scene as if it were an image painted by God himself. I felt the warmth of God's presence that day, but I had to turn back to the shelter of the solitary cabin. I did not know then that the journey ahead would be hard and long. Yet wherever life took me, I carried with me that image as sustenance for those times when I would experience hunger and thirst.

Have you journeyed to the springs of the sea or walked in the recesses of the deep? Have the gates of death been shown to you? Have you seen the gates of the shadow of death? Have you comprehended the vast expanses of the earth? Tell me, if you know all this.

—Job 38:16–18

EXTENDING OUR KNOWLEDGE

"Have you comprehended the vast expanses of the earth?" Oswald Chambers gave a very interesting answer to that question: "The Bible reveals that the force behind everything is the Great Spirit of God. A great change has come over what is called material science. In the early days when people tried to explain the material world, they said that it was made up of molecules; then they found that those molecules could be split up, and the split-up elements were called atoms; then they found that the atoms were made of neutrons, protons, and electrons; then they discovered that these particles themselves are like whole solar systems."[5]

Material science has extended our knowledge of the world, but it has also pried open a box of infinite mystery and infinite possibilities.

There is a time for everything, and a season for every activity under heaven: a time to be born and a time to die, a time to plant and a time to uproot, a time to kill and a time to heal, a time to tear down and a time to build, a time to weep and a time to laugh, a time to mourn and a time to dance, a time to scatter stones and a time to gather them, a time to embrace and a time to refrain, a time to search and a time to give up, a time to keep and a time to throw away, a time to tear and a time to mend, a time to be silent and a time to speak, a time to love and a time to hate, a time for war and a time for peace.

—Ecclesiastes 3:1–8

THE GOD OF NEAR AND FAR

One of the advantages of being older is the perspective that the accumulation of time and experience can give.

When he wrote Ecclesiastes, Solomon, was an old man. When we read these verses, it feels like we are being guided to the top of a big mountain to be shown a view of all of earthly existence with all the patterns that make up the varied heights and depths of human life.

But the advantages of perspective must be weighed against the disadvantages of missing the taste and texture of existence. If we choose to look at things from a vast distance, then we lose the fine details that are just as important and just as real.

Being mere mortals, we humans must often decide which view to take, the near or the far. But God is different, for he can do both simultaneously. And herein is a paradox.

God is so big, so powerful and so vast in scope that He can create the entire universe. But at the same time, He never loses sight of the smallest, most insignificant details of everyday life. He is the God of the vast and the microscopic. He brought the whole universe into being, yet He cares intimately about you and about me. He is truly the God of love.

My son, do not despise the LORD'S discipline and do not resent his rebuke, because the LORD disciplines those he loves, as a father the son he delights in.

—Proverbs 3:11–12

CHARIOTS OF FIRE

Frequently, we hear people speak about receiving a "wake up call," but rarely do they imply that the call has a supernatural caller at the other end of the line. Instead, they mean that some change in circumstance or fortune forced them to rethink what they were doing and may have helped them out of a tight situation.

Many years ago, I received one of those calls. I was being buffeted around by a financial storm that had grown out of control. In the end, I found a safe harbor, but by then, I knew that my own efforts would never have been enough to save me. I experienced personal salvation from ruin at that time. But I was not quite ready to admit that I had witnessed a supernatural act of God in my own life. Eventually, though, my eyes opened to the host of angels that had led me through the danger. (2 Kings 6:17) Finally, I could see that the crisis had a divine purpose behind it.

Sometimes God's love feels like pain, but in reality, it is nothing more than an opening to get back the life He wants for us. "One thing God has spoken, two things have I heard: that you, O God, are strong, and that you, O Lord are loving." (Psalm 62:11-12)

My heart is not proud, O LORD, my eyes are not haughty; I do not concern myself with great matters or things too wonderful for me. But I have stilled and quieted my soul; like a weaned child with its mother, like a weaned child is my soul within me. O Israel, put your hope in the LORD both now and forevermore.

—Psalm 131:1–3

GOD OPPOSES THE PROUD

When we step out in front of God, we ignite a desire to be great in the eyes of the world; at the same time, we damp down the ability to live in genuine humility. We unleash pride, which is lethal for our ability to maintain our relationship with God. We substitute a love of God with a love for self.

Self-love puffs up and distorts our relationship not only to God but also to others. "All of you, clothe yourselves with humility toward one another because God opposes the proud but gives grace to the humble. Humble yourselves, therefore, under God's mighty hand, that he may lift you up in due time." (1 Peter 5:5-6)

Consider what God has done: Who can straighten what he has made crooked? When times are good, be happy; but when times are bad, consider: God has made the one as well as the other. Therefore, a man cannot discover anything about his future.

—Ecclesiastes 7:13–14

RISK IT

For many, this is a very uncomfortable saying. So much of our time is spent attempting to control every aspect of our existence from the upbringing of our children to the next five-year plan for our business. We try to control our time, our environment, our future, our health and our weight, as if our desire for an outcome is the same as reality itself.

Much of the impulse for control is based on a fear-driven life; we fear the worst and therefore try to design our actions and behavior in a way that will avoid risk.

Solomon tells us that this kind of living is not living at all. Because we cannot "discover anything about (our) future," (v14) we should live a life deliberately dependent on God. Jesus tells us the same thing in the Sermon on the Mount: "Therefore do not worry about tomorrow, for tomorrow will worry about itself. Each day has enough trouble of its own." (Matthew 6:34)

For I am about to fall, and my pain is ever with me. I confess my iniquity; I am troubled by my sin. Many are those who are my vigorous enemies; those who hate me without reason are numerous. Those who repay my good with evil slander me when I pursue what is good.

—Psalm 38:17–20

THE REALITY OF EVIL

The possibility that evil might exist beyond the realm of our own reasoning disturbs many people. They do not accept biblical revelation and therefore pursue "scientific" causes for the existence of evil. The biblical explanation is rejected as irrelevant because the Bible faces the existence of evil head on: "our struggle is not against flesh and blood, but against the rulers, against the authorities, against the powers of this dark world and against the spiritual forces of evil in the heavenly realms."(Ephesians 6:20)

If we are forced to restrict our understanding of evil to modern explanations, then we render ourselves incapable of perceiving the spiritual dimension to evil's existence. And by limiting ourselves to naturalistic explanations, we will not be able to arrive at the truth behind the surface realities of life. Evil becomes merely an event to be rationalized away. When we engage in mere naturalistic logic, we will remain blind to the mortal danger that exists on every side of us and within.

There are three things that are too amazing for me, four that I do not understand: the way of an eagle in the sky, the way of a snake on a rock, the way of a ship on the high seas, and the way of a man with a maiden.

—Proverbs 30:18–19

THE MYSTERIOUS EAGLE

Why does the eagle fascinate us? The Bible gives us one reason: "…like an eagle that stirs up its nest and hovers over its young, that spreads its wings to catch them and carries them on its pinions." (Deuteronomy 32:10-11)

The young eagles stay in the nest and are cared for until it is time for them to learn to fly on their own. They need to be taught, though, and they are reluctant to climb out of the safety of the nest. So they are pushed out and begin to fall toward the ground until the parent eagle swoops under the chick and catches it on its wings before it is too late. This continues until the young eagle gains enough confidence and strength to soar away on its own.

How did this come to be? The magnificent eagle is also the mysterious eagle that seems to have a wisdom all its own.

Do not withhold discipline from a child; if you punish him with the rod, he will not die. Punish him with the rod and save his soul from death.

—*Proverbs 23:13–14*

DISCIPLINE

Discipline is a fact of life. If you are not disciplined early in life by a loving parent, you will be disciplined later by an indifferent world. Today, parents often think that punishment is equivalent to harm and permanent damage, but children require direction. If they do not learn at a young age that certain actions will have adverse consequences, then they will be defenseless against temptations when they are old enough to make up their own minds.

The parent's purpose is to raise godly children who are aware that Satan does not discriminate by age.

Praise be to the LORD, for he has heard my cry for mercy. The LORD is my strength and my shield; my heart trusts in him, and I am helped. My heart leaps for joy and I will give thanks to him in song. The LORD is the strength of his people, a fortress of salvation for his anointed one. Save your people and bless your inheritance; be their shepherd and carry them forever.

—*Psalm 28:6–9*

I AM THE GOOD SHEPHERD

When David was called by Samuel to be anointed, he was tending sheep for his father Jesse. David was a shepherd, foreshadowing the shepherd to come who would claim, "I am the good shepherd. The good shepherd lays down his life for the sheep. The hired hand is not the shepherd who owns the sheep. So when he sees the wolf coming, he abandons the sheep and runs away." (John 10:11-12)

Jesus, the good shepherd, has "heard my cry for mercy." He is my strength; "my heart trusts him" and "leaps for joy" when I hear his voice. The good shepherd is "a fortress of salvation" and he will save us from the wolf that has come to attack and devour. David, the good shepherd of Israel, prepared the way for the good shepherd of all the people.

Turn to me and be gracious to me, for I am lonely and afflicted. The troubles of my heart have multiplied; free me from my anguish. Look upon my affliction and my distress and take away all my sins. See how my enemies have increased and how fiercely they hate me! Guard my life and rescue me; let me not be put to shame, for I take refuge in you. May integrity and uprightness protect me, because my hope is in you.

—Psalm 25:16–21

MY HOPE IS IN YOU

When finally we admit to being lonely and afflicted, we often try to medicate our way back to health. But at the heart of this distress and shame is a word that has been nearly banished from our contemporary vocabulary: sin.

The Bible tells us that it is the sinful nature that separates us from God and leaves us vulnerable to the vagaries of this world. Sin afflicts us with the weight of guilt and regret from the accumulated memories of past acts. Alone, we cannot bear the burden. We must unload it or we will be crushed. We fear the future and anguish over what is to come. Our days become crowded with worries and we lose all sense of joy. This is why David turns to one who can bring real healing. "...I take refuge in you... my hope is in you." (v21)

One man pretends to be rich, yet has nothing; another pretends to be poor, yet has great wealth. A man's riches may ransom his life, but a poor man hears no threat.

—Proverbs 13:7–8

RICH AND POOR

A man can be rich and have nothing and a poor man can want for everything and yet be rich. When we open our hearts to the Holy Spirit, God saturates our whole being, which releases us from the prison of circumstance and frees us to enjoy the presence of God in everything. "...as servants of God we commend ourselves in every way...through glory and dishonor, bad report and good report; genuine, yet regarded as impostors; known, yet regarded as unknown; dying, and yet we live on; beaten, yet not killed; sorrowful, yet making many rich; having nothing, and yet possessing everything." (2 Corinthians 6:4, 8-10)

The world cannot begin to comprehend this paradox; it evaluates riches and richness as merely the one-dimensional accumulation of things of this life. The frustration experienced by the worldly man grows out of the fleeting nature of time and the awareness of mortality.

And yet we would do well to cleave to the warning Jesus gives in the Sermon on the Mount: "Do not store up for yourselves treasures on earth, where moth and rust destroy, and where thieves break in and steal. But store up for yourselves treasures in heaven, where moth and rust do not destroy, and where thieves do not break in and steal. For where your treasure is, there your heart will be also." (Matthew 6:19-21)

At the window of my house I looked out through the lattice. I saw among the simple, I noticed among the young men, a youth who lacked judgment. He was going down the street near her corner, walking along in the direction of her house at twilight, as the day was fading, as the dark of night set in.

—Proverbs 7:6–9

GUIDE ME, LORD

Here the young man departs the company of his friends and opens the way for temptation: "As the day was fading, as the dark of night set in," he moves away from the safety of the town square to the intrigue of the things of the night.

This reminds us that danger is everywhere and no one is exempt. We should constantly pray: "Father help me to withstand temptation; deliver me from the hands of the evil one; help me to walk in your path; let your light illuminate the way so that I will not become lost. Guide me, Lord, for without your presence, my passage through this world would be hopelessly dangerous."

I lift up my eyes to you, to you whose throne is in heaven. As the eyes of slaves look to the hand of their master, as the eyes of a maid look to the hand of her mistress, so our eyes look to the LORD our God, till he shows us his mercy. Have mercy on us, O LORD, have mercy on us, for we have endured much contempt. We have endured much ridicule from the proud, much contempt from the arrogant.

—Psalm 123:1–4

THE STUDENT AND HIS TEACHER

When we think of our relationship with God, do we really think of a slave's relationship to a master or a maid's to her mistress? It is hard to imagine that we would because contemporary thought finds such thinking repugnant. For many, nothing less than being equal is unacceptable, even if there is no reality to back up our claim. So we transform God to fit our diminished idea of Him.

But in reality, it is God who calls us to transformation, asking us to relinquish love of self for the love of God. Jesus defines a right relationship with God this way: "A student is not above his teacher, nor a servant above his master." (Matthew 10:24) Furthermore, he says, "…whoever wants to become great among you must be your servant, and whoever wants to be first must be your slave—just as the Son of Man did not come to be served, but to serve, and to give his life as a ransom for many." (Matthew 20:26-28)

My son, pay attention to what I say; listen closely to my words. Do not let them out of your sight, keep them within your heart; for they are life to those who find them and health to a man's whole body. Above all else, guard your heart, for it is the wellspring of life. Put away perversity from your mouth; keep corrupt talk far from your lips. Let your eyes look straight ahead, fix your gaze directly before you. Make level paths for your feet and take only ways that are firm. Do not swerve to the right or the left; keep your foot from evil.

—*Proverbs 4:20–27*

A PARENT'S WISDOM

Oh, how we wish our wise words could penetrate the hearts of our children so that they might walk a straighter and narrower path than we did in our own youth. As parents, we desire that our children will avoid our mistakes, but if we are wise to the ways of this world, we know that they will invent new pits we never dreamt existed.

In this verse the father is commanding attention, but he is not demanding strict compliance. The father has great wisdom and knows it is important to warn his son that danger lies to the left and the right. If we refrain from warning our children of the real dangers of life, they will blindly proceed ahead and discover too late that they have not guarded their hearts and have not kept their feet from evil.

Pray for your children. Guard their steps with persistent prayers and ask for good guidance as parents.

Does not man have hard service on earth? Are not his days like those of a hired man? Like a slave longing for the evening shadows, or a hired man waiting eagerly for his wages, so I have been allotted months of futility, and nights of misery have been assigned to me. When I lie down I think, "How long before I get up?" The night drags on, and I toss till dawn. My body is clothed with worms and scabs, my skin is broken and festering.

—Job 7:1–5

A CROOKED AND EVIL TIME

If you remove the Christianity of Christ from life and describe raw existence as it really is, you will come up with the picture Job paints here. Without Christ, life is much like the hard service of a hired hand.

In a world where Jesus never existed, one would be forced to adopt a strategy based on either stoicism or its reverse, hedonism. Life in such a world would indeed be nasty, brutish and short, to paraphrase the philosopher Thomas Hobbes.

But in a world where Christ lives through the Holy Spirit, the issue of hard service and suffering is transformed into joyful and willing service no matter the cost. Christ asks those who serve to be strong and persevere, whatever the circumstance. He tells us that to suffer as Christians in a crooked and evil time is a blessed honor that will reap rewards for all eternity. "Blessed are you when people insult you, persecute you and falsely say all kinds of evil against you because of me."

And he then gives the reason for hope: "Rejoice and be glad, because great is your reward in heaven, for in the same way they persecuted the prophets who were before you." (Matthew 5:11-12)

Out of the depths I cry to you, O LORD; O Lord, hear my voice. Let your ears be attentive to my cry for mercy. If you, O LORD, kept a record of sins, O Lord, who could stand? But with you there is forgiveness; therefore you are feared. I wait for the LORD, my soul waits, and in his word I put my hope. My soul waits for the Lord more than watchmen wait for the morning, more than watchmen wait for the morning.

—Psalm 130:1–6

THE PROMISE FULFLLED

The psalmist understands that his dilemma has been caused by a "record of sins." He knows that he cannot cure himself, but must rest his case on the mercy of God. And then he says, "My soul waits for the Lord more than watchmen wait for the morning, more than watchmen wait for the morning."

Repeating the last line puts a special emphasis on his longing for a Savior who will provide the way for the forgiveness of sins and new life through God's grace. It is almost as if he is waiting for the one who "will save his people from their sins." (Matthew 1:21)

And now the Savior has come and has washed away all our sins through the cross; all we need to do is respond as Nathanael did when he realized who Jesus was: "Rabbi, you are the Son of God; you are the King of Israel." (John 1:49) The wait is over; new life is the promise fulfilled.

A scoundrel and villain, who goes about with a corrupt mouth, who winks with his eye, signals with his feet and motions with his fingers, who plots evil with deceit in his heart— he always stirs up dissension. Therefore disaster will overtake him in an instant; he will suddenly be destroyed—without remedy.

—Proverbs 6:12–15

OUT OF MEN'S HEARTS

Doesn't this passage remind you of those early movies where the villain always wore black leaving absolutely no doubt about who the bad guy really was? It is as if the moviemakers took their cue from Proverbs by inventing their villains right out of this play book.

But there is a serious dimension to this passage that should not be overlooked. The scoundrel might speak with a corrupt mouth, wink with his eye and signal with his feet, but all of those external indications of evil come from within, for we are told that he plots deceit in his heart. In the movies, evil is just evil. It is not explained or even properly understood in terms of its cosmic implications. The Bible tells us that evil is an infection that comes out of the unredeemed human heart: "For from within, out of men's hearts, come evil thoughts, sexual immorality, theft, murder, adultery, greed, malice....All these evils come from inside and make a man 'unclean.'" (Mark 7:20-23)

The sea looked and fled, the Jordan turned back; the mountains skipped like rams, the hills like lambs. Why was it, O sea, that you fled, O Jordan, that you turned back, you mountains, that you skipped like rams, you hills, like lambs? Tremble, O earth, at the presence of the Lord, at the presence of the God of Jacob, who turned the rock into a pool, the hard rock into springs of water.

—*Psalm 114:3–8*

MIRACULOUS POSSIBILITIES

Have we been diminished by our obsessive pursuit of the literal? Have we strained out the possibility of the miraculous through the filter of the factual?

It is a fact that the earth moves around the sun at a speed of almost 67,000 miles per hour. And it is a fact that the earth, with a circumference of 24,902 miles, rotates on its axis at approximately 1038 miles per hour to create the 24-hour day. And it is a certainty that a slight change in any of these physical facts would mean for us instant death by fire or by ice.

How did these life-friendly facts come to be without a creator? How would we have any facts at all without the miracle of creation? If we look at all this wondrous creation through the filter of the Spirit of God, we come to a very different and much more fertile interpretation of the "facts" of the miracle of the created universe.

Here is Oswald Chambers on the reasonableness of miracles: "The miracles which our Lord performed (a miracle simply means the public power of God) transcend human reason, but not one of them contradicts human reason. For example, our Lord turned water into wine, but the same thing is done every year all over the world in process of time: water is sucked up through the stem of the vine and turned into grapes. Why should it be considered more of a miracle when it is done suddenly by the same Being who does it gradually?"[6] Opening the eyes of our hearts and unfettering our minds to the reality of the miraculous opens our lives to miraculous possibilities.

The highway of the upright avoids evil; he who guards his way guards his life. Pride goes before destruction, a haughty spirit before a fall. There is a way that seems right to a man, but in the end it leads to death.

—Proverbs 16:17, 18, 25

IN EVERY CORNER OF THE WORLD

A father often will express pride in his son or daughter and a worker will be proud of a task well done, but this is not the pride of "a haughty spirit" nor is it the pride that "goes before destruction."

The seeds of the pride that kills can be found in the earliest chapters of Genesis where the serpent persuades Eve to defy God's warning not to eat of the tree of knowledge of good and evil. The serpent tells her that if she eats of this tree, she "will be like God." (Genesis 3:5) Both Adam and Eve put themselves first by defying God. By wanting to be like God, they deny their own human nature as created by God and fall into the self-consciousness of self-love.

The pattern was set at the very beginning of human history: man's disastrous tendency to deny God by exalting self. The so-called agnostics may not be certain about the existence of God, but they surely put a huge emphasis on self. They repeat the self-destructive mistake of our earliest ancestors.

When you defy God, you *deny* God and thereby make yourself into a false god to fill the void. It is hard to miss this, for evidence abounds on every street in every city in every corner of the world.

My son, if you accept my words and store up my commands within you, turning your ear to wisdom and applying your heart to understanding, and if you call out for insight and cry aloud for understanding, and if you look for it as for silver and search for it as for hidden treasure, then you will understand the fear of the LORD and find the knowledge of God.

—Proverbs 2:1–5

A JOURNEY

When we hear people say that "life is a journey," they are almost always implying that the journey will be from darkness to light, from bad to good and from sin to salvation. This, of course, can be true, but my own experience would suggest that life is more like a very bumpy road, filled with unexpected turns, strange dead ends and ambiguous intersections. It is a journey where we often have no idea where we are going, and rather than admit to our own lack of knowledge, we fake it, pull out the map and point to exactly where we think we might be at any given moment.

Fathers who have been on that uncharted road, have experienced a thing or two and they have a great desire to impart advice about right and wrong ways to their own sons. Will the son hear and avoid wrong turns or will he behave like the lost son in Jesus' parable? "Not long after that, the younger son got together all he had, set off for a distant country and there squandered his wealth in wild living." (Luke 15:13) His journey is just as likely as the upbeat version. The father is right to put up warning signs, but still the son must set forth on his own, deciding which way he will go.

The righteous will see and fear; they will laugh at him, saying, "Here now is the man who did not make God his stronghold but trusted in his great wealth and grew strong by destroying others!" But I am like an olive tree flourishing in the house of God; I trust in God's unfailing love for ever and ever. I will praise you forever for what you have done; in your name I will hope, for your name is good. I will praise you in the presence of your saints.

—Psalm 52:6–9

THE GIFT OF THE HOLY SPIRIT

Philosopher and theologian Thomas Aquinas says: "For no one can truly love God, unless he has the Holy Spirit abiding in his soul, for we do not come to God before the grace of God, but it comes to us first."

Transformation comes when we accept the gift of grace and turn away from our natural disposition to worship self. Then the depth and dimension of the revealed truth of scripture begins to crystallize and we begin to see and feel and understand with new eyes and a new heart: "I love those who love me, and those who seek me find me."(Proverbs 8:17)

Discerning the love of God comes from the Spirit of God that is placed within the heart as a deposit, which then allows us to say with Paul, "We have not received the spirit of the world but the Spirit who is from God that we may understand what God has freely given us." (1 Corinthians 2:12)

When justice is done, it brings joy to the righteous but terror to evildoers. A man who strays from the path of understanding comes to rest in the company of the dead. He who loves pleasure will become poor; whoever loves wine and oil will never be rich. The wicked become a ransom for the righteous, and the unfaithful for the upright. Better to live in a desert than with a quarrelsome and ill-tempered wife. In the house of the wise are stores of choice food and oil, but a foolish man devours all he has. He who pursues righteousness and love finds life, prosperity and honor.

—Proverbs 21:15–21

CHOOSE LIFE

It is easy to skim over words of wisdom because they seem so normal. Everyone is for justice, right? And we all know that straying from the right path can cause disaster.

But what if the entire culture begins to wander away from the norm, when "[t]he wicked freely strut about when what is vile is honored among men." (Psalm 12:8)

God has a norm and he builds a longing for that norm in every human heart. When we are right with God, we understand and love justice and we abhor every injustice when we see it. We understand that there is a way that leads to death and we avoid it. We plan and make provision for the future and try not to squander our wealth on foolish things. God's norm is a pathway that leads to life; when the reverse is honored, then we find ourselves enslaved in a culture of death.

God says this to the people of the promise as they prepare to cross the Jordan River to enter the new land: "This day I call heaven and earth as witnesses against you that I have set before you life and death, blessings and curses. Now choose life, so that you and your children may live and that you may love the Lord your God, listen to his voice, and hold fast to him. For the Lord is your life, and he will give you many years in the land he swore to give to your fathers, Abraham, Isaac and Jacob." (Deuteronomy 30:19-20)

What does the worker gain from his toil? I have seen the burden God has laid on men. He has made everything beautiful in its time. He has also set eternity in the hearts of men; yet they cannot fathom what God has done from beginning to end.

—Ecclesiastes 3:9–11

THIS IS ETERNAL LIFE

To have everything is never enough. We strive, we attain and we strive again, reaching ever higher but never high enough.

Solomon tells us that this persistent yearning is a gift from God, but we should be warned that this desire for the eternal can be corrupted when we take our focus off God and, instead, substitute a longing for worldly gain.

Jesus speaks of this heart-centered inclination when he explains the meaning of his parable of the sower: "Still others, like seed sown among thorns, hear the word; but the worries of this life, the deceitfulness of wealth and the desires for other things come in and choke the word, making it unfruitful."

God planted "eternity in the hearts of men" so that we could be His ambassadors in this world, and "like seed sown on good soil, hear the word, accept it, and produce a crop-thirty, sixty or even a hundred times what was sown." (Mark 4:18-20) The gift has been given to each of us; how we use it is a question each one of us must answer.

Come, let us sing for joy to the LORD; let us shout aloud to the Rock of our salvation. Let us come before him with thanksgiving and extol him with music and song. For the LORD is the great God, the great King above all gods. In his hand are the depths of the earth, and the mountain peaks belong to him. The sea is his, for he made it, and his hands formed the dry land. Come, let us bow down in worship, let us kneel before the LORD our Maker; for he is our God and we are the people of his pasture, the flock under his care.

—Psalm 95:1–7

SING AND MAKE MUSIC

Worship is so much more than a Sunday event. It is the everyday expression of our gratitude to the Author of all creation and for the amazing provision that we experience each day. Genuine worship wells up from the heart and transforms the mind so that we see and feel God's presence everywhere.

With Paul we can see the world with new eyes: "For since the creation of the world God's invisible qualities-his eternal power and divine nature-have been clearly seen, being understood from what has been made..." (Romans 1:20)

And so we come to sing for joy to the Lord. We rejoice, shouting aloud to the Rock of our salvation. Paul tells the Ephesians what perfect worship looks like: "...be filled with the Spirit. Speak to one another with psalms, hymns and spiritual songs. Sing and make music in your heart to the Lord, always giving thanks to God the Father for everything, in the name of our Lord Jesus Christ." (Ephesians 5:18-20)

In spite of all this, they kept on sinning; in spite of his wonders, they did not believe. So he ended their days in futility and their years in terror. Whenever God slew them, they would seek him; they eagerly turned to him again. They remembered that God was their Rock, that God Most High was their Redeemer. But then they would flatter him with their mouths, lying to him with their tongues; their hearts were not loyal to him, they were not faithful to his covenant. Yet he was merciful; he forgave their iniquities and did not destroy them. Time after time he restrained his anger and did not stir up his full wrath. He remembered that they were but flesh, a passing breeze that does not return.

—Psalm 78:32–39

GOD IS FAITHFUL

The people of Israel had, by the grace of God, been brought out of slavery in Egypt with the promise that they would be led to a land of "milk and honey." To get there they needed to travel across the Sinai Desert. But as the hardships of the journey increased, they turned against Moses and their leaders and against God because "they did not believe." (v32) God in His graciousness had liberated them from the hardship and humiliation of bondage, but their unfaithfulness led them deeper into the desert wilderness where their "days ended in futility and their years in terror." (v33)

When we consider faithfulness, we should remember that God is always faithful; we, on the other hand, are the ones who are like infants "tossed back and forth by the waves and blown here and there by every wind of teaching...." (Ephesians 4:14) We should take heart that we have a merciful and loving God, but we, who have been delivered out of the bondage of sin, should remember that we are called to follow Him, even when it is hard to do so.

Like a muddied spring or a polluted well is a righteous man who gives way to the wicked.

—*Proverbs 25:26*

JUDAS

A man who once walked with God, but then turns away and walks alone, not only betrays God, but also betrays the Holy Spirit. This person suffers a terrible depth of despair.

Judas, an apostle who walked with the Lord, turned on his master and betrayed him for thirty pieces of silver. Judas was seemingly a righteous man who served the Lord, but when doubt crept in, he gave way to temptation, took the money, led the guards to the Garden of Gethsemane and identified Jesus with a kiss. At that moment, the darkness of despair entered his soul and he began to experience deep regret which became remorse and finally, utter hopelessness.

"When Judas, who had betrayed him, saw that Jesus was condemned, he was seized with remorse and returned the thirty silver coins to the chief priests and the elders. 'I have sinned,' he said, 'for I have betrayed innocent blood.' 'What is that to us?' they replied. 'That's your responsibility.' So Judas threw the money into the temple and left. Then he went away and hanged himself." (Matthew 27:3-5)

But as for me, my feet had almost slipped; I had nearly lost my foothold. For I envied the arrogant when I saw the prosperity of the wicked. They have no struggles; their bodies are healthy and strong. They are free from the burdens common to man; they are not plagued by human ills. Therefore pride is their necklace; they clothe themselves with violence. From their callous hearts comes iniquity; the evil conceits of their minds know no limits. They scoff, and speak with malice; in their arrogance they threaten oppression. Their mouths lay claim to heaven, and their tongues take possession of the earth. Therefore their people turn to them and drink up waters in abundance. They say, "How can God know? Does the Most High have knowledge?" This is what the wicked are like— always carefree, they increase in wealth. Surely in vain have I kept my heart pure; in vain have I washed my hands in innocence. All day long I have been plagued; I have been punished every morning.

—Psalm 73:2–14

ALL IN VAIN?

Does it make any sense to say, "in vain have I kept my heart pure; in vain have I washed my hands in innocence?" (v13)

If we look at events strictly from the world's point of view, we can sympathize with people who mourn the fact that the spoils seem to go to the wicked, the arrogant and the powerful.

Referring to religious hypocrites who love to show off their power and position, Jesus gives us a different perspective: "I tell you the truth, they have received their reward in full." (Matthew 6:5) He makes a distinction that needs to be repeated every day: rewards in this life do not necessarily lead to the reward of eternal life; likewise, the reward of eternal life is often preceded by great suffering in this life. What appears to be victory for the wicked in this world may be a prelude to something very different in the next.

Like snow in summer or rain in harvest, honor is not fitting for a fool. Like a fluttering sparrow or a darting swallow, an undeserved curse does not come to rest. A whip for the horse, a halter for the donkey, and a rod for the backs of fools! Do not answer a fool according to his folly, or you will be like him yourself.

—Proverbs 26:1–4

A FOOL FOR GOD

A fool engages in self-destructive tendencies that seem irrational to most people. Does the Bible tell us what causes people to act in ways that are harmful to their own well being?

Yes. In Psalm 14, it says, "The fool says in his heart, 'There is no God.'" The psalmist tells us the fool begins his strange odyssey by denying the existence of God. By rejecting God, the fool frees himself to do anything he wants. The fool lives without boundaries even as he comes up against boundaries every day. For we are free to reject God and we are free to act in destructive ways.

The freedom that allows us to become a fool is a gift of God. But God wants us freely to embrace the wisdom of trusting Him. He wants us to choose to follow in His way, thus becoming a fool (in the opinion of the world) for God. "For the foolishness of God is wiser than man's wisdom, and the weakness of God is stronger than man's strength." (1 Corinthians 1:25)

The LORD will extend your mighty scepter from Zion; you will rule in the midst of your enemies. Your troops will be willing on your day of battle. Arrayed in holy majesty, from the womb of the dawn you will receive the dew of your youth.

—Psalm 110:2–3

FRIENDS AT OUR SIDE

In the midst of the chaos of battle, the outcome always remains in doubt. We fight from minute to minute and depend upon split second decisions that may lead to disaster or triumph. But war is merely everyday life accelerated.

When life is lived at the normal pace, we seem to have time to deliberate in order to arrive at the right decision about the next move. In this condition, we also have the luxury of living within a pattern of repetitive experiences that allow us to makes many decisions as if we were on automatic pilot.

But we delude ourselves if we live as if tomorrow is predictable and certain. Whether we are at war or peace, the principles remain the same: We must choose to act on the information we have at that moment. We must turn to the right or to the left, aware that one way may lead us to the mountain while the other may lead us to the swamp. Therefore, we must depend on more than our own intuition and judgment.

We need reliable friends at our side because it is better that decisions not be made in isolation. And where we put our full trust in God, we always have a friend at our side helping us in all our decisions. For without Him, the battle will be lost and the soldiers will be unwilling: "Therefore, you kings, be wise; be warned, you rulers of the earth. Serve the Lord with fear and rejoice with trembling." (Psalm 2:10-11)

As you do not know the path of the wind, or how the body is formed in a mother's womb, so you cannot understand the work of God, the Maker of all things.

—Ecclesiastes 11:5

CLEVERNESS WITHOUT COMPASS

Wisdom is often thought of as a product of the intellect. If we can only come to know enough, we are told, then we will become wise. But often mere intellect is cleverness without compass. God did not call us to love Him only with our minds; He said, "Love the Lord your God with all your heart and with all your soul and with all your strength." (Deuteronomy 6:5) To know God intellectually leads to futility because the mind can analyze and compute, but it cannot love. If we think of God only as an aspect of our theology, we are already in opposition to God's greatest commandment. God commanded us to love Him; He did not command us to think about loving Him. "The reason people disbelieve God is not because they do not understand with their heads-we understand very few things with our heads-but because they have turned their hearts in another direction."[7] Man's pride may be seated in his intellectual prowess, but his righteousness grows out of a true and faithful heart.

Can you pull in the leviathan with a fishhook or tie down his tongue with a rope? Can you put a cord through his nose or pierce his jaw with a hook? Will he keep begging you for mercy? Will he speak to you with gentle words? Will he make an agreement with you for you to take him as your slave for life? Can you make a pet of him like a bird or put him on a leash for your girls? Will traders barter for him? Will they divide him up among the merchants? Can you fill his hide with harpoons or his head with fishing spears? If you lay a hand on him, you will remember the struggle and never do it again! Any hope of subduing him is false; the mere sight of him is overpowering. No one is fierce enough to rouse him. Who then is able to stand against me? Who has a claim against me that I must pay? Everything under heaven belongs to me.

—Job 41:1–11

FISHING FOR LEVIATHAN

Leviathan, or the great whale, is not a fish you would try to catch with an ordinary fishing pole. Yet God tells Job that mankind has been doing just that by trying to capture God with our imagined idea of who God is.

We are fishing for leviathan when we try to limit God by defining Him down to a size that will allow us to believe that we are in control of every aspect of life. We are surprised when we find leviathan at the other end of the line. But as with leviathan so with God: "If you lay a hand on him, you will remember the struggle and never do it again!"(v8)

It is very common to try to bring God down to our own size, but the endeavor will fail utterly, as it failed when mankind tried to build a tower that would reach heaven. "As the heavens are higher than the earth, so are my ways higher than your ways and my thoughts than your thoughts." (Isaiah 55:8-9)

Rather than the futility of fishing for leviathan, Jesus turned the tables completely around. In the early days of his three-year ministry, he called to meek fishermen to be his followers and he made them a promise; he would transform each of them into a different kind of fisherman. "'Come", follow me,' Jesus said," 'and I will make you fishers of men.'" (Matthew 4:19) Man fishing for leviathan is foolish arrogance. God fishing for men is the very embodiment of hope and love that flows through faith in Jesus Christ.

Not only was the Teacher wise, but also he imparted knowledge to the people. He pondered and searched out and set in order many proverbs. The Teacher searched to find just the right words, and what he wrote was upright and true. The words of the wise are like goads, their collected sayings like firmly embedded nails—given by one Shepherd. Be warned, my son, of anything in addition to them. Of making many books there is no end, and much study wearies the body.

—Ecclesiastes 12:9–12

THE LANGUAGE OF GOD

How do we become literate in the language of the spirit of God? What are the "right words" given by "one Shepherd?"

Jesus is that "one Shepherd," but when he spoke, he was often misunderstood because he spoke in the figurative language of the Holy Spirit. Nicodemus came to Jesus with a literal spirit, and so, was bewildered when Jesus told him, "I tell you the truth, no one can see the kingdom of God unless he is born again." (John 3:3) Likewise, the Samaritan woman is blinded at first by her ethnic literalism: "You are a Jew and I am a Samaritan woman. How can you ask me for a drink?" (John 4:9) But Jesus speaks of another kind of water that never fails and that wells "up to eternal life." (John 4:14)

Then Jesus speaks of a time when all barriers will be broken down and one language will be spoken: "Yet a time is coming and has now come when the true worshippers will worship the Father in spirit and truth, for they are the kind of worshippers the Father seeks. God is spirit, and his worshippers must worship in spirit and in truth." (John 4:23-24)

If we are bound by a spiritual literalism, then we should pray that our Emmaus moment will come: "And beginning with Moses and all the Prophets, he explained to them what was said in all the Scriptures concerning himself...Then their eyes were opened and they recognized him, and he disappeared from their sight. They asked each other, 'Were not our hearts burning within us while he talked with us on the road and opened the Scriptures to us?'" (Luke 24:27-32)

Rescue me, O LORD, from evil men; protect me from men of violence, who devise evil plans in their hearts and stir up war every day. They make their tongues as sharp as a serpent's; the poison of vipers is on their lips. Keep me, O LORD, from the hands of the wicked; protect me from men of violence who plan to trip my feet. Proud men have hidden a snare for me; they have spread out the cords of their net and have set traps for me along my path.

—Psalm 140:1–5

THE RIGHTEOUS WILL PREVAIL

Here we have the prayer of a righteous man. Evildoers surround him and he is in great danger. Those opposing him "devise evil plans" and "stir up war every day"; their words are poisonous and they lie in wait to snare their victim. In other words, both the prophet and the disciple are guaranteed active and treacherous opposition.

When Jesus embarked on his three-year ministry, he encountered strong resistance from religious and political authorities. From his first teaching in Nazareth where "All the people in the synagogue were furious" at what they heard (Luke 4:28) to the final treachery of Judas, Jesus is attacked by the very same forces that threatened David. But take heart, for the righteous will prevail: "Rejoice and be glad" because great is your reward in heaven, for in the same way they persecuted the prophets who were before you." (Matthew 5:12)

The wicked lie in wait for the righteous, seeking their very lives; but the LORD will not leave them in their power or let them be condemned when brought to trial.

—Psalm 37:32–33

THE LORD WILL NOT ABANDON THEM

Does the presence of evil in the world invalidate the reality of the existence of God? Some would say so. Why does God permit evil and injustice to exist? Why do innocent people fall prey to violent men? "(God) causes the sun to rise on the evil and the good, and sends rain on the righteous and the unrighteous." (Matthew 5:45)

And yet today's verse tells us that justice will always prevail for those who are righteous before God: "...the Lord will not leave them in their power or let them be condemned when brought to trial." (v33)

My days are swifter than a weaver's shuttle, and they come to an end without hope. Remember, O God, that my life is but a breath; my eyes will never see happiness again. The eye that now sees me will see me no longer; you will look for me, but I will be no more. As a cloud vanishes and is gone, so he who goes down to the grave does not return. He will never come to his house again; his place will know him no more.

—Job 7:6–10

THE WHOLE DUTY OF MAN

Contemporary caregivers might diagnose Job as being depressed and prescribe medicine to relieve his symptoms. But do pills fix the problem or do they just cover it up?

Job's lamentation is appealing because he describes a reality all people face: "You sweep men away in the sleep of death; they are like the new grass of the morning-though in the morning it springs up new, by evening it is dry and withered." (Psalm 90:5-6)

If this life is all there is, then depression would not be an inappropriate response. Solomon called such a life "meaningless:" And Job summarizes the stark facts of such an existence this way: "For this is your lot in life and in your toilsome labor under the sun. Whatever your hand finds to do, do it with all your might, for in the grave, where you are going, there is neither working nor planning nor knowledge nor wisdom."(Job 9:9-10)

Yet neither Job nor Solomon fall into the trap of succumbing to the view that there is no God and that life is full of sound and fury signifying nothing. The ways of God may not always seem brilliantly clear, but this is not cause for abandoning God. In the end, Job says, "I know my Redeemer lives, and in the end he will stand upon the earth. And after my skin has been destroyed, yet in my flesh I will see God." (Job 19:25-26) And Solomon says this: "Now all has been heard; here is the conclusion of the matter: Fear God and keep his commandments, for this is the whole duty of man."(Ecclesiastes 12:13)

Who is this coming up from the desert leaning on her lover? Under the apple tree I roused you; there your mother conceived you, there she who was in labor gave you birth. Place me like a seal over your heart, like a seal on your arm; for love is as strong as death, its jealousy unyielding as the grave. It burns like blazing fire, like a mighty flame. Many waters cannot quench love; rivers cannot wash it away. If one were to give all the wealth of his house for love, it would be utterly scorned.

—*Song of Songs 8:5–7*

THE MEANING OF LOVE

God's love for man, even wayward man, is the central truth of the Bible. Reestablishing the original relationship between man and God is the central purpose of the life and death of Jesus Christ. "We love because He (God, the Father) first loved us." (1 John 4:19) "No, the Father himself loves you because you have loved me and have believed that I came from God." (John 16:27) "My command is this: Love each other as I have loved you. Greater love has no one than this, that he lay down his life for his friends. You are my friends if you do what I command." (John 15:12) "God is love. Whoever lives in love lives in God, and God in him." (1 John 4:16)

Paul says this: "Love is patient, love is kind. It does not envy, it does not boast, it is not proud. It is not rude, it is not self-seeking, it is not easily angered, it keeps no record of wrongs. Love does not delight in evil, but rejoices with the truth. It always protects, always trusts, always hopes, always perseveres." (1 Corinthians 13:4-7)

Give thanks to the LORD, call on his name; make known among the nations what he has done. Sing to him, sing praise to him; tell of all his wonderful acts. Glory in his holy name; let the hearts of those who seek the LORD rejoice. Look to the LORD and his strength; seek his face always. Remember the wonders he has done, his miracles, and the judgments he pronounced.

—Psalm 105:1–5

SOME VERY RELIGIOUS PEOPLE

One weekend not long ago, I was invited to speak to a group of people who were very spiritual. They spoke of the "spirit," but the spirit they talked about seemed foreign to the Holy Spirit as described in the Bible. When they tried to explain their beliefs, they would return to the Almighty Self as the source of all their joy, their hopes and their faith.

It was as if in rejecting the religion of their youth and in pursuing the desires of their own hearts, they were afraid to reject God altogether and so, hedging their bets, they made up a brand new faith that spoke to their individual needs and aspirations. In fact, the believers were so various in their beliefs that it seemed as if I had entered a spiritual Babel.

The particulars of their many philosophies I will not try to recount. However, I was struck by the sense of sheer desperation because their faith seemed to be built on near total subjectivity: "God is real if He/She is real to me. I am the author of my own life and it is my right to define God in any way that I want to. Furthermore, I love everyone, except those I believe are enemies." And on and on.

I was reminded of Paul in Athens (all the Athenians and the foreigners who lived there spent their time doing nothing but talking about and listening to the latest ideas): "…Men of Athens! I see that in every way you are very religious. For as I walked around and looked at your objects of worship, I even found an altar with this inscription: To An Unknown God." (Acts 17:21-23)

Apparently, it is possible to be both religious and idolatrous. I witnessed it.

Listen, my son, and be wise, and keep your heart on the right path. Do not join those who drink too much wine or gorge themselves on meat, for drunkards and gluttons become poor, and drowsiness clothes them in rags.

—Proverbs 23:19–21

REDEMPTION

An unredeemed world is an arid place where the iron law of inevitable consequences prevails. It is a world of predictable outcomes, a place free of mystery and miracles, a world devoid of hope.

So when the father addresses the son in the proverb and he speaks of the consequences of deviating from the "right path," (v19) he speaks of wisdom apart from redemption.

But, elsewhere, Job prophetically speaks of a redeeming God, one who loves His lost children enough to bring them back through the sacrifice of His one and only son, Jesus Christ. Through the power of the cross, the most craven criminal can break the chains of inevitability to find new life and hope through the One who died for all. "For he (God, the Father) has rescued us from the dominion of darkness and brought us into the kingdom of the Son he loves, in whom we have redemption, the forgiveness of sins." (Colossians 1:13-14)

You are not a God who takes pleasure in evil; with you the wicked cannot dwell. The arrogant cannot stand in your presence; you hate all who do wrong. You destroy those who tell lies; bloodthirsty and deceitful men the LORD abhors.

—Psalm 5:4–6

A GOD OF WRATH?

The God of the Old Testament has a reputation of being a wrathful God, which this passage would seem to support: "You hate all who do wrong. You destroy those who tell lies...." (v5, 6)

But do we have the mirror pointed in the right direction? This verse does not say that God hates his children; rather it points to those who have rejected God and have become wicked, arrogant, bloodthirsty and deceitful. It is not God who has turned away. It is His children who have abandoned their inheritance for worthless things. They have become rebellious and treacherous to the One who loves them, forgetting all the while that God is also a God of judgment: "...the Lord knows how to rescue godly men from trials and to hold the unrighteous for the day of judgment, while continuing their punishment. This is especially true of those who follow the corrupt desire of the sinful nature and despise authority." (2 Peter 2:9-10)

Job continued his discourse: "How I long for the months gone by, for the days when God watched over me, when his lamp shone upon my head and by his light I walked through darkness! Oh, for the days when I was in my prime, when God's intimate friendship blessed my house, when the Almighty was still with me and my children were around me, when my path was drenched with cream and the rock poured out for me streams of olive oil."

—Job 29:1–6

ADAM'S CHOICE

As we journey through life, we seem to experience the loss of something precious, but we cannot quite put our finger on what it is. Job says, "How I long...for the days when God watched over me...Oh, for the days when I was in my prime, when God's intimate friendship blessed my house...."

This universal sense of loss was reversed on Calvary, but up until that moment in history, the human story was written by the choice of Adam, the first man. He too walked with God: "The Lord God took the man and put him in the Garden of Eden to work and take care of it." (Genesis 2:15) "In the middle of the garden were the tree of life and the tree of knowledge of good and evil." (Genesis 2:9)

Adam was commanded not to eat of the second tree or he would die and lose access to the tree of life. But he disobeyed, and forever after, until the advent of Christ, we have all felt the sting of Adam's sin. "So the Lord God banished him from the Garden of Eden to work the ground from which he had been taken. After he drove the man out, he placed on the east side of the Garden of Eden cherubim and a flaming sword flashing back and forth to guard the way to the tree of life." (Genesis 3:23-24)

From that time until Calvary, all men and women were born exiles; all experienced the same sense of loss and all longed to find a path "drenched with cream" and rocks that "poured out for (us) streams of olive oil."(v6)

Let the sea resound, and everything in it, the world, and all who live in it. Let the rivers clap their hands, let the mountains sing together for joy; let them sing before the LORD, for he comes to judge the earth. He will judge the world in righteousness and the peoples with equity.

—*Psalm 98:7–9*

MUSIC IN THE HEAVENLY SPHERES

It is tragic when men attempt to reduce the world to a collection of "objective" facts. Can we really claim objectivity when we are so intimately dependent on the very world we wish to know? We breathe it, we feel it, we move in it as it relentlessly moves. The rational mind rejects this intimacy, depending instead on the selective power of reason to achieve understanding and knowledge.

Wisdom, though, requires the attention of our hearts as well as our heads. Our minds alone cannot hear "the rivers clap their hands," nor can the mind alone hear "the mountains sing together for joy...." But when we walk in faith, trusting in the Lord as the creator of the very world we wish to know, then the whole world becomes a symphony making music before the Lord and all his creation, singing praise to His glorious name: "Sing to the Lord a new song, for he has done marvelous things...." (Psalm 98:1)

You are a garden locked up, my sister, my bride; you are a spring enclosed, a sealed fountain. Your plants are an orchard of pomegranates with choice fruits, with henna and nard, nard and saffron, calamus and cinnamon, with every kind of incense tree, with myrrh and aloes and all the finest spices. You are a garden fountain, a well of flowing water streaming down from Lebanon.

—Song of Songs 4:12–15

A COPY OF THE ORIGINAL

Song of Songs is an extended love poem; here it describes the passion a man has for a woman, ("How beautiful you are, my darling! Oh, how beautiful!") as well as the love a woman has for a man. ("Let him kiss me with the kisses of his mouth-for your love is more delightful than wine.")

But Solomon is speaking of something beyond physical desire. The lover is compared to a garden fed by a spring of "flowing water," a garden abundantly provided with every kind of fruit and sustenance. This place, so fair and plentiful, resembles the original garden, Eden, where the first man and woman lived in harmony with God and with nature. It was a place created in love and for love, the love between God, the creator, and man, the one He created.

The love of a man for a woman should be understood as a copy of the original; we long to be in a place where love and abundance abide: this garden is "an orchard of pomegranates with choice fruits, with henna and nard, nard and saffron, calamus and cinnamon, with every kind of incense tree, with myrrh and aloes and all the finest spices." (v13-14)

A wife of noble character who can find? She is worth far more than rubies. Her husband has full confidence in her and lacks nothing of value. She brings him good, not harm, all the days of her life. She selects wool and flax and works with eager hands. She is like the merchant ships, bringing her food from afar. She gets up while it is still dark; she provides food for her family and portions for her servant girls. She considers a field and buys it; out of her earnings she plants a vineyard. She sets about her work vigorously; her arms are strong for her tasks. She sees that her trading is profitable, and her lamp does not go out at night. In her hand she holds the distaff and grasps the spindle with her fingers. She opens her arms to the poor and extends her hands to the needy. When it snows, she has no fear for her household; for all of them are clothed in scarlet. She makes coverings for her bed; she is clothed in fine linen and purple. Her husband is respected at the city gate, where he takes his seat among the elders of the land.

—Proverbs 31:10–23

THE POWER OF TWO

The wife described here is of noble character because she knows that she is a partner in a great joint venture and the success of the enterprise will very much depend on her: "She is worth far more than rubies. Her husband has full confidence in her and lacks nothing of value." (v10)This is the way God intended it. "The Lord God said, 'It is not good for the man to be alone. I will make a helper suitable for him." (Genesis 2:18)

And Paul reminds us how God wants us to be with our wives: "In the same way, husbands ought to love their wives as their own bodies. He who loves his wife loves himself...For this reason a man will leave his father and mother and be united to his wife, and the two will become one flesh." (Ephesians 5:28, 31) Joined together as one, we become stronger than if we stand alone: "Two are better than one, because they have good return for their work....But pity the man who falls and has no one to help him up!" (Ecclesiastes 4:9-10)

He sends his command to the earth; his word runs swiftly. He spreads the snow like wool and scatters the frost like ashes. He hurls down his hail like pebbles. Who can withstand his icy blast? He sends his word and melts them; he stirs up his breezes, and the waters flow.

—Psalm 147:15–18

GENUINE THIRST

I was hiking in the Selway-Bitterroot Wilderness in Montana several years ago when I took a wrong turn. I thought I was on the right track and I was comforted by the fact that the map showed a small body of water up ahead so I continued on.

But as I climbed higher, the land grew dryer; trees and vegetation gave way to dust and unrelenting heat and my supply of water quickly dwindled to a few drops. I thought of turning back, but I foolishly decided to forge ahead to what became even dryer and more isolated ground.

Within an hour, the water on the map became a longing, then an obsession, then an urgent necessity. I was becoming desperate when I finally stumbled upon a shallow pool of still water. Without hesitation, I drank it as if it was the sweetest water I had ever tasted. I experienced great relief and great joy at something as common as water because my body desperately needed replenishment.

What is true for the body depleted of life-giving water is just as true for the soul of any person wandering in a spiritual wasteland. David says, "As a deer pants for streams of water, so my soul pants for you, O God. My soul thirsts for God, for the living God." (Psalm 42:1-2) And elsewhere, he says, "O God, you are my God, earnestly I seek you; my soul thirsts for you, my body longs for you, in a dry and weary land where there is no water." (Psalm 63:1)

Our physical thirst mirrors a thirst deep within the human heart. Will we turn and find drink to quench this thirst or will we continue farther into the dry land where there is little water to be found?

Take heed, you senseless ones among the people; you fools, when will you become wise? Does he who implanted the ear not hear? Does he who formed the eye not see? Does he who disciplines nations not punish? Does he who teaches man lack knowledge? The LORD knows the thoughts of man; he knows that they are futile.

—*Psalm 94:8–11*

CONSIDER THE EYE

Yes, consider the eye. We marvel at images created by cameras. We are amazed at the technological power of film and the pictures they produce. We sit transfixed before a television set or the big screen of a movie theatre, but do we ever consider the original technology that surpasses all the imagery generated by the hand of man?

Consider the eye with its ability to translate trillions of particles of light into images instantly comprehensible to the human brain. "Does he who formed the eye not see?"(v9) We may be able to dissect the eye and explain its function, but can we explain how the eye came to be in the first place? We may marvel at technology, but it is the far greater work of God that deserves our attention and our wonder.

Hope deferred makes the heart sick, but a longing fulfilled is a tree of life.

—Proverbs 13:12

I PRESS ON

In war, we long for peace; in sickness, we long for health; when we are lonely, we seek friends and when we are away, we yearn for home and family. The present moment never seems to be enough; we are restless and wish to satisfy a powerful drive for something better. For many, this need expresses itself through the desire to recover something lost. In others, it translates into a quest for a better life here and now.

The Christian is also striving, but with a difference: As his faith grows stronger, his longing becomes a desire to know and follow Jesus as an intimate friend. "I want to know Christ and the power of his resurrection....Not that I have already obtained all this, or have already been made perfect, but I press on to take hold of that for which Christ Jesus took hold of me....One thing I do: Forgetting what is behind and straining toward what is ahead, I press on toward the goal to win the prize for which God has called me heavenward in Christ Jesus." (Philippians 3:10, 12-14)

Those living far away fear your wonders; where morning dawns and evening fades you call forth songs of joy. You care for the land and water it; you enrich it abundantly. The streams of God are filled with water to provide the people with grain, for so you have ordained it. You drench its furrows and level its ridges; you soften it with showers and bless its crops. You crown the year with your bounty, and your carts overflow with abundance. The grasslands of the desert overflow; the hills are clothed with gladness. The meadows are covered with flocks and the valleys are mantled with grain; they shout for joy and sing.

—Psalm 65:8–13

AN UNLIKELY SAVIOR

Picture the Shire in Tolkien's *Lord of the Rings*: It is a gentle and bounteous place where "the hills are clothed with gladness. The meadows are covered with flocks and the valleys are mantled with grain."(v11, 13)

But right below the surface of this peaceful and pleasant image lies an ominous presence that threatens the very existence of the idyllic Shire. The gathering menace promises the desolation described by the prophet Jeremiah: "The ruined city lies desolate; the entrance to every house is barred. In the streets they cry out for wine; all joy turns to gloom, all gaiety is banished from the earth. The city is left in ruins, its gate is battered to pieces. So it will be on the earth and among the nations...."(Jeremiah 24:10-13)

But Tolkien wrote an epic of salvation and hope where the peaceful Shire is saved through the quest of the most unlikely heroes. The prophets of Israel also tell of a savior to come who will restore peace and joy to the land and who will invite us join the battle in his name. And he too will be just as unlikely as the fictional hobbits: "He had no beauty or majesty to attract us to him, nothing in his appearance that we should desire him. He was despised and rejected by men, a man of sorrows, and familiar with suffering." (Isaiah 53:2-3)

Some trust in chariots and some in horses, but we trust in the name of the LORD our God. They are brought to their knees and fall, but we rise up and stand firm. O LORD, save the king! Answer us when we call!

—Psalm 20:7–9

TRUST IN THE LORD

Let's start with the fundamentals: It is impossible to function successfully in life without a strong dose of trust. Think about it: If we were able to exist independently of every one else, we might be able to achieve a state of total self-reliance.

But from the time we are conceived, we are intimately involved in the lives of other people, beginning with our own mothers and fathers. As we emerge from childhood, we become aware of our interdependence with the world at large. When we play sports, we join teams and when we begin to work, we join organizations. Libraries are filled with books on "networking" and "teamwork."

But to live in this world without trust would inject us into a world of suspicion, intrigue and paranoia. We would be incapable of acting because we would see threatening forces behind every tree and hidden in every office. Trust, therefore, is an essential component of our human nature. We need to trust to live effective, healthy lives, but even then, we need to discern who is and who is not worthy of our trust: "Some trust in chariots and some in horses, but we trust in the name of the Lord our God." (v9)

Pay attention and listen to the sayings of the wise; apply your heart to what I teach, for it is pleasing when you keep them in your heart and have all of them ready on your lips. So that your trust may be in the LORD, I teach you today, even you. Have I not written thirty sayings for you, sayings of counsel and knowledge, teaching you true and reliable words, so that you can give sound answers to him who sent you?

—Proverbs 22:17–21

BE TEACHERS OF YOUR CHILDREN

Fathers, do not be discouraged. Though it often seems that our children are heading off to a distant country equipped only with a wild and unrestrained heart, they have heard your "sayings of counsel and knowledge" which have made an impression and which they will carry with them wherever they go.

As fathers, we are called to be teachers and all important teaching begins at home. And here are the words of wisdom that transcend time and place: "Hear, O Israel: The Lord our God, the Lord is one. Love the Lord your God with all your heart and with all your soul and with all your strength. These commandments that I give you today are to be upon your hearts. Impress them on your children. Talk about them when you sit at home and when you walk along the road, when you lie down and when you get up." (Deuteronomy 6:4-7)

"But when you teach, teach with your life, not with mere words that are undermined by contradictory behavior: "Fathers, do not exasperate your children; instead, bring them up in the training and instruction of the Lord." (Ephesians 6:4)

I cried out to God for help; I cried out to God to hear me. When I was in distress, I sought the Lord; at night I stretched out untiring hands and my soul refused to be comforted. I remembered you, O God, and I groaned; I mused, and my spirit grew faint. You kept my eyes from closing; I was too troubled to speak. I thought about the former days, the years of long ago; I remembered my songs in the night. My heart mused and my spirit inquired: "Will the Lord reject forever? Will he never show his favor again? Has his unfailing love vanished forever? Has his promise failed for all time? Has God forgotten to be merciful? Has he in anger withheld his compassion?"

—Psalm 77:1–9

AN UNBEARABLE LOSS

Implanted within the soul of every person is a longing for something lost. This is true even of young people, but it becomes acutely evident as we move through the middle years and become dragged down by circumstance and trouble. We look over our shoulders and with the psalmist, we lament: "I thought about the former days, the years of long ago; I remembered my songs in the night." (v5, 6)

It is as if the biblical story of the Garden of Eden is somehow an intertwined part of who we were and what we long to recapture. It is when the loss becomes unbearable that we cry out to God for help; we cry out to God to hear us and understand our lament.

Though the LORD is on high, he looks upon the lowly, but the proud he knows from afar. Though I walk in the midst of trouble, you preserve my life; you stretch out your hand against the anger of my foes, with your right hand you save me. The LORD will fulfill his purpose for me; your love, O LORD, endures forever—do not abandon the works of your hands.

—Psalm 138:6–8

IN THE MIDST OF TROUBLE

Have you ever read a passage from a book and suddenly a line or word or phrase leaps right off the page and grabs you?

Sometimes you will read a verse and it glances right off your consciousness. You may absorb it, but it doesn't stop you in your tracks. Then, for no apparent reason, that same passage becomes electric and now you see it and feel it for the first time ever.

That happened to me with this verse: "Though I walk in the midst of trouble, you preserve my life." In twelve short words, I finally saw the truth of what had happened to me several years before.

It would be easy to say that when trouble befell me, I met the challenge and conquered the foe. I could have claimed victory, but my heart told me that the victory wasn't mine. I had walked in the midst of desperate trouble, but the trouble never seemed to touch me. I walked through it and survived. This verse told me why I survived. It was not my will, but God's will that it should be so. Recognizing that truth changed everything.

This is the way of an adulteress: She eats and wipes her mouth and says, "I've done nothing wrong."

—*Proverbs 30:20*

SELF-JUSTIFICATION

Denying our own sinfulness is as old as human history itself. After succumbing to temptation, Adam and Eve come up with every unsupportable excuse in the book to explain why they recklessly betrayed God's commandment. Eve said, "The serpent deceived me and I ate." And the man said, "The woman...gave me some fruit from the tree, and I ate." (Genesis 3:13, 12)

When we indulge our sinful nature and give way to temptation, we immediately default to self-justification and excuse making. But behind the assertion that "I've done nothing wrong" is the uneasy knowledge that I have done something *very* wrong and my weak claim to innocence will not wash away my very real guilt and shame.

O LORD, you have searched me and you know me. You know when I sit and when I rise; you perceive my thoughts from afar. You discern my going out and my lying down; you are familiar with all my ways. Before a word is on my tongue you know it completely, O LORD.

—Psalm 139:1–4

DARKNESS IS AS LIGHT TO YOU

We can deceive our friends, we can even deceive ourselves, but can we successfully hide from the presence of God?

If we say that God cannot know everything about us, then we are diminishing His power and elevating our own. We put ourselves first, making God an afterthought in the conduct of our lives. David sees it differently: "When I was woven together in the depths of the earth, your eyes saw my unformed body. All the days ordained for me were written in your book before one of them came to be." (Psalm 139:15-16)

Acknowledging God only when it is convenient diminishes the reality of His presence in our life from the moment we are conceived to the time of our death. This includes even the most secret and hidden parts of our life: "If I say, 'Surely the darkness will hide me and the light become night around me,' even the darkness will not be dark to you; the night will shine like the day, for the darkness is as light to you." (Psalm 139:11-12)

Be sure of this: The wicked will not go unpunished, but those who are righteous will go free. Like a gold ring in a pig's snout is a beautiful woman who shows no discretion. The desire of the righteous ends only in good, but the hope of the wicked only in wrath. One man gives freely, yet gains even more; another withholds unduly, but comes to poverty. A generous man will prosper; he who refreshes others will himself be refreshed. People curse the man who hoards grain, but blessing crowns him who is willing to sell. He who seeks good finds goodwill, but evil comes to him who searches for it.

—Proverbs 11:21–27

SQUANDERED BEAUTY

Ancient Scripture tells us that swine were considered unclean creatures, unfit for eating or handling. (Leviticus 11:7-8) So it would have been an appalling and unimaginable waste to place "a gold ring in a pig's snout." (v22)

When men and women choose to disregard God, when they thoughtlessly give into "the sinful desires of their hearts…for the degrading of their bodies with one another," (Romans 1:24) then they have wasted the gift just as surely as the gold ring has been wasted on the swine.

Instead, in everything we say and do, we should want to reflect the glory of God: "One thing I ask of the Lord…that I may dwell in the house of the Lord all the days of my life, to gaze upon the beauty of the Lord and seek him in his temple." (Psalm 27:4)

Hear me, O God, as I voice my complaint; protect my life from the threat of the enemy. Hide me from the conspiracy of the wicked, from that noisy crowd of evildoers. They sharpen their tongues like swords and aim their words like deadly arrows. They shoot from ambush at the innocent man; they shoot at him suddenly, without fear. They encourage each other in evil plans, they talk about hiding their snares; they say, "Who will see them?" They plot injustice and say, "We have devised a perfect plan!' Surely the mind and heart of man are cunning."

—Psalm 64:1–6

THE TIDE OF DARKNESS

You have to avert your eyes not to see that "the mind and heart of man are cunning." Jesus always saw clearly, describing the unredeemed world as an "adulterous and sinful generation," as well as an "unbelieving and perverse generation."

When men free themselves from God, the tide of darkness rolls in, covering the landscape with the evils of malice, conspiracy, and conflict. "There is no one righteous, not even one; there is no one who understands, no one who seeks God. All have turned away, they have together worthless; there is no one who does good, not even one." (Romans 3:10-12)

So David raises his voice in prayer and supplication: "protect my life from the threat of the enemy." (v1) Ultimately, God gave his children the armor of the love of Jesus Christ to vanquish the author of sin and death.

When the righteous triumph, there is great elation; but when the wicked rise to power, men go into hiding. Like a roaring lion or a charging bear is a wicked man ruling over a helpless people. A tyrannical ruler lacks judgment, but he who hates ill-gotten gain will enjoy a long life.

—Proverbs 28:12, 15-16

THEY CALL FOR A KING

In the days of the prophet Samuel, Israel did not have a king. Eventually, the people demanded that a king be appointed to rule over them: "You are old, and your sons do not walk in your ways; now appoint a king to lead us, such as all the other nations have." (1 Samuel 8:5)

Samuel asks God what he should do and he receives this reply: "it is not you they have rejected, but they have rejected me as their king." (1 Samuel 8:7) And then God tells Samuel to warn the people of the terrible dangers that will come with an earthly king. "...warn them solemnly and let them know what the king who will reign over them will do." (1 Samuel 8:9)

To this very day, people argue over the question of what makes a good ruler. It is clear from this verse that great suffering will come when we turn to wicked men to rule over us, which is why we should always say, "In God we Trust." Or as David states it in Psalm 118: "It is better to take refuge in the Lord than to trust in man. It is better to take refuge in the Lord than to trust in princes." (Psalm 118:8-9)

The wings of the ostrich flap joyfully, but they cannot compare with the pinions and feathers of the stork. She lays her eggs on the ground and lets them warm in the sand, unmindful that a foot may crush them, that some wild animal may trample them. She treats her young harshly, as if they were not hers; she cares not that her labor was in vain, for God did not endow her with wisdom or give her a share of good sense. Yet when she spreads her feathers to run, she laughs at horse and rider.

—Job 39:13–18

CONTENDING WITH THE ALMIGHTY

Toward the end of the Book of Job, God "answered Job out of the storm" saying, "Who is this that darkens my counsel with words without knowledge?" (Job 38:1-2)

God then asks a series of questions that shatters the intellectual pride of those who would have us believe that they hold the knowledge of God in their hands. He asks, "Where were you when I laid the earth's foundation?" (v4) "Have you ever given orders to the morning, or shown the dawn its place...?" (v12) "Have you journeyed to the springs of the sea or walked in the recesses of the deep?" (v16) "Have you comprehended the vast expanses of the earth? Tell, me, if you know all this." (v18)

Finally, he says to Job (and to us), "Will the one who contends with the Almighty correct him? Let him who accuses God answer him!" (Job 40:2)

In his arrogance the wicked man hunts down the weak, who are caught in the schemes he devises. He boasts of the cravings of his heart; he blesses the greedy and reviles the LORD. In his pride the wicked does not seek him; in all his thoughts there is no room for God. His ways are always prosperous; he is haughty and your laws are far from him; he sneers at all his enemies.

—Psalm 10:2–5

GOD WILL NEVER QUIT

How do we successfully satisfy the cravings of our heart? If we assume that all our impulses are godly, then every desire should be expressed through action.

But notice what this Psalm actually says: *In order to follow the impulses of the heart, we must leave "no room for God."* Is that possible?

The truth is that every human heart is a hidden battlefield with eternal life hanging in the balance. Even the arrogant and wicked man has not fully given himself over to his own wicked schemes. He has not fully expelled God from the field of his plotting as he goes about his business. But when the rebellious desires of the heart are dominant, we push God aside, creating great sorrow in heaven. God will never quit on anyone, but if we insist on pursuing the path of our own desires, we will join the legions who bless the greedy and revile the Lord." (v3)

Do not make friends with a hot-tempered man, do not associate with one easily angered, or you may learn his ways and get yourself ensnared.

—*Proverbs 22:24–25*

THE PRICE OF ANGER

Anger is a fire that consumes everything in its path…and it is contagious. It may start in the heart of one man, but it soon spreads, causing confusion and havoc. "A fool gives full vent to his anger, but a wise man keeps himself under control." (Proverbs 29:11) An angry man is a fool because he may harm others, but he first harms himself.

When circumstances shift against us and we are tempted to lash out in anger, we should remember to follow the example given to us by God Himself who is "slow to anger and abounding in love and forgiving sin and rebellion." (Numbers 14:18)

Anger is possible for anyone; the *impulse* of anger should be avoided by everyone. Instead, "Do not let the sun go down while you are still angry, and do not give the devil a foothold." (Ephesians 4:26-27)

To have a fool for a son brings grief; there is no joy for the father of a fool. A cheerful heart is good medicine, but a crushed spirit dries up the bones. A wicked man accepts a bribe in secret to pervert the course of justice. A discerning man keeps wisdom in view, but a fool's eyes wander to the ends of the earth. A foolish son brings grief to his father and bitterness to the one who bore him.

—Proverbs 17:21–25

A LOST SON

A good and righteous father can raise a rebellious and wicked son. Isaac's son Esau sold his birthright for a pot of stew. Eli, the chief priest of the Temple and the man who raises Samuel, the prophet, has two sons who "were wicked men; they had no regard for the Lord." (1 Samuel 2:12)

Samuel's own "sons did not walk in his ways. They turned aside after dishonest gain and accepted bribes and perverted justice." (1 Samuel 8:3) King David's son, Absalom, rebels against his father and almost kills him, but even so, when Absalom is killed in battle, David is left inconsolable. (2 Samuel 18:33)

We pray that our sons will hear the voice of God and follow the right path, but we also must be aware that they are being pulled in many directions. Pray, therefore, that your own children will have a discerning heart that will keep "wisdom in view."

I cry out to you, O God, but you do not answer; I stand up, but you merely look at me. You turn on me ruthlessly; with the might of your hand you attack me. You snatch me up and drive me before the wind; you toss me about in the storm. I know you will bring me down to death, to the place appointed for all the living.

—Job 30:20–23

THE COST OF DISCIPLESHIP

Job's suffering causes him to cry out to God. He is experiencing the worst pain and misery imaginable, but he cannot fathom why this is happening to him.

We, on the other hand, see a fuller picture. We witness the beginning of this drama when "the angels came to present themselves before the Lord, and Satan also came with them." (Job 1:6) We see Satan challenge God's claim that Job is "blameless and upright, a man who fears God and shuns evil." (Job 1:8) And we see how Satan brings catastrophe upon catastrophe to Job to prove that there is no genuinely righteous man walking the earth.

To Job, it seems that God has abandoned him. For us, there is an echo of the cry of despair that will be heard everywhere throughout the world: "My God, My God, why have you forsaken me?" (Psalm 22:1) It is the cry of another righteous man, Jesus of Nazareth, who has been nailed to a cross on a small hill called Calvary, outside of the gates of Jerusalem.

God's purpose behind this horror is redemption and restoration, but it can only begin when His one and only son takes all the sin of the world upon himself. "You see, at just the right time, when we were still powerless, Christ died for the ungodly...While we were still sinners, Christ died for us." (Romans 5:6, 8) When we consider Job's suffering and all that it implies, we see a foreshadowing of the cross of the suffering servant, Christ, for the redemption of a world separated from God.

Praise the LORD, O my soul, and forget not all his benefits— who forgives all your sins and heals all your diseases, who redeems your life from the pit and crowns you with love and compassion, who satisfies your desires with good things so that your youth is renewed like the eagle's.

—Psalm 103:2–5

HE WILL SHARE ALL HIS BENEFITS

In our time, health and youthfulness trump practically every other virtue. It is considered a liability to appear old, and we will go to great lengths to delay the inevitable physical decline that we are destined to experience.

So we invent new remedies to erase the ravages of time: new vitamins, new diets, new forms of cosmetic surgery. We turn to a new solution a day, but we keep coming up empty and become anxiety ridden because delaying the inevitable has never been a cure.

In this passage, David provides us with an answer that is a gift for the asking. God can open the way to eternal life ("your youth is renewed like the eagle's"). He can do this because only God can forgive sins and thereby heal you and redeem you from the penalty of death. He does this because He is a God of love and compassion. If we turn to Him, we can partake of all of His benefits and find enduring satisfaction even during this fleeting time in this world.

I know that everything God does will endure forever; nothing can be added to it and nothing taken from it. God does it so that men will revere him. Whatever is has already been, and what will be has been before; and God will call the past to account.

—Ecclesiastes 3:14–15

REGAINING OUR LIGHTNESS OF BEING

Have you ever noticed that as people age, they lose the lightness of their step? They begin to walk around slightly stooped over with their faces down, as if they were burdened with an enormous weight resting awkwardly on their shoulders.

Could it be that the accumulated weight of the past has finally caught up with them? Could our own past be catching up with us? For we may be able to deny the past, but we cannot escape it; if we choose to let the poison of sin remain untreated, we will slowly become weighed down and lose the lightness of our being.

The way of the world is to medicate, but does this reach to the source of the problem? Here is the truth: "All of us also lived among them at one time, gratifying the cravings of the sinful nature and following its desires and thoughts. Like the rest, we were by nature objects of wrath." (Ephesians 2:3) Yet it need not remain this way: "But because of his great love for us, God, who is rich in mercy, made us alive with Christ even when we were dead in transgressions-it is by grace you have been saved." (Ephesians 2: 4, 5)

The LORD is righteous, yet I rebelled against his command. Listen, all you peoples; look upon my suffering. My young men and maidens have gone into exile. I called to my allies but they betrayed me. My priests and my elders perished in the city while they searched for food to keep themselves alive.

—Lamentations 1:18–19

INVITED TO STAY?

The Lord is righteous. I am not righteous, but by rebelling, I claim righteousness as my own. As with Satan, in my defiance, I claim equality with God and I begin to construct my own counterfeit kingdom. "'Let us break their chains,' they say 'and throw off their fetters.'" (Psalm 2:3)

As rebels against God, we live to satisfy the darker desires of our sinful nature, but we prefer not to do this in the open light of day. Our rebellion is built on lies and stealth. We make up our justifications as we go, little knowing that our denial of God is drawing us ever closer to the disaster of eternal darkness.

"Then the king told the attendants, 'Tie him hand and foot, and throw him outside, into the darkness, where there will be weeping and gnashing of teeth.'" (Matthew 22:13) These are the words of Jesus as he tells the parable of the wedding banquet. Will we be invited to stay? Or will we be cast out into the deepest darkness?

I lift up my eyes to the hills—where does my help come from? My help comes from the LORD, the Maker of heaven and earth. He will not let your foot slip—he who watches over you will not slumber; indeed, he who watches over Israel will neither slumber nor sleep. The LORD watches over you—the LORD is your shade at your right hand; the sun will not harm you by day, nor the moon by night. The LORD will keep you from all harm—he will watch over your life; the LORD will watch over your coming and going both now and forevermore.

—Psalm 121:1–8

A FELLOW PASSENGER

Years ago—I do not remember how many—I was sitting on an airplane heading for Nashville, and like almost everyone else, quietly minding my own business. But I did notice the lady sitting by the window on my aisle; she was holding a Bible in her hands. She was an older black woman and she seemed to possess a quiet dignity.

At some point in the flight we began to talk about usual things, but I wanted to know about her Bible, as I had begun reading Scripture several years before. I don't remember most of the details of our conversation but I was struck when she said, "I am a missionary from Africa working here in the United States. I often do not know where I will go or who I will meet, but God has blessed my life in so many ways. The verse that guides me everyday, wherever I am and wherever I go, is 'I lift my eyes to the mountains—where does my help come from? My help comes from the Lord, the Maker of heaven and earth.'"(v1)

I have never forgotten that brief conversation. I had never thought of missionaries coming *from* Africa to work in the vineyards of America, but it was not the mission that impressed me. It was the person. She was a child of God doing God's business in a way that would not attract notice, but still had that unique concentrated power that changes the world… one person at a time.

What is man that you make so much of him, that you give him so much attention, that you examine him every morning and test him every moment? Will you never look away from me, or let me alone even for an instant? If I have sinned, what have I done to you, O watcher of men? Why have you made me your target? Have I become a burden to you? Why do you not pardon my offenses and forgive my sins? For I will soon lie down in the dust; you will search for me, but I will be no more.

—Job 7:17–21

HERE IS THE MAN!

What is man, indeed?

Job seems to be saying that man is no more than a plaything of God, but later he repents and says, "Surely I spoke of things I did not understand, things too wonderful for me to know." (Job 42:3)

Ages later, another man, wearing a crown of thorns and a purple robe, paradoxically represents the complete answer to Job's question. This man stands before an angry mob that does not recognize him for who he truly is and, instead of worshipping him, they mock and insult him and call for him to be put to death on a cross.

Pilate, the human figure of authority, stands by his side and says to the frenzied crowd: "Here is the man!" (John 19:5) Yes, here is the man who "took up our infirmities and carried our sorrows…" "…he was pierced for our transgressions, he was crushed for our iniquities; the punishment that brought us peace was upon him, and by his wounds we are healed. We all, like sheep, have gone astray, each of us has turned to his own way; and the Lord has laid on him the iniquity of us all." (Isaiah 53:4-6)

Behold the man. Ecce Homo.

Sing joyfully to the LORD, you righteous; it is fitting for the upright to praise him. Praise the LORD with the harp; make music to him on the ten-stringed lyre. Sing to him a new song; play skillfully, and shout for joy. For the word of the LORD is right and true; he is faithful in all he does. The LORD loves righteousness and justice; the earth is full of his unfailing love.

—Psalm 33:1–5

ALL CREATURES GREAT AND SMALL

Not long ago, I walked 43 miles of the Appalachian Trail in central Pennsylvania. You need to walk the earth to experience the marvels that inhabit it. Whole worlds of tiny beings going about their mysterious business catch your attention with every passing step.

The big things like the mighty Susquehanna River, or the powerful midnight storm, or even the rolling hills of cultivated farmland cause one to stop in wonder, but it is the small things of the land, the insects and small animals that suggest design and purpose and affirm the glorious truth of David's song: "By the word of the Lord were the heavens made, their starry host by the breath of his mouth....For he spoke and it came to be; he commanded, and it stood firm." (v6, 9)

My son, keep my words and store up my commands within you. Keep my commands and you will live; guard my teachings as the apple of your eye. Bind them on your fingers; write them on the tablet of your heart. Say to wisdom, "You are my sister," and call understanding your kinsman; they will keep you from the adulteress, from the wayward wife with her seductive words.

—Proverbs 7:1–5

THE BEGINNING OF WISDOM

If all wisdom comes from God, then our foolish desire to engage in foolish and self-destructive behavior may have its origin in our own disbelief. The Bible explicitly says that "The fool says in his heart, 'There is no God.'" (Psalm 14:1)

Once a man pushes God aside, sin has free reign to grow and prosper within his heart. Boundaries begin to evaporate, and he begins to justify behavior that cannot be justified and so lies pile on top of lies creating an intolerable burden.

The Bible clearly defines the one and only place where wisdom can be found: "The fear of the Lord is the beginning of wisdom." (Psalm 111:10) The well-spent life begins with the Lord; we are told to store up his commands, guard his teachings and "write them on the tablet of your heart." (v3)

Without God's strong and steady hand, men are blown back and forth by every temptation and the inevitable descent follows: "Then, after desire has conceived, it gives birth to sin, and sin, when it is full-grown, gives birth to death." (James 1:15)

Can a corrupt throne be allied with you— one that brings on misery by its decrees? They band together against the righteous and condemn the innocent to death. But the LORD has become my fortress, and my God the rock in whom I take refuge. He will repay them for their sins and destroy them for their wickedness; the LORD our God will destroy them.

—Psalm 94:20–23

A CORRUPT RULER POLLUTES THE LAND

The framers of the American Constitution knew that kings matter. They knew biblical history and they understood that tyranny, corruption and misery were more often the historical norm rather than the exception. A corrupt king matters because everything he does and says is magnified and therefore ripples to every corner of the land: "A king's wrath is like the roar of a lion; he who angers him forfeits his life." (Proverbs 20:2)

From the beginning, Israel is warned about the dangers a king will bring to the people: "This is what the king who will reign over you will do: He will take your sons and make them serve with his chariots and horses...He will take your daughters to be perfumers and cooks and bakers. He will take the best of your fields and vineyards and olive groves and give them to his attendants.... He will take a tenth of your flocks, and you yourselves will become his slaves." (1 Samuel 8:11-17)

The abuse of power and privilege at the top infects the entire kingdom and all the people suffer: "The wicked freely strut about when what is vile is honored among men." (Psalm 12:8)

May the peoples praise you, O God; may all the peoples praise you.
May the nations be glad and sing for joy, for you rule the peoples justly
and guide the nations of the earth. May the peoples praise you, O God;
may all the peoples praise you. Then the land will yield its harvest, and
God, our God, will bless us. God will bless us, and all the ends of the
earth will fear him.

—Psalm 67:3–7

MY HEART WILL SING TO YOU

What happens when the people stop praising God? What happens when the people scorn God's abundant grace and they break free to do whatever they want?

Whenever this happens, in recent or ancient times, such as in Nazi Germany or Soviet Russia, a spiritual famine spreads throughout the land, leaving poverty, sickness and brutality in its wake. Without the blessings of God's grace, we revert to the elemental truth of our nature: "every inclination of (man's) heart is evil from birth." (Genesis 8:21)

The absence of God's blessings is unendurable because our unbridled nature will unleash devastation and terror throughout the earth. Without God's blessings, the situation is hopeless. But God is the giver of abundant life and it is dangerous to forget God, as we pursue our own well being.

Therefore, we should praise the Lord mightily because His grace is life. It is by God's grace that we are saved from our terrible dilemma. We praise God because we intuit the truth about our nature and we know that we do not merit His blessings. "O Lord my God (we say with all sincerity of heart), I called to you for help and you healed me." (Psalm 30:2) Therefore, I will praise your holy name because "You turned my wailing into dancing; you removed my sackcloth and clothed me with joy, that my heart may sing to you and not be silent. O Lord my God, I will give you thanks forever." (Psalm 30:11-12)

Who can say, I have kept my heart pure; I am clean and without sin?

—Proverbs 20:9

A WORLD OF INTENTIONAL INDIFFERENCE

Many may not say it, but people do believe that they are free of sin and are fairly pure in the eyes of God. We usually hear them say, "I am really a good person," which is a way of raising the bar high enough for them to walk right under it.

We all do it, but we should pause and be honest. By saying we are good, we engage in self-deception, which eventually will bring us to grief. To truly "know thyself" we need to acknowledge that we do not have a pure heart; that we are not clean and that we sin against God and neighbor everyday. Jesus tells the rich ruler, "No one is good—except God alone." (Luke 18:19)

If we are blind to the nature of the disease that is killing us, how can we know that we even need a cure? Jesus tells the parable of the Good Samaritan to a self-righteous expert in the law. It is important to understand that the man stripped, beaten and left for dead is each one of us.

I am that man and so are you. We need someone to come and lift us out of the dust, and to love us and heal us. Sin is what got us there. It is Jesus who crosses the road to bring us the healing we so desperately need. While the world passes by with intentional indifference, God stops to care for us because God is love.

I am under vows to you, O God; I will present my thank offerings to you. For you have delivered me from death and my feet from stumbling, that I may walk before God in the light of life.

—Psalm 56:12–13

LOVE, LIGHT, LIFE

What does David mean when he says that he will "walk in the light of life"?

In one sense, he is prefiguring the very nature of the one who is to come: "One of your descendants [who] I will place on your throne." (Psalm 132:11) The Gospel tells us that Jesus is the promised descendant who has come to restore access to eternal life for all who will accept him. In Jesus, the love of God, the light of the world and eternal life come together in one person.

Jesus says, "I am the light of the world. Whoever follows me will never walk in darkness, but will have the light of life." (John 8:12) Elsewhere, Jesus says, "I am the resurrection and the life. He who believes in me will live, even though he dies; and whoever lives and believes in me will never die." (John 11:25-26) And John the apostle proclaims, "God is love. Whoever lives in love lives in God, and God in him." (1 John 4:16)

Indeed, to believe in Jesus Christ is to open wide the door to God's love, to His light and to eternal life.

The sluggard says, "There is a lion in the road, a fierce lion roaming the streets!" As a door turns on its hinges, so a sluggard turns on his bed. The sluggard buries his hand in the dish; he is too lazy to bring it back to his mouth. The sluggard is wiser in his own eyes than seven men who answer discreetly.

—Proverbs 26:13–16

BE STRONG AND COURAGEOUS

Laziness is not what you might think it is. Notice that the sluggard cries out that there is a frightening obstacle in his path. The implication is that nothing but a fervid imagination stands in his way.

The truth is that unreasonable fear holds him back. He is free to move forward, but something inside, some fear, stops him cold. Laziness, therefore, may be just another name for fear.

If we live in fear, taking the next step, any step will become increasingly difficult until the day arrives when we are so paralyzed that we cannot even emerge from our own beds or lift a spoon to our own mouths.

Laziness is sinful because we are too immobilized to answer the call of God. God says this to Joshua and to all men: "Be strong and courageous. Do not be terrified; do not be discouraged, for the Lord your God will be with you wherever you go." (Joshua 1:9)

O LORD, the God who saves me, day and night I cry out before you. May my prayer come before you; turn your ear to my cry. For my soul is full of trouble and my life draws near the grave. I am counted among those who go down to the pit; I am like a man without strength. I am set apart with the dead, like the slain who lie in the grave, whom you remember no more, who are cut off from your care.

—Psalm 88:1–5

I AM IN CONTROL!

How do we react when we find that we are in a dangerous situation? For example, many of us have gone through the terrible experience of sitting comfortably in an airplane when a violent storm strikes, sending the plane into convulsions. In the midst of such moments, do we say, "I'm okay. Nothing can harm me because I am in control," or do we say a silent prayer, asking for God's help because we know that we are suddenly vulnerable to forces far greater than our ability to control them?

And when the plane finally lands without incident, do we forget our feeling of powerlessness, returning to the illusionary sense of invulnerability that normally informs our behavior?

The truth is we are always traveling through life in need of God's saving hand. To believe that we do not need God at all times is to believe that we are more than mere mortals, that we, in fact, have superhuman powers that defy all the forces of evil that may invade our world at any given time.

I, for one, prefer to stand with David who understood that all his blessings and all his favor came from God and from nowhere else: "O Lord, the God who saves me, day and night I cry out before you. May my prayer come before you; turn your ear to my cry." (v1-2)

He chose David his servant and took him from the sheep pens; from tending the sheep he brought him to be the shepherd of his people Jacob, of Israel his inheritance. And David shepherded them with integrity of heart; with skillful hands he led them.

—Psalm 78:70–72

HIS ORIGINS ARE FROM OF OLD

Though three thousand years have passed since he reigned, David still lives through the covenant God made with him. Nathan, the prophet, gives David God's promise: "'The Lord declared to you that the Lord himself will establish a house for you: When your days are over and you rest with your fathers, I will raise up your offspring to succeed you, who will come from your own body, and I will establish his kingdom...and I will establish the throne of his kingdom forever. I will be his father, and he will be my son...Your house and your kingdom will endure forever before me; your throne will be established forever.'" (2 Samuel 7:11-16)

One thousand years later, in David's city of Bethlehem, a child is born near an inn. He is of the lineage of David and his birth is the fulfillment of Nathan's prophecy: "But you, Bethlehem Ephrathah, though you are small among the clans of Judah, out of you will come for me one who will be ruler over Israel, whose origins are from of old, from ancient times." (Micah 5:2)

Like cutting off one's feet or drinking violence is the sending of a message by the hand of a fool. Like a lame man's legs that hang limp is a proverb in the mouth of a fool. Like tying a stone in a sling is the giving of honor to a fool.

—*Proverbs 26:6–8*

THE FOOL

The "fool" of Proverbs lacks spiritual intelligence. He is an aimless talker (10:10), a slanderer (10:18) who is hotheaded and reckless. (14:16) He spurns discipline (15:5), misuses money and brings grief to his parents. (17:16, 21) In this passage, the fool shows himself to be ineffective, powerless and undependable. He has no character and he is a danger to anyone in his company.

On the other hand, the saint may have started out as a fool, but rather than remain in a state of spiritual stupor, he has been transformed into a character builder. The saint is a striver, not for self, but for service to the God whom he loves. He sees his all in all in Jesus Christ, the very one who called him out of foolishness and despair. For "(Christ's) divine power has given us everything we need for life and godliness through our knowledge of him who called us by his own glory and goodness." (2 Peter 1:3)

Test me, O LORD, and try me, examine my heart and my mind; for your love is ever before me, and I walk continually in your truth. I do not sit with deceitful men, nor do I consort with hypocrites; I abhor the assembly of evildoers and refuse to sit with the wicked.

—Psalm 26:2–5

WHO DO I LOVE?

Because the "heart is deceitful above all things," (Jeremiah 17:9) it is important to undergo a thorough and frequent heart checkup. But this is hard and often inconvenient, so we spend valuable time finding excuses for avoiding what might be unpleasant news.

If we refuse to undergo a daily "heart exam," we might consider wearing a sign around our neck similar to the one found on the side of cigarette packs: "Caution: This heart may kill you!"

Left untreated by God, the human heart is the center of great turmoil and raging conflict. Our affections shift like an altimeter in a storm; one moment we yearn to follow the right way, then the next moment we turn our back on the Lord just as Peter did three times immediately after claiming eternal allegiance to him. The battle we face everyday is over the constancy of our wavering hearts.

In the end, the question for each of us is about one thing: whom do I love with all my heart? We can deceive ourselves into believing that we have been exempted from this conflict, but when we do, we are implicitly admitting that the other side has already taken over.

Do not wear yourself out to get rich; have the wisdom to show restraint. Cast but a glance at riches, and they are gone, for they will surely sprout wings and fly off to the sky like an eagle.

—Proverbs 23:4–5

THE LAST MOURNFUL NOTE

Why are so many of us obsessed with money and everything it can buy? At one level, gold *does* glitter. The lavish parties of the rich are impressive for their momentary splendor.

For an instant, everything appears to be perfect, but just as quickly, time ripples over the scene and all that remains in the end is a wrecked vestige of what was before. The band has played its last mournful note, the guests have departed, and the despoiled tables have lost their ordered elegance.

Money has the power to withhold the ravages of time for an instant, which makes it a poor substitute for the real thing. If we stake everything on the power of money, we will always feel the cold breath of mortality passing through the room, for behind all the pomp and circumstance we know in our hearts that "our days are like a fleeting shadow" (Psalm 144:4) that "vanish like smoke." (Psalm 102:3) Thus wisdom dictates, "Though your riches increase, do not set your hearts on them."(Psalm 62:10)

My companion attacks his friends; he violates his covenant. His speech is smooth as butter, yet war is in his heart.

—Psalm 55:20–21

A WORLD ABSENT OF GOD

If you are looking for a strong dose of reality, then immerse yourself in the 55th Psalm. David is in anguish, confronted with the "terrors of death" and filled with "fear and trembling...for (he) see(s) violence and strife in the city. Day and night they prowl about on its walls; malice and abuse are within it. Destructive forces are at work in the city; threats and lies never leave its streets." (v4-11)

It is in such a world that even friends betray their companions. Here is the bad news: David is describing a world that has abandoned God and so men have reverted to their natural state of depravity and corruption.

This is the very same world that Jesus entered on a cold night in the small town of Bethlehem. Soon the kings of the earth, and their agents, would set out to destroy this child and eventually, they would crucify him outside the walls of Jerusalem.

But little did any of them know that this one death would set a multitude free. We cannot understand this saving act until we come to understand what we have been saved from. David paints a vivid picture of what the world looks like absent of God. It is a world in desperate need of His saving hand.

Wisdom has built her house; she has hewn out its seven pillars. She has prepared her meat and mixed her wine; she has also set her table. She has sent out her maids, and she calls from the highest point of the city. "Let all who are simple come in here!" she says to those who lack judgment. "Come, eat my food and drink the wine I have mixed. Leave your simple ways and you will live; walk in the way of understanding."

—Proverbs 9:1–6

A HOUSE BUILT ON ROCK

Wisdom is a house built *with* stone and *on* stone and supported by seven pillars. This is the house that Jesus describes at the end of his Sermon on the Mount. It is a house that can withstand the worst storm: "The rain came down, the streams rose, and the winds blow and beat against that house; yet it did not fall, because it had its foundation on the rock." (Matthew 7:24-25)

But there is another kind of house built to entrap the simple and the foolish. It is the kind of house that leads to destruction. "At the window of my house I looked out through the lattice. I saw among the simple, I noticed among the young men, a youth who lacked judgment. He was going down the street near her corner, walking along in the direction of her house…(Proverbs 7:6-8) All at once he followed her…little knowing it will cost him his life." (Proverbs 7:22-23)

God invites each of us to enter His house of seven pillars. Other houses, and there are many, are prisons filled with sorrow and regret. Beware of entering such places.

Listen, my son, accept what I say, and the years of your life will be many. I guide you in the way of wisdom and lead you along straight paths. When you walk, your steps will not be hampered; when you run, you will not stumble. Hold on to instruction, do not let it go; guard it well, for it is your life. Do not set foot on the path of the wicked or walk in the way of evil men. Avoid it, do not travel on it; turn from it and go on your way.

—Proverbs 4:10–15

HIS BOUNDLESS LOVE

"Listen my son, accept what I say…" Here we have every good father speaking words of wisdom and advice to his son out of natural love. Every good father, we would say, wants only the best for his own child. It is so natural that we do not even think about it.

In a parable, Jesus uses this natural relationship between father and son to make a more profound point: "Which of you fathers, if your son asks for a fish, will give him a snake instead? Or if he asks for an egg, will give him a scorpion? If you then, though you are evil, know how to give good gifts to your children, how much more will your Father in heaven give the Holy Spirit to those who ask?" (Luke 11:11-13)

Jesus is telling us a truth that we often find hard to believe. Just as it is natural that a father will give good things to his son because he loves him, so it is true that God the Father will give good things to His children out of his boundless love for them. So when as children of God we pray to our Father in heaven, we can expect Him to respond in love.

Under three things the earth trembles, under four it cannot bear up: a servant who becomes king, a fool who is full of food, an unloved woman who is married, and a maidservant who displaces her mistress.

—Proverbs 30:21-23

GOD'S ORIGINAL DESIGN

Marriage absent love is a shipwreck. God's original design did not contemplate an unloved wife.

The first man and the first woman were made to complement one another, reflecting the harmony built into everything God created. "This is now bone of my bone and flesh of my flesh..." said Adam. "For this reason a man will leave his father and mother and be united to his wife, and they will become one flesh. The man and his wife were both naked, and they felt no shame."(Genesis 2:21-25)

But with the Fall came sin and death, fracturing the original order and turning marriage into a vestige of the relationship of love God intended. Instead of the ideals of patience, kindness, protection, trust, hope and perseverance, we often find envy, pride, rudeness, selfishness and anger. (1 Corinthians 13:4-7) Paul reminds men that they need to live within God's original purpose: "Husbands, love your wives, just as Christ loves the church..." (Ephesians 5:25)

When my heart was grieved and my spirit embittered, I was senseless and ignorant; I was a brute beast before you. Yet I am always with you; you hold me by my right hand. You guide me with your counsel, and afterward you will take me into glory. Whom have I in heaven but you? And earth has nothing I desire besides you. My flesh and my heart may fail, but God is the strength of my heart and my portion forever.

—Psalm 73:21–26

DO NOT BE GRIEVED

David's heart is grieved and his spirit embittered, not by external afflictions, but by a corrosive envy of others, which is a source of alienation and frustration. He says that his own heart had become impure because "I envied the arrogant when I saw the prosperity of the wicked." (Psalm 73:3)

David also says that the wicked seem to be rewarded in this life, raising the question of justice. "They have no struggles; their bodies are healthy and strong. They are free from the burdens common to man; they are not plagued by human ills." (v4-5) Who has not wondered about the purpose of life when they see the wicked prospering all around? But then David has a revelation from God that reminds him that, while His ways may seem inscrutable at times, God holds those who are faithful by their "right hand" and will not abandon His children. "When I tried to understand all this, it was oppressive to me till I entered the sanctuary of God; then I understood their final destiny." (v16-17)

When we enter the sanctuary of the Holy Spirit, we begin to see with the wisdom of God as given to us in the words of Christ: "…pray for those who persecute you, that you may be sons of your Father in heaven. He causes his sun to rise on the evil and the good and sends rain on the righteous and the unrighteous. If you love those who love you, what reward will you get? Are not even the tax collectors doing that?" (Matthew 5:44-46)

We are called to live in the power of God's love. When we do, envy and frustration evaporate and our life becomes characterized by abundance.

Who is this that appears like the dawn, fair as the moon, bright as the sun, majestic as the stars in procession?

—Song of Songs 6:10

THE BRIGHT MORNING STAR

Song of Songs provides some of the finest love poetry the world has ever seen, but there is more. The love between a man and a woman is but a pale reflection of the love that the Lord has for each one of His children. "Who is this that appears like the dawn...?" (v10)

It is the maker of heaven and earth, the very one who brought the world into being through love and who gave his one and only Son that we might be one with the Father as the Son is one with the Father: "As the Father has loved me, so have I loved you. Now remain in my love." (John 15:9) Who is this that appears at the dawn? "I, Jesus,...am the Root and the Offspring of David, and the bright Morning Star." (Revelation 22:16)

Four things on earth are small, yet they are extremely wise: Ants are creatures of little strength, yet they store up their food in the summer; coneys are creatures of little power, yet they make their home in the crags; locusts have no king, yet they advance together in ranks; a lizard can be caught with the hand, yet it is found in kings' palaces.

—Proverbs 30:24–28

NOTHING IS IMPOSSIBLE WITH GOD

As with the ant, or locusts, or a little lizard, we too are small when compared to the unimaginable size of the universe. When seen from the perspective of infinite time and space, we can become frozen into hopeless inaction because we ask how God could care for someone as small and insignificant as we are.

Indeed, it is a mystery, but it is a mystery that the Bible confronts time and again. We read stories in almost every book of Scripture telling how God uses a seemingly insignificant person to accomplish His own purpose. Here is Moses, exiled from his people, being called back to lead them out of the bondage of Egypt. Here is Sarah, old and without children, being told that she would bear a child who would be the child of a promise. Here is Esther, who summons all the courage she has to stand in the way of the total destruction of her people. And here is Mary, a young virgin, who is visited by an angel of God and is told she will give birth to a child to be named Jesus who "will be great and will be called the son of the Most High." (Matthew 1:31-32)

When Mary questions the visitor, she is told a truth that should lift our hearts: No matter how impossible, difficult and terrible our situation might be, "nothing is impossible with God." (Luke 1:37) When God calls us to His purpose, our answer should be the same as Mary's: "My soul glorifies the Lord and my spirit rejoices in God my savior, for he has been mindful of the humble state of his servant." (Luke 1:46-48)

Who may ascend the hill of the LORD? Who may stand in his holy place? He who has clean hands and a pure heart, who does not lift up his soul to an idol or swear by what is false. He will receive blessing from the LORD and vindication from God his Savior. Such is the generation of those who seek him, who seek your face, O God of Jacob.

—Psalm 24:3–6

THE SERVANT OF THE VALLEY

Moses received the Ten Commandments on Mount Sinai; Jesus gave his sermon on a hill; and his disciples witnessed the transfiguration on a mountaintop.

Yet while Moses was with God, the people of Israel abandoned God to worship a man-made golden calf. They were living in the valley of the shadow of death. And when Jesus completed his sermon, he returned to the valley where he was immediately confronted by a man suffering with leprosy who begged that he would be cured. When Jesus, Peter, James and John descended the mountain after the transfiguration, they encountered another man whose son was possessed with epilepsy.

The valley is the place Jesus needed to be. Jesus never stayed on the mountaintop; nor did Moses. Their ministry was always to be in the valley where the greatest need existed. Both had ascended the mountain of God, but both were genuine servants.

With Jesus it is said that though he was "in very nature God, (he) did not consider equality with God something to be grasped, but made himself nothing, taking on the very nature of a servant." (Philippians 2:6-7) God may have called His servants to the mountaintop, but he always sent them back to the valley to accomplish the plan He had for them.

Where can I go from your Spirit? Where can I flee from your presence? If I go up to the heavens, you are there; if I make my bed in the depths, you are there. If I rise on the wings of the dawn, if I settle on the far side of the sea, even there your hand will guide me, your right hand will hold me fast.

—Psalm 139:7–10

HE WILL NOT ABANDON

Have you been hunting for God lately?

Many claim to be searching high and low, proclaiming all the while that God just can't be found anywhere. But what if this claim is bogus and the opposite is true? What if, instead of seeking God, we have been steadfastly avoiding Him? What if we actually fear coming face to face with Him because that would hamper our strong inclination to live free of Him?

This Psalm tells us that the quest for independence is delusional and futile. "Where can I go from your Spirit?" Where can I flee from your presence?" (v7)

The truth is that it is impossible to flee from the presence of God. We can deny God, but our denial does not cause God to turn away. Peter proclaimed that he would defend Jesus unto death and then flees in the face of danger. In one way or another, Peter is all of us, but God remains ever present and ever true and does not abandon Peter and He does not abandon us just because we are weak.

We abandon God in our weakness, yet He remains present and faithful.

And I saw something else under the sun: In the place of judgment—
wickedness was there, in the place of justice—wickedness was there. I
thought in my heart, "God will bring to judgment both the righteous
and the wicked, for there will be a time for every activity, a time for
every deed."

—Ecclesiastes 3:16–17

SETTLING OUR ACCOUNT

Solomon scanned the world and described what he found: "In the
place of judgment—wickedness was there, in the place of justice—
wickedness was there."(v16)

To imagine a world without justice and judgment is contrary to our
deepest convictions of how the world needs to work. Yet experience tells
us that in this world crime is rampant and justice is often absent.

Jesus also speaks of justice and judgment, but with a panoramic lens.
He knows that if we confine our understanding to what we experience
in this world alone, as many people do, we will never comprehend God's
great plan. Here is the way Jesus describes God's justice and judgment:
"The good man brings good things out of the good stored up in him, and
the evil man brings evil things out of the evil stored up in him. But I tell
you that men will have to give account on the Day of Judgment for every
careless word they have spoken. For by your words you will be acquitted,
and by your words you will be condemned."(Matthew 12:35-37)

As for God, his way is perfect; the word of the LORD is flawless. He is a shield for all who take refuge in him. For who is God besides the LORD? And who is the Rock except our God? It is God who arms me with strength and makes my way perfect. He makes my feet like the feet of a deer; he enables me to stand on the heights. He trains my hands for battle; my arms can bend a bow of bronze. You give me your shield of victory, and your right hand sustains me; you stoop down to make me great. You broaden the path beneath me, so that my ankles do not turn.

—Psalm 18:30–36

ALL THINGS ARE POSSIBLE WITH GOD

If we depend only on our own resources, we will fail. While God's way is perfect, our way is not. "It is God who arms me with strength and makes my way perfect." (v32)

Our strength and our success all come from the Lord. When we forget this and attribute success to our own abilities, we inevitably turn away from God to fight our own battles and travel on our own path based on our own standards.

But Jesus tells us it is fatal to fight alone. Every battle will weaken us a little more, preparing the way for our ultimate collapse. Paul understands that we do not stand a chance unless we are fully armed with the Holy Spirit against the devil's schemes. (Ephesians 6:10-20) Then and only then are we equipped to do the Lord's work; only then will the odds turn in favor of salvation and what seemed impossible before, now is possible.

Go to the ant, you sluggard; consider its ways and be wise! It has no commander, no overseer or ruler, yet it stores its provisions in summer and gathers its food at harvest. How long will you lie there, you sluggard? When will you get up from your sleep? A little sleep, a little slumber, a little folding of the hands to rest— and poverty will come on you like a bandit and scarcity like an armed man.

—Proverbs 6:6–11

A SPIRITUAL PENALTY BOX

Here we have the contrast between the small but industrious ant who seems to have inborn wisdom to gather while time allows and an indolent man who will not lift a hand to stave off scarcity and poverty.

The irony is clear. While the ant is merely an insect, man was made "a little lower than the heavenly beings and crowned...with glory and honor." (Psalm 8:5) When our behavior is below that of an ant, we dishonor the God who made us and, therefore, we end up living in a kind of spiritual penalty box until we choose to live up to the nature that God blessed us with.

Does the hawk take flight by your wisdom and spread his wings toward the south? Does the eagle soar at your command and build his nest on high? He dwells on a cliff and stays there at night; a rocky crag is his stronghold. From there he seeks out his food; his eyes detect it from afar. His young ones feast on blood, and where the slain are, there is he.

—Job 39:26–30

THE RIGHT PERSPECTIVE

Men command armies; they build corporations; they amass fortunes. Men design supersonic jets and engineer bridges and tunnels. They send rockets into the heavens and measure everything great and small.

But does the wisdom of man tell the hawk how to fly? And can we command the eagle? God asks Job dozens of questions and to each question, Job has no answer. (Job 38:16-17)

When men applaud their own ingenuity for building cities and civilizations, they might stop to consider the unanswerable questions addressed to Job (Job 38), for perhaps we are not the genuine architects after all. And this might help us put all human accomplishments in the proper perspective.

Be merciful to me, O LORD, for I am in distress; my eyes grow weak with sorrow, my soul and my body with grief. My life is consumed by anguish and my years by groaning; my strength fails because of my affliction, and my bones grow weak.

—Psalm 31:9–10

RELY ON GOD'S MERCY ALWAYS

David is in distress. "Because of all my enemies...there is terror on every side; they conspire against me and plot to take my life." (Psalm 31: v11-13) These words could just as well have been the words of Jesus as his tormentors pursued him with "hatred beyond reason."

This Psalm is a prayer for every righteous man because this fallen world desires to attack and punish him. Even the saint is not exempt from the terrible reality of opposition from the captives of the sinful nature.

One of the seven words Jesus spoke from the cross is uttered here by David: "Since you are my rock and my fortress, for the sake of your name lead and guide me.... Into your hands I commit my spirit. Redeem me, O Lord, the God of truth." (Psalm 31:3, 5)

As children of God, we have been called by God to be His agents in transforming the world into what He intended it to be in both small and large ways. And as children of God, we know we must rely on God in all things and call on His mercy for everything. He is our hope and our salvation.

I said, "O LORD, have mercy on me; heal me, for I have sinned against you."

—*Psalm 41:4*

GENUINE HEALTH

Is it possible that this single line from Psalm 41 sums up the greatest problem afflicting all of mankind?

Most of us travel through life in a semi-conscious state of spiritual blindness to our fractured relationship with God. If we prosper, we attribute success to our own abilities and think no more about it. Or if we are troubled with difficulties and problems, we attribute it to bad luck or bad circumstances or to someone else.

But in this passage the psalmist says something fundamentally different. He says, "I have sinned against God." As a result, he is sick and cannot cure himself. His conscience is stricken and he can only plead for mercy.

Oswald Chambers says that "conscience is the innate law in nature whereby man knows he is known."[8] When we come to that place where we know that we are known by God, then the true state of our unhealthiness is placed in stark contrast to the holiness of God. We recognize, perhaps for the first time, that we are not as good as we think we are. In fact, we finally see that we exist apart from God in an unholy state and that we are in desperate need of God's mercy.

My heart is steadfast, O God; I will sing and make music with all my soul. Awake, harp and lyre! I will awaken the dawn. I will praise you, O LORD, among the nations; I will sing of you among the peoples. For great is your love, higher than the heavens; your faithfulness reaches to the skies. Be exalted, O God, above the heavens, and let your glory be over all the earth.

—Psalm 108:1–5

THE SWEET POWER OF MUSIC

Music has enormous power over our souls because it is able to open our hearts to intimations of the original state of harmony of God's universe. When we sing songs of praise to God, our hearts are lifted up into the company of angels choiring in heaven. Holy music speaks to us about the presence of God in all dimensions of creation, both at the beginning and even now.

Music is God's universal language that speaks even to wild animals that intuit the natural harmony of the universe: "For do but note a wild and wanton herd, or race of youthful and unhandled colts, fetching mad bounds, bellowing and neighing loud, which is the hot condition of their blood; if they but hear perchance a trumpet sound, or any air of music touch their ears, you shall perceive them make a mutual stand, their savage eyes turn'd to modest gaze by the sweet power of music."[9]

A despairing man should have the devotion of his friends, even though he forsakes the fear of the Almighty. But my brothers are as undependable as intermittent streams, as the streams that overflow when darkened by thawing ice and swollen with melting snow, but that cease to flow in the dry season, and in the heat vanish from their channels.

—Job 6:14–17

THE TIES THAT BIND

Friendship, as the world defines it, is never enough to withstand the temptation of betrayal. The world with its passions and pressures will wear down the ties that bind people together, inevitably leading to conflict, sorrow and separation. David addresses this in one of his Psalms: "My companion attacks his friends; he violates his covenant. His speech is smooth as butter, yet war is in his heart; his words are more soothing than oil, yet they are drawn swords." (Psalm 55:21-22)

Friendships cannot survive unless they are bound together by the principle of the love that originates with God. "God is love," says John. "Whoever lives in love lives in God and God in him." (1 John 4:16) Jesus is even more precise: "As the Father has loved me, so have I loved you. Now remain in my love...Love each other as I have loved you. Greater love has no one than this, that he lay down his life for his friends. You are my friends if you do as I command." (John 15:9, 12-14)

Who will rise up for me against the wicked? Who will take a stand for me against evildoers? Unless the LORD had given me help, I would soon have dwelt in the silence of death. When I said, "My foot is slipping," your love, O LORD, supported me. When anxiety was great within me, your consolation brought joy to my soul.

—Psalm 94:16–19

LIKE SODOM, LIKE GOMORRAH

Who will rise up for me against the wicked? (v16) "'I will rise up against them,' declares the Lord Almighty." (Isaiah 14:22)

The battle is fierce; the outcome seems uncertain. Even the righteous are brought down low. The world itself seems to be rising up against the Lord and all of his children: "Why do the nations conspire and the peoples plot in vain? The kings of the earth take their stand and the rulers gather together against the Lord and against his Anointed One." (Psalm 2:1-2) The shining city on a hill has been transformed into the sties of Sodom and Gomorrah.

The truth is that without the strong but gentle hand of God, our footing will always be unsure and the anxiety of war, near and far, will always afflict us. It is the Holy Spirit of God that supports us and brings consolation. Otherwise, "we would have become like Sodom, we would have been like Gomorrah." (Romans 9:29)

I find more bitter than death the woman who is a snare, whose heart is a trap and whose hands are chains. The man who pleases God will escape her, but the sinner she will ensnare.

—Ecclesiastes 7:26

SEDUCTION

Seduction is not a word that finds its way into polite conversation, but just because we pretend that all relationships are motivated by understandable and controllable emotions does not mean that seduction has been eradicated like some dreaded virus.

The truth is that all men suffer from faulty judgment and when we fall in love with a beautiful woman, our vision may easily be clouded by what the apostle John calls "the cravings of sinful man, the lust of his eyes and the boasting of what he has and does (which) comes not from the Father, but from the world." (1 John 2:16)

So when teaching our sons about the ways of the world, we must be wise and realistic. It is easier than ever to enter into relationships that bind in chains. Women and men are meant to complement and bless one another, not trap and destroy.

*But I call to God, and the LORD saves me. Evening, morning and noon
I cry out in distress, and he hears my voice. He ransoms me unharmed
from the battle waged against me, even though many oppose me. God,
who is enthroned forever, will hear them and afflict them— men who
never change their ways and have no fear of God.*

—*Psalm 55:16–19*

THE GOD OF THE RIGHTEOUS

King David has placed his life in the hands of a faithful God. He
kneels at the foot of the throne of the One who hears his voice and who
saves him from the battle being waged on his left and his right.

In another psalm David says, "In my anguish I cried to the Lord, and
he answered by setting me free. The Lord is with me: I will not be afraid.
What can man do to me? The Lord is with me: he is my helper. I will look
in triumph on my enemies." (Psalm 118:5-7)

Compare the deep faith of David to the pallid claims of some of our
modern enlightened leaders who stake everything on the belief that man
can save man. These contemporary leaders give lip service to God, but
their genuine faith seems to be built on the premise that mankind has
progressed to a point in history where we are better off acting as if the
God of David did not exist at all. For many of our leaders, God represents
a stumbling block to their use of intellect, technology and political power
to erect monuments to their own greatness.

But is the enlightened leader really modern or does he represent
nothing more than mankind's ancient and ongoing rebellion against
God? "Son of man, say to the ruler of Tyre, 'This is what the Sovereign
Lord says: In the pride of your heart, you say, *I am a god; I sit on the throne
of a god in the heart of the seas. But you are not a god, though you think you
are as wise as a god.*'" (Ezekiel 28:2)

Have the leaders of our time fallen for the same old promise offered to
our ancestors that we "will be like God, knowing good and evil"? If this
is so, then their monuments of pride are nothing more than a handful
of dust.

Like a thornbush in a drunkard's hand is a proverb in the mouth of a fool. Like an archer who wounds at random is he who hires a fool or any passer-by. As a dog returns to its vomit, so a fool repeats his folly. Do you see a man wise in his own eyes? There is more hope for a fool than for him.

—Proverbs 26:9-12

PUT CHILDISH WAYS ASIDE

Have you ever wished to be something you clearly are not?

Children are constantly dreaming of being something they cannot possibly be during their youth, but when they grow older, these dreams, when unrealistic, become fantasies and quickly lose their charm.

A fool chases childhood dreams when he should have arrived at a realistic assessment of his abilities and his life. A fool looks in the mirror and sees the reflection of a king; he wishes to be greater than he is and thus his folly is his pride. "When I was a child, I talked like a child, I thought like a child, I reasoned like a child. When I became a man, I put childish ways behind me." (1 Corinthians 13:11) We finally become adult men and women when we look at our reflection through the eyes of God.

My heart is in anguish within me; the terrors of death assail me. Fear and trembling have beset me; horror has overwhelmed me. I said, "Oh, that I had the wings of a dove! I would fly away and be at rest— I would flee far away and stay in the desert; I would hurry to my place of shelter, far from the tempest and storm."

—*Psalm 55:4–8*

CARRYING THE LIGHT

It would be wonderful to "fly away" and be at rest "far from the tempest and the storm," for there are times when the forces of this world seem to close in, leaving no apparent room for escape. We find ourselves cornered and our condition is all but hopeless.

This was the situation that King David found himself in; his friends had betrayed him and Jerusalem was under attack on all sides. But David was favored and God said to him: "...call upon me in the day of trouble; I will deliver you, and you will honor me." (Psalm 50:15)

In our own day of trouble, we should never forget that God wants us to call out to Him. He has promised that we will be delivered, but we must never forget that we are to give over our life to Him so that we can be effective ambassadors as God originally intended. God wants us to be "blameless and pure, children of God without fault in a crooked and depraved generation, in which you shine like stars in the universe as you hold out the word of life...." (Philippians 2:15-16) For no matter what the circumstance, whether in chains or free, we are called to carry his light in our hearts and in our lives.

Trust in the LORD with all your heart and lean not on your own understanding; in all your ways acknowledge him, and he will make your paths straight.

—*Proverbs 3:5–6*

SEEK GUIDANCE

Here we have sound advice, but it is rarely followed. We seem to believe we have a self-appointed board of directors bouncing around in our heads, always permitting us to do whatever we want to do.

However, we should beware of engaging in this amusing form of self-deception because this is a board that will be nothing more than a rubber stamp to our most momentary whims. Therefore, stop fooling yourself and "lean not on your own understanding." (v5) Rather, a wise man seeks guidance through good and trustworthy council.

By the word of the LORD were the heavens made, their starry host by the breath of his mouth. He gathers the waters of the sea into jars; he puts the deep into storehouses. Let all the earth fear the LORD; let all the people of the world revere him. For he spoke, and it came to be; he commanded, and it stood firm. The LORD foils the plans of the nations; he thwarts the purposes of the peoples. But the plans of the LORD stand firm forever, the purposes of his heart through all generations.

—Psalm 33:6–11

SATAN'S FALSE QUESTION

What makes the naturalistic understanding of the origin of the universe more reliable than the Biblical account from Genesis? Actually, the motives behind much of scientific thinking may be more Biblical than many suspect.

Biblical history reveals that men have been trying to cancel out God from the very beginning; we have been in a state of continuous rebellion against God since a certain tragic question was asked of our first ancestors: "Did God really say, 'You must not eat from any tree in the garden?'" (Genesis 3:1) The answer was as false as the promise that followed: "...you will be like God, knowing good and evil." (Genesis 3:5)

To become like God is not to make mankind greater, but to make God less. The serpent in the Garden would like each one of us to believe that we can be gods by knowing what God knows. However, consider the source.

Do not boast about tomorrow, for you do not know what a day may bring forth.

—Proverbs 27:1

ENGAGING THE MOMENT

All of us stand precariously between past and future, and so, many respond to this unsteady state by seeking false security. We may try to protect ourselves with wealth or excessive activity or living in denial, but all of this, no matter what the form, is defensive in nature. We look to the future with a fear-filled heart, seeking a false security when, in fact, we do not know if the next minute will be our last: "for you do not know what a day may bring forth." (v1)

The man who puts his faith in God does not need to address the future with anything but hope. Jesus summarizes this attitude in the Sermon on the Mount: "So do not worry, saying 'What shall we eat?' or 'What shall we drink?' or 'What shall we wear?' For the pagans run after all these things, and your heavenly Father knows that you need them. But seek first His kingdom and His righteousness, and all these things will be given to you as well." (Matthew 6:31-33)

The way we deal with the present moment should tell us everything we need to know about the condition of our faith. Are we fear driven, thus missing the opportunities before us or do we engage in the moment letting the hand of God lead us forward into the future?

I will sing of your love and justice; to you, O LORD, I will sing praise. I will be careful to lead a blameless life— when will you come to me? I will walk in my house with blameless heart. I will set before my eyes no vile thing. The deeds of faithless men I hate; they will not cling to me. Men of perverse heart shall be far from me; I will have nothing to do with evil.

—Psalm 101:1–4

FIGHT THE GOOD FIGHT

David is speaking about a man who has a heart for God. The "blameless heart" loves God before all things, even before loving oneself.

But the blameless man is warned to live thoughtfully. Virtue can be attacked and compromised. "I will have nothing to do with evil." (v4) We are cautioned to do even more because the threat is real and dangerous: "Flee from sexual immorality." (1 Corinthians 6:18) "Flee from idolatry." (1 Corinthians 10:14) "But you, man of God, flee from all this, and pursue righteousness, godliness, faith, love, endurance and gentleness. Fight the good fight of the faith...." (1 Timothy 6:11-12)

Righteous men will always face conflict, for the world itself is inhabited by a host of the faithless and perverse of heart.

The heavens declare the glory of God; the skies proclaim the work of his hands. Day after day they pour forth speech; night after night they display knowledge. There is no speech or language where their voice is not heard. Their voice goes out into all the earth, their words to the ends of the world.

—Psalm 19:1–4

GOD'S INVISIBLE QUALITIES

Jesus asks, "Why is my language not clear to you?" (John 8:43) To another he asks, "But what about you? Who do you say I am?" (Mark 8:29) And to another: "You do not know me or my Father...If you knew me, you would know my Father also." (John 8:19)

We are like foolish men wandering through a beautiful garden complaining about the insects. God stands before our very eyes and we see...nothing. Ever since we departed that first garden, we have been afflicted by a spiritual blindness that passes down from one generation to the next.

God keeps calling out to us to open the eyes of our hearts (Ephesians 1:18) just as Elisha prayed that God would open the eyes of his servant so that he could see the power of God all around him. (2 Kings 6:17) If we insist on remaining blind, we do it through our own choice. For God makes Himself evident throughout all of creation: "For since the creation of the world God's invisible qualities-his eternal power and divine nature-have been clearly seen, being understood from what has been made...." (Romans 1:20)

The poor are shunned even by their neighbors, but the rich have many friends. He who despises his neighbor sins, but blessed is he who is kind to the needy. He who oppresses the poor shows contempt for their Maker, but whoever is kind to the needy honors God.

—Proverbs 14:20, 21, 31

THE WEIGHT OF OUR COINS

Jesus walked among the rich and poor alike, but his teaching never praised or judged people by their station in this life. He always looked beyond the normal lines of demarcation that seem to pit men against men and men against God.

The rich young man, for example, is virtuous by human standards, but he turns his back on Jesus because he cannot discard the treasure he sees for a treasure he cannot see. Also, in the parable of the Rich Man and Lazarus, the poor man dies but goes to rest with Abraham, while the rich man in the end is carried off to perdition.

In both cases, rich men reject the true eternal treasure for the "treasure on earth, where moth and rust destroy." (Matthew 6:19) This is what the Rich Man is told in the parable: "But Abraham replied, 'Son, remember that in your lifetime you received your good things, while Lazarus received bad things, but now he is comforted here and you are in agony.'" (Luke 16:25)

We should be careful about how we judge our own condition, as well as the condition of others, both rich and poor, because God does not weigh our righteousness by the weight of the coins in our pocket.

You answer us with awesome deeds of righteousness, O God our Savior, the hope of all the ends of the earth and of the farthest seas, who formed the mountains by your power, having armed yourself with strength, who stilled the roaring of the seas, the roaring of their waves, and the turmoil of the nations. Those living far away fear your wonders; where morning dawns and evening fades you call forth songs of joy.

—Psalm 65:5–8

EVER PRESENT, NEVER ABSENT

God is ever present, never absent. He formed the mountains, stilled the roaring sea and even quieted the turmoil of the nations. Without God's presence, the sun would rise on hopelessness and despair. Wars and rumors of wars would be commonplace and the lament of Job would be on every person's lips: "If only there were someone to arbitrate between us..." (Job 9:33)

God heard the cry of this righteous man and in good time He sent His son into the world to reconcile each one of us to Himself. The joy of the morning and the evening is the resurrected Christ: "I am the Alpha and the Omega, the First and the Last, the Beginning and the End. Blessed are those who wash their robes, that they may have the right to the tree of life and may go through the gates into the city...I am the Root and the Off-spring of David, and the bright Morning Star." (Revelation 22:13, 14, 16)

He who works his land will have abundant food, but he who chases fantasies lacks judgment.

—Proverbs 12:11

A FACT OF LIFE

Whom are we working for when we subscribe to the fantasy that we don't have to work? Work is a fact of life and has been part of the human condition since the earliest days of existence: "By the sweat of your brow you will eat your food until you return to the ground..."(Genesis 3:19) No creature in nature survives without diligent work; even the tiny ant "stores its provisions in summer and gathers its food at harvest." (Proverbs 6:8)

On the other hand, "a sluggard does not plow in season; so at harvest time he looks but finds nothing." (Proverbs 20:4) No, to shun work is to buy into a lie that comes as a subtle whisper from the original purveyor of lies, Satan. We always work, even if we choose to be indolent. The only question is: Whom are you working for?

Oh, how I love your law! I meditate on it all day long. Your commands make me wiser than my enemies, for they are ever with me. I have more insight than all my teachers, for I meditate on your statutes. I have more understanding than the elders, for I obey your precepts. I have kept my feet from every evil path so that I might obey your word. I have not departed from your laws, for you yourself have taught me. How sweet are your words to my taste, sweeter than honey to my mouth! I gain understanding from your precepts; therefore, I hate every wrong path.

—Psalm 119:97–104

OBEYING GOD'S LAW

This Psalm begins with a description of those who are blessed: "Blessed are they whose ways are blameless, who walk according to the law of the Lord." (Psalm 119:1) But what about those who hate the Lord's law, who never meditate on it, who disregard teachers and obey no one?

God cannot be mocked. Either we love His law and desire to obey Him or we turn our backs on Him even while we put on an extraordinary show of goodness and virtue.

The psalmist is speaking from his heart: I love the Lord and everything about him. When you love, obedience is never a chore; it is a strong desire to do the right thing for the one you love. If you disregard some aspect of the Lord, for whatever reason, you are saying with your very life that you love something more than God Himself.

Give ear to my words, O LORD, consider my sighing. Listen to my cry for help, my King and my God, for to you I pray. In the morning, O LORD, you hear my voice; in the morning I lay my requests before you and wait in expectation.

—Psalm 5:1–3

NEW EVERY MORNING

Darkness giving way to gentle light is the hint of warmth and hope that is the dawning of a new day. We awake as the sun begins to paint the earth in vibrant colors and we rise to expectations of new opportunities and chances.

But we should never attack the new day; rather, we should embrace it because God wants us to begin by appreciating and acknowledging Him.

In my own life, the glory of the day is built on the foundation of spending time in the Word of God. It has come to the point that everything other than the Word must wait, for there comes a time when the truth and power of God's word exceeds even the beauty of the most glorious sunrise. "Because of the Lord's great love we are not consumed, for his compassions never fail. They are new every morning; great is your faithfulness. I say to myself, 'The Lord is my portion; therefore I will wait for him.'" (Lamentations 3:22-24)

My eyes are dim with grief. I call to you, O LORD, every day; I spread out my hands to you. Do you show your wonders to the dead? Do those who are dead rise up and praise you? Is your love declared in the grave, your faithfulness in Destruction? Are your wonders known in the place of darkness, or your righteous deeds in the land of oblivion? But I cry to you for help, O LORD; in the morning my prayer comes before you.

—*Psalm 88:9–13*

AN ANSWERED PRAYER

Arthur, my sixteen-year-old son, and I were sixteen miles into a eighteen mile day on the Appalachian Trail in Pennsylvania. We started early that morning in the small river town of Duncannon. We crossed the Susquehanna on a well-travelled bridge, ascended a moderate ridge and then began the long, rocky trek north. The temperature was mild for August, but the long miles began to wear me down.

A few days before we started out on this journey, I had arranged to have a man pick us up at an isolated trail crossing in the middle of state forestland, as we would need a ride back to Duncannon. But as the miles passed by and it became time to call to connect with my ride, the phone failed. The day was drawing to a close and my heart began to sink as I descended the ridge.

Would we have to spend an uncomfortable night in the woods or worse, would we be forced to walk back? It is in moments like this that we know the truth of our own vulnerability and our eyes become "dim with grief." (v9) But as I approached the road, I began to hear voices.

Like a guardian angel, the stranger and his wife had kept their appointment. Just as the cloud of anxiety of being stranded colored every step I took, I was suddenly blessed by feeling gratitude and joy at the gracious generosity and kindness of the two people who were there to greet us at the end of an arduous day. At that moment, I felt a small touch of God's presence and His goodness and I could say in my heart "in the morning (and in the evening) my prayer comes before you." (v13)

Remember your word to your servant, for you have given me hope. My comfort in my suffering is this: Your promise preserves my life. The arrogant mock me without restraint, but I do not turn from your law. I remember your ancient laws, O LORD, and I find comfort in them. Indignation grips me because of the wicked, who have forsaken your law. Your decrees are the theme of my song wherever I lodge. In the night I remember your name, O LORD, and I will keep your law. This has been my practice: I obey your precepts.

—Psalm 119:49–56

YOU STEADY US

God's "ancient laws" were a reminder to a wayward people that there are boundaries and we wander away at our own risk. "Do not move an ancient boundary stone" (Proverbs 23:10) means that the spiritual path has been laid out and marked by God and it leads to eternal life.

But we cannot embrace the law and disregard the creator of that law. The psalmist can say he has hope and feels comfort and obeys because he has it fixed in his heart that God is all and everything. Without God the law would be empty and without power. "There is no holiness, O Lord, if You withdraw your comforting hand...When you are not with us, we sink and perish, but when You visit us we rise up and live again. Of ourselves we are unstable, but You steady us; we are lukewarm, but You set us on fire."[10]

Surely no one lays a hand on a broken man when he cries for help in his distress. Have I not wept for those in trouble? Has not my soul grieved for the poor? Yet when I hoped for good, evil came; when I looked for light, then came darkness. The churning inside me never stops; days of suffering confront me. I go about blackened, but not by the sun; I stand up in the assembly and cry for help. I have become a brother of jackals, a companion of owls. My skin grows black and peels; my body burns with fever. My harp is tuned to mourning, and my flute to the sound of wailing.

—Job 30:24–31

YOU CLOTHED ME WITH JOY

Severe affliction has visited Job with the force of an unexpected and overwhelming storm. Has he brought this suffering on himself or has he, in some way, offended God so that he must endure the due penalty of his iniquity?

Job cannot explain what has happened; he lived as a righteous man and even when first tested by trouble "Job did not sin by charging God with wrongdoing." (Job 1:22)

When his trial becomes unendurable, Job's wife says, 'Are you still holding on to your integrity? Curse God and die!' He replied, 'You are talking like a foolish woman. Shall we accept good from God and not trouble?' In all this, Job did not sin in what he said." (Job 2:9-10)

We live in a world where we cannot possibly control all events. It is foolish to believe we can construct walls against all adversity: "...when I hoped for good, evil came."(v26) This is a truth common to all humanity; no one is exempt; yet, no matter what comes our way, we can keep our integrity and not curse God. Instead, we should pray for God's mercy that He may be present in our lives: "Hear, O Lord, be my help. You turned my wailing into dancing; you removed my sackcloth and clothed me with joy, that my heart may sing to you and not be silent." (Psalm 30:10-12)

Lowborn men are but a breath, the highborn are but a lie; if weighed on a balance, they are nothing; together they are only a breath. Do not trust in extortion or take pride in stolen goods; though your riches increase, do not set your heart on them. One thing God has spoken, two things have I heard: that you, O God, are strong, and that you, O Lord, are loving. Surely you will reward each person according to what he has done.

—Psalm 62:9–12

VICTORY OVER DEATH

Our relationship with God determines our relationship with time. When we attempt to live without God, we begin to battle time as we grow older and become conscious that, for each of us, time is a finite commodity. We begin to fear everything because time is slipping through our fingers like so much dust: "Man is a mere phantom as he goes to and fro: He bustles about, but only in vain; he heaps up wealth, not knowing who will get it." (Psalm 39:6)

Whether rich or poor, all men are propelled toward death, unless... unless we accept the promise of a "strong" and "loving" God. We have heard the promise: "For God so loved the world that he gave his one and only Son that whoever believes in him shall not perish but have eternal life." (John 3:16) Acknowledging the love of God through the gift of His Son opens the way to the gift that defeats time and death: "When the perishable has been clothed with the imperishable, and the mortal with immortality, then the saying that is written will come true: "Death has been swallowed up in victory." (1 Corinthians 15:54)

The law of the LORD is perfect, reviving the soul. The statutes of the LORD are trustworthy, making wise the simple. The precepts of the LORD are right, giving joy to the heart. The commands of the LORD are radiant, giving light to the eyes. The fear of the LORD is pure, enduring forever. The ordinances of the LORD are sure and altogether righteous. They are more precious than gold, than much pure gold; they are sweeter than honey, than honey from the comb. By them is your servant warned; in keeping them there is great reward.

—*Psalm 19:7–11*

HIS INCREDIBLE GIFT

We are told, "Be perfect, therefore, as your heavenly Father is perfect." (Matthew 5:48) But how do we ever achieve perfection if, in fact, all people sin?

Sin is so powerful that most of us struggle against it without success. We wonder if we can ever get back to the ideal we long for, knowing that the way back is harder than the way ahead. So we feel stuck and depressed.

Listen, though, to David. He is pointing to the way that is perfect, trustworthy, wise and simple. He is speaking of a heart filled with joy. He is praising someone who has infinitely more value than gold. He is speaking of the one who will come after him to recover a people lost wandering in life's desert regions.

He is speaking of Jesus, the healer of all wounds, the giver of hope, the way to life eternal, the Son of God. Jesus asks only one thing in return for the incredible gift he wants to bestow: "Do you love me?" (John 21:17) If we have it in our hearts to say yes to the question he asks of each of us, then we will also love the laws, commands and precepts of God.

The visions of your prophets were false and worthless; they did not expose your sin to ward off your captivity. The oracles they gave you were false and misleading. All who pass your way clap their hands at you; they scoff and shake their heads at the Daughter of Jerusalem: "Is this the city that was called the perfection of beauty, the joy of the whole earth?" All your enemies open their mouths wide against you; they scoff and gnash their teeth and say, "We have swallowed her up. This is the day we have waited for; we have lived to see it."

—Lamentations 2:14–16

REJECTING FALSE PROPHETS

We live in dangerous times. And false prophets are preaching everywhere. Whether radical clerics in the Middle East or the notorious Jim Jones in Guyana in the 1970's, false prophets are declaring death to infidels or claiming the world has entered end times.

The phenomenon is not new. False prophets are found throughout the Bible. Jesus warns, "Watch out for false prophets. They come to you in sheep's clothing, but inwardly they are ferocious wolves." (Matthew 7:15)

Over 600 years before Jesus, Jeremiah speaks about how the false prophets and priests have brought corruption and trouble to the land: "'The prophets follow an evil course and use their power unjustly. Both prophet and priest are godless; even in my temple I find their wickedness,' declares the Lord." (Jeremiah 23:10-11)

In times like these, it is especially difficult to filter the false from the true. We hear so many claims, many sounding legitimate, but John in his first letter does tell us how to test the spirit of truth. "This is how you can recognize the Spirit of God: Every spirit that acknowledges that Jesus Christ has come in the flesh is from God, but every spirit that does not acknowledge Jesus is not from God. This is the spirit of the antichrist, which you have heard is coming and even now is already in the world." (1 John 4:2-3)

Blessed is the man who finds wisdom, The man who gains understanding, For she is more profitable than silver And yields better returns than gold. She is more precious than rubies; Nothing you desire can compare with her. Long life is in her right hand; In her left hand are riches and honor. Her ways are pleasant ways, And all her paths are peace. She is a tree of life to those who embrace her; Those who lay hold of her will be blessed.

—Proverbs 3:13-18

THE POWER OF GOD

Those who claim to possess a special "insider" knowledge of the *mind* of God are in danger of placing themselves in opposition to the *will* of God. Instead of walking in step with God, they jump out in front of Him in an attempt to get God to walk behind them. But this raises a question: Can the abundant and good life be built on a foundation of rebellion?

If we are to find the pleasant ways that lead to peace, and if we desire to gain access to the tree of life, then our wisdom will come through reconciliation, not rebellion.

Christians believe that this reconciliation comes only through the cross of Christ and the blood of the Lamb: "For God was pleased to have all his fullness dwell in him, and through him to reconcile to himself all things, whether things on earth or things in heaven, by making peace through his blood shed on the cross." (Colossians 1:19-20)

To the world, the cross of Christ is foolishness, but to those who believe, it is the wisdom of God: "For the message of the cross is foolishness to those who are perishing, but to those of us who are being saved it is the power of God." (1 Corinthians 1:18)

Men do not despise a thief if he steals to satisfy his hunger when he is starving. Yet if he is caught, he must pay sevenfold, though it costs him all the wealth of his house. But a man who commits adultery lacks judgment; whoever does so destroys himself. Blows and disgrace are his lot, and his shame will never be wiped away; for jealousy arouses a husband's fury, and he will show no mercy when he takes revenge. He will not accept any compensation; he will refuse the bribe, however great it is.

—*Proverbs 6:30–35*

THE ONLY GENUINE FRUIT OF LOVE

Stealing and adultery are both forms of theft, but the degree of seriousness of the two crimes are worlds apart. If caught, the thief must face punishment, offering restitution to the victim sevenfold. But it also says that "men will not despise (him) if he steals to satisfy his hunger when he is starving." (v33)

No such quarter, however, is given the one who steals a wife. The adulterer may offer excuses, but he "lacks judgment" and his crime will lead to lies, dissension and sometimes even murder. Adultery fractures; it does not unite.

How often do we hear the sad lament of the adulterer who, amidst the ruins of his life, claims that he did it all for love? But if this is true, why does "the eye of the adulterer watch for dusk?" Why does he think, "No eye will see me?" And why does he keep "his face concealed?" (Job 24:15)

Love is never about betrayal or stealing. The fruit of love is patience, kindness, protection, trust, hope and perseverance. Adultery is about theft; the only genuine fruit it produces is misery and strife.

Unless the LORD builds the house, its builders labor in vain. Unless the LORD watches over the city, the watchmen stand guard in vain. In vain you rise early and stay up late, toiling for food to eat—for he grants sleep to those he loves.

—Psalm 127:1–2

WHAT ABOUT YOU? WHAT ABOUT ME?

Saul is a righteous Jew, a Pharisee, instructed in the letter of the law. He has decided that he must destroy the troublesome Christian sect that is causing so much turmoil in Jerusalem and beyond. He has gained the permission of the high priests to go to Damascus to find and arrest the agitators and bring them in chains back to Jerusalem.

Saul has the authority of the high priests behind him. He has the force of the Hebrew law supporting him, but he is fruitlessly laboring against the will of God. On the way to Damascus, he is stopped by a blinding light and he hears a voice: "Saul, Saul, why do you persecute me?" (Acts 9:4)

From that time on, Saul (who would become known as Paul), begins to labor mightily in God's vineyard. Until that flash of light near Damascus, Saul was a "builder laboring in vain." He was the watchman standing guard over Judaism in vain.

God had a purpose for Paul as He has a purpose for each one of us. But to work within that purpose, we need to stop working against the will of God. Paul was transformed into an Apostle by his encounter with Jesus.

What about you? What about me? Are we like Saul, "builder(s) laboring in vain? Or are we fulfilling God's purpose by working within His will rather than against it?

The elders are gone from the city gate; the young men have stopped their music. Joy is gone from our hearts; our dancing has turned to mourning. The crown has fallen from our head. Woe to us, for we have sinned! Because of this our hearts are faint, because of these things our eyes grow dim for Mount Zion, which lies desolate, with jackals prowling over it.

—Lamentations 5:14–18

CITY OF GOD, CITY OF MAN

Jerusalem "lies desolate with jackals prowling over it."

Why has David's city fallen into the hands of its enemies? The answer is clear: "…we have sinned!" This great city, so favored by God, has turned away in favor of violence and strife. "Destructive forces are at work in the city; threats and lies never leave its streets." (Psalm 55:11)

Isaiah warns: "Woe to those who make unjust laws, to those who issue oppressive decrees, to deprive the poor of their rights and withhold justice from the oppressed of my people, making widows their prey and robbing the fatherless." (Isaiah 10: 1,2) To those who pervert justice he says, "What will you do on the day of reckoning, when disaster comes from afar? To whom will you run for help? Where will you leave your riches?" (Isaiah 10:3)

The leaders of Jerusalem had abandoned the law and the prophets. Through Moses, God gave the people a promise and a warning: "See, I set before you today life and prosperity, death and destruction…This day I call heaven and earth as witnesses against you that I have set before you life and death, blessings and curses. Now choose life, so that you and your children may live and that you may love the Lord your God, listen to his voice and hold fast to him. For the Lord is your life…" (Deuteronomy 30:15-16, 19-20)

When the Lord is cast aside, the city of God must become the city of man. And when this happens, desolation, death and exile cannot be far off.

No king is saved by the size of his army; no warrior escapes by his great strength. A horse is a vain hope for deliverance; despite all its great strength it cannot save. But the eyes of the LORD are on those who fear him, on those whose hope is in his unfailing love, to deliver them from death and keep them alive in famine.

—Psalm 33:16–19

THE LORD IS MY STRENGTH

It is difficult not to be impressed by the stature of a prince or king or president. He is surrounded by his armies and protected by his guards. When he speaks, the nation listens; when he is angered, people tremble.

And yet the strongest leader in the greatest nation is nothing compared to the strength of God: "For the foolishness of God is wiser than man's wisdom, and the weakness of God is stronger than man's strength." (1 Corinthians 1:25) David says, "It is God who arms me with strength and makes my way perfect." (2 Samuel 22:33)

We easily confuse the strength God confers on men with a *man's* strength. Stalin, at the height of his power in the Soviet Union, reportedly asked with great sarcasm, "Where are the Pope's armies?" We might ask the same question today, but only in reverse: "Where is Stalin? Where is the Soviet Union and where are *his* armies?"

David gives us another perspective. "It is better to take refuge in the Lord than to trust in man. It is better to take refuge in the Lord than to trust in princes." (Psalm 118:8-9) David, even at the height of his power, attributed his worldly strength to God: "I was pushed back and about to fall, but the Lord helped me. The Lord is my strength and my song; he has become my salvation." (Psalm 118:13-14)

Two are better than one, because they have a good return for their work: If one falls down, his friend can help him up. But pity the man who falls and has no one to help him up! Also, if two lie down together, they will keep warm. But how can one keep warm alone? Though one may be overpowered, two can defend themselves. A cord of three strands is not quickly broken.

—Ecclesiastes 4:9–12

THE COMPANION

I often enjoy hiking in the woods alone. On one particular trip, the trail took me up to a ridge on a low-lying mountain range in central Pennsylvania. On such trips, the familiar noises of civilization can often be heard: the distant rumble of a passing freight train or the subtle hum of an interstate or just the low-grade sounds of distant activity filtering up to the trail.

But on this day everything was different, for as I moved further along the rocky path, I began to notice the absence of sound. It seemed as if I had walked into a vacuum chamber. The feeling of isolation became palpable and the sense of sudden vulnerability was haunting.

It is at times like this that you feel a deep appreciation for the power of two. If I had fallen while alone, I would have been in trouble, but if a companion had been with me, I would have been helped. If I had become lost, my friend would have assisted finding the way back to the trail. Alone, my chances of success would have been greatly diminished.

This noiseless world, beautiful and intriguing as it was, left me with a feeling of aloneness. It seemed like a world outside of God's design for us. So, while the walk was memorable, I was relieved, in the end, to hear all the familiar sounds of human activity once again. For to me these noises were the sound of companionship, friendship and most importantly, the sound of love.

It felt good to be back.

My eyes will be on the faithful in the land, that they may dwell with me; he whose walk is blameless will minister to me. No one who practices deceit will dwell in my house; no one who speaks falsely will stand in my presence.

—Psalm 101:6–7

KNOWING GOD

Genuine faith is a lived faith; it is not an abstract concept. Here faith refers directly to our relationship with God. If we live faithful lives, we live in obedience to the will of God above everything else.

Our human relationships, therefore, are triangular. As we love another person, we are expressing to that person the love that God has for us. When another person loves us, we are being shown the very nature of God as expressed through that love.

If we flaunt our own will, defying God's will through our own loveless acts and perverse desires, then we are denying the life God intended for us. The model is Jesus, "Who, being in very nature God, did not consider equality with God something to be grasped, but he made himself nothing, taking on the very nature of a servant." (Philippians 2:6-7)

The faithless man disdains being thought of as a servant; his pride lifts him high above the field of battle and he gathers the entire strength of his heart to humble others rather than being humble himself. But by doing so, he breaks the bond of love with God and replaces it with a bond of justice: "Whoever slanders his neighbor in secret, him I will put to silence; whoever has haughty eyes and a proud heart, him will I not endure." (Psalm 101:5)

Speak up for those who cannot speak for themselves, for the rights of all who are destitute. Speak up and judge fairly; defend the rights of the poor and needy.

—Proverbs 31:8–9

THE RIGHTEOUS KING'S EXAMPLE

This proverb can be a lethal weapon in the hands of a politician. For they proclaim an interest in the welfare of the poor and needy by attacking the wickedness of the wealthy. But if they are not careful, and many are not, they become demigods and hypocrites because they embrace the very things they claim to hate—money and power.

Solomon is describing how an ideal king should rule. The king should model his conduct on the righteousness and justice of God Himself because he is a servant of God. And what applies to the righteous king applies to us as well: "Be careful not to do your acts of righteousness before men to be seen by them. If you do, you will have no reward from your Father in heaven. So when you give to the needy, do not announce it with trumpets, as the hypocrites do in the synagogues and on the streets, to be honored by men. I tell you the truth, they have received their reward in full." (Matthew 6:1-2)

The LORD is my shepherd, I shall not be in want. He makes me lie down in green pastures, he leads me beside quiet waters, he restores my soul. He guides me in paths of righteousness for his name's sake. Even though I walk through the valley of the shadow of death, I will fear no evil, for you are with me; your rod and your staff, they comfort me. You prepare a table before me in the presence of my enemies. You anoint my head with oil; my cup overflows. Surely goodness and love will follow me all the days of my life, and I will dwell in the house of the LORD forever.

—Psalm 23:1–6

THE VALLEY OF THE SHADOW OF DEATH

Until one bright September morning in 2001, it would be fair to say that America had taken a short vacation from history. The smaller matters of everyday life were paramount with the nature of evil receding to an irrelevance, as chasing wealth seemed to become the only obsession. America seemed to float in a sea of cascading distractions until nineteen men exploded our revelry in an instant.

By the end of that day, people were praying everywhere, and while it cannot be known for sure, thousands, if not millions, of people were saying aloud and in their hearts the 23rd Psalm. "Even though I walk through the valley of the shadow of death, I will fear no evil, for you are with me; your rod and your staff they comfort me."(4)

Individually, and as a nation, we awake as if from a dream and call out to the shepherd who promises to guide and restore us.

My eyes fail from weeping, I am in torment within, my heart is poured out on the ground because my people are destroyed, because children and infants faint in the streets of the city. They say to their mothers, "Where is bread and wine?" as they faint like wounded men in the streets of the city, as their lives ebb away in their mothers' arms. What can I say for you? With what can I compare you, O Daughter of Jerusalem? To what can I liken you, that I may comfort you, O Virgin Daughter of Zion? Your wound is as deep as the sea. Who can heal you?

—Lamentations 2:11–13

THE PEOPLE WOULD NOT LISTEN

In 586 B.C., the fierce and powerful armies of Nebuchadnezzar finally overwhelmed the last of the defenders of the city of David. Those who were not slaughtered immediately were led away in chains to live in exile in Babylon. A small and poor remnant was left behind but the magnificent temple build by King Solomon was reduced to rubble.

The tragedy was not inevitable, however. The leaders and people of Jerusalem had heard the prophetic messages of Isaiah, Jeremiah and others, but they stubbornly disregarded God's warnings and continued to adhere to their own misguided and treacherous ways. Speaking through Jeremiah, the Lord says, "There is a conspiracy among the people of Judah and those who live in Jerusalem. They have returned to the sins of their forefathers, who refused to listen to my words. They have followed other gods to serve them. Both the house of Israel and the house of Judah have broken the covenant I made with their forefathers." (Jeremiah 11:9-10)

The people of Jerusalem tragically disregarded the blessing of the promise to embrace the curse by abandoning the God of Abraham, Isaac and Jacob. The city of David fell because the people of Judah broke the covenant with God by turning to worship other gods. They turned away from the prophets saying, "Do not prophesy in the name of the Lord or you will die by our hands..." (Jeremiah 11:21) From that time on, the city was no longer safe from attack and destuction from the barbarous armies of the night.

For men are not cast off by the Lord forever. Though he brings grief, he will show compassion, so great is his unfailing love. For he does not willingly bring affliction or grief to the children of men. To crush underfoot all prisoners in the land, to deny a man his rights before the Most High, to deprive a man of justice— would not the Lord see such things?

—Lamentations 3:31–36

SEIZE THE MOMENT

No grief equals the grief of being separated from God.

After murdering his brother Abel, Cain is condemned and becomes "a restless wanderer of the earth." (Genesis 4:12) Cain cries out that this punishment of exile is more than he can bear: "...I will be hidden from your presence." (Genesis 4:14)

Time and again, we hear the cry of despair of those who believe they cannot receive God's forgiveness. Peter breaks down in tears after denying the Lord the third time. Judas hangs himself after attempting to give back the thirty silver coins to the chief priests: "'I have sinned,' he said, 'for I have betrayed innocent blood.'" (Matthew 27:4)

Of these three, Peter, in his remorse, seeks the Lord's forgiveness, and is forgiven. While all men sin, God is gracious to those who genuinely seek His forgiveness.

David prays, "Have mercy on me, O God, according to your unfailing love, according to your great compassion blot out my transgressions.... Against you, you only, have I sinned and done what is evil in your sight...." (Psalm 51:1, 4) David's prayer should be on every man's lips everyday. God hears our plea and His compassions are new every morning. (Lamentations 3:22, 23)

Every morning we have a chance to renew our relationship with God. But we must seize the moment.

Whoever loves money never has money enough; whoever loves wealth is never satisfied with his income. This too is meaningless. As goods increase, so do those who consume them. And what benefit are they to the owner except to feast his eyes on them? The sleep of a laborer is sweet, whether he eats little or much, but the abundance of a rich man permits him no sleep.

—Ecclesiastes 5:10–12

COME NEAR TO GOD

It might be said that whoever lusts after anything will never have enough. What begins as an inclination soon becomes a passion and finally ends as a consuming fire.

C. S. Lewis has spoken of hell as an act or desire that begins as something very small, but, with time, expands into something that overwhelms the whole person to the point where there is no other reality. Once Satan has gained a foothold, it is exceedingly difficult to shake him off.

It is not wealth or money that corrupts and destroys; it is the lust for money that squeezes out the capacity to love anything else, especially God. Our sin becomes our sole obsession.

While we were created to enjoy fellowship with God, sin will block that relationship. When we turn away from God to gain the treasures offered by this world, we flee into the arms of the adversary. "Resist the devil, and he will flee from you. Come near to God and he will come near to you." (James 4:7-8)

Listen to your father, who gave you life, and do not despise your mother when she is old. Buy the truth and do not sell it; get wisdom, discipline and understanding. The father of a righteous man has great joy; he who has a wise son delights in him. May your father and mother be glad; may she who gave you birth rejoice!

—Proverbs 23:22–25

WHAT GOD WANTS FOR YOUR CHILDREN

What do parents want for their children? Is it enough to desire that your child be obedient or successful in school or a star on the fields of dreams? A better question might be: What does *God* want your child to be? A clue to the answer might be found in the following verse: "The father of a righteous man has great joy; he who has a wise son delights in him." (v24)

God does not ask parents to produce persuasive lawyers or great scholars or star athletes; this is what the *culture* wants. God calls us to raise children that will want to be right with God, to love the Lord with all their heart, strength and mind and to love their neighbor as well. Paul instructs Timothy as a father would a son: "...pursue righteousness, godliness, faith, love, endurance and gentleness. Fight the good fight of the faith. Take hold of the eternal life to which you were called when you made your good confession in the presence of many witnesses." (1 Timothy 6:11-12)

Precious in the sight of the LORD is the death of his saints. O LORD, truly I am your servant; I am your servant, the son of your maidservant; you have freed me from my chains.

—Psalm 116:15–16

A DANGEROUS MISSION

Before we shrink back from the statement that "Precious in the sight of the LORD is the death of his saints," we need to acknowledge that sooner or later all men are destined to die. But even before we experience physical death, as children of God, we must die to the cravings and passions for the things of this world. "If anyone would come after me, he must deny himself and take up his cross daily and follow me. For whoever wants to save his life will lose it, but whoever loses his life for me will save it." (Luke 9:23-24)

If we do not experience death to the impulses of the sinful nature, then we will be driven by fear of physical death and our journey will resemble Jonah's flight from God. The Christian life calls us to overcome all fear; to be "strong and courageous" (Joshua 1:6); and to "stand [our] ground, and after [we] have done everything, to stand." (Ephesians 6:14)

When we become disciples, we are embarking on a great and dangerous mission, but we are not alone: In God we place our trust. And it gives us comfort to know that "[our] brothers throughout the world are undergoing the same kind of sufferings." (1 Peter 5:9)

If I have denied justice to my menservants and maidservants when they had a grievance against me, what will I do when God confronts me? What will I answer when called to account? Did not he who made me in the womb make them? Did not the same one form us both within our mothers?

—*Job 31:13-15*

CONFRONTED BY GOD

"Do not be deceived. God cannot be mocked." (Galatians 6:7) Yet we live as if we were not being watched. We believe we can cover up our petty crimes in the darkness of night, where eyes cannot see nor ears hear the work of our folly. But while we can deceive ourselves into believing that we are independent of God, we cannot deceive the one who made us: "From heaven the Lord looks down and sees all mankind; from his dwelling place he watches all who live on earth-he who forms the heart of all, who considers everything they do." (Psalm 33:13-15)

So much of anxiety, stress and sorrow come from the misapprehension that we are free to perpetrate our favorite crimes. We say in our hearts, "who will see us, who will hear us, who will know?" Instead, we might ask Job's question: "...what will I do when God confronts me?" (v14)

The woman Folly is loud; she is undisciplined and without knowledge. She sits at the door of her house, on a seat at the highest point of the city, calling out to those who pass by, who go straight on their way. "Let all who are simple come in here!" she says to those who lack judgment. "Stolen water is sweet; food eaten in secret is delicious!" But little do they know that the dead are there, that her guests are in the depths of the grave.

—Proverbs 9:13-18

BEING STALKED

Some might interpret the comparison between women and folly as a slur, but this would miss the point completely. The fool does not seek a woman of noble character; rather, he would prefer to keep the company of prostitutes. He does not hear the call of wisdom that cries out: "To you, O men, I call out; I raise my voice to all mankind. You who are simple, gain prudence; you who are foolish, gain understanding...My mouth speaks what is true, for my lips detest wickedness." (Proverbs 8: 4-5, 7)

The fool abandons God for the sweetness of "stolen water" and the delicious taste of "food eaten in secret." And in abandoning God, who is forever calling out to every hidden corner of the earth, the fool turns away to embrace that which will only bring him death. The folly of the fool is to discount the dangers lurking all around him. He stalks his prey unarmed, not realizing that it is he who is being stalked. Recognizing the danger is the first step toward wisdom. "I love those who love me, and those who seek me find me." (Proverbs 8:17)

Listen to my prayer, O God, do not ignore my plea; hear me and answer me. My thoughts trouble me and I am distraught at the voice of the enemy, at the stares of the wicked; for they bring down suffering upon me and revile me in their anger.

—Psalm 55:1–3

ELIJAH

The man of God lives under a constant threat of danger and strife. Elijah is one of the great prophets, a true man of God, but Ahab, the king, calls him a "troubler of Israel." (1 Kings 18:17)

The king has married Jezebel who worships Baal, and she has set out to kill all the prophets of the Lord. When Elijah confronts her and exposes her four hundred and fifty corrupt prophets for who they are, Jezebel swears an oath on his life: "May the gods deal with me, be it ever so severely, if by this time tomorrow I do not make your life like that of one of them." (1 Kings 19:2)

Elijah escapes, but, in the desert, he despairs and prays to God to take his life. It is then that a miracle happens. At his lowest moment, an angel appears and tells him to eat and gain strength and then go to Horeb, the mountain of God. Shortly after this, he hears the voice of God as a gentle whisper in the wind. And it is then that he is told to go and find Elisha so that together they can continue to do God's work of restoring the Lord's place in Israel.

In fulfilling the purpose of God as children of God, we are promised difficulties, hardships and even persecution: "Blessed are those who are persecuted because of righteousness, for theirs is the kingdom of heaven. Blessed are you when people insult you, persecute you and falsely say all kinds of evil against you because of me." (Matthew 5:10-11) No matter what the circumstance may be, we are called to persevere.

There are three things that are stately in their stride, four that move with stately bearing: a lion, mighty among beasts, who retreats before nothing; a strutting rooster, a he-goat, and a king with his army around him.

—Proverbs 30:29–31

KING OF KINGS

Here is the king with his powerful army, clad in his armor, surrounded by his generals and lieutenants and ready for war. When confronted with such a spectacle, we respond with a sense of awe, fear and respect. The king is powerful and he impresses with his stately bearing. Any other image of the king would seem to be inappropriate, unless, of course, the king shattered our preconception of what it means to be a genuine king.

In fact, another king *does* appear who does not have "a stately bearing." He may be "KING OF KINGS and LORD OF LORDS," (Revelation 19:16) but "He had no beauty or majesty to attract us to him, nothing in his appearance that we should desire him. He was despised and rejected by men, a man of sorrows, and familiar with suffering. Like one from whom men hide their faces he was despised, and we esteemed him not." (Isaiah 53:2-3)

He is the King who says, "If anyone wants to be first, he must be the very last, and the servant of all." (Mark 9:35) He is the King who "made himself nothing," and who "humbled himself and became obedient to death—even death on a cross." (Philippians 2:6, 7)

The truth is that this is a King who can give us something that no earthly king can give—eternal life. Here is a king that has descended into an "unbelieving and perverse generation," (Matthew 17:17) not to condemn the world, but to save it.

How many are your works, O LORD! In wisdom you made them all;
the earth is full of your creatures. There is the sea, vast and spacious,
teeming with creatures beyond number— living things both large and
small. There the ships go to and fro, and the leviathan, which you
formed to frolic there.

—Psalm 104:24–26

THINGS TOO WONDERFUL FOR ME

How easy it is to look at the world and see only as far as the narrowness of our own imaginations will allow! Rather than the stress and strain of mystery, we chose the safety of simplicity, transforming a brilliant full color picture into plain black and white.

In this passage, intimations of the complexities of the canvas are suggested: "There is the sea, vast and spacious, teeming with creatures beyond number—living things both large and small." (v25) When the element of mystery is removed, we are reduced to "explanations" that elucidate nothing. Our rational approach to the world would suggest that the human mind can formulate a theory of everything, whereas the truth can only be approached if we abide in the mystery of creation and the mystery of the creator.

"The Lord answered Job out of the storm. He said: 'Who is this that darkens my counsel with words without knowledge. Brace yourself like a man; I will question you, and you will answer me. Where were you when I laid the earth's foundation? Tell me, if you understand.'" (Job 38:2-4)

After being presented with countless unanswerable questions, Job submits to the Lord: "Surely I spoke of things I did not understand, things too wonderful for me to know." (Job 42:3)

Wisdom begins by acknowledging the mystery that exists at the center of life and of our lives. "It is the glory of God to conceal a matter…" (Proverbs 25:2)

There is not a righteous man on earth who does what is right and never sins.

—*Ecclesiastes 7:20*

THE SELF-RIGHTEOUS HOLY MAN

Solomon reveals a hard truth: all men sin, including the best and brightest among us. No one is exempt, and to argue otherwise is to deny the reality of biblical revelation. Yet we persist in the blindness of our own pride by proclaiming our own righteousness to anyone who will listen.

Jesus tells the parable of the holy man and the tax collector. Whereas the tax collector simply prays "God, have mercy on me a sinner," the holy man looks down his imperious nose and declares: "God, I thank you that I am not like other men—robbers, evildoers, adulterers—or even like this tax collector. I fast twice a week and give a tenth of all I get." (Luke 18:10-13)

The holy man is not righteous in the eyes of God, but *self*-righteous. He is denying the reality of sin in his own life, yet sees sin in others.

Jesus always sees the difference and says so to his disciples: "I tell you that this man (the tax collector) went home justified before God. For everyone who exalts himself will be humbled, and he who humbles himself will be exalted." (Luke 18:14)

*My days are swifter than a runner; they fly away without a glimpse
of joy. They skim past like boats of papyrus, like eagles swooping down
on their prey.*

—*Job 9:25–26*

RENEWED DAY BY DAY

Do we ever stop to consider what we are doing with our time? Do we
wonder what time is doing to us?

One strategy used to avoid these questions is to schedule every waking
minute, leaving little time for reflection and thought. It is as if we need
a framework for pushing away the anxiety that would rush in if we were
faced with a moment of down time.

But super-structuring our time succeeds at keeping our anxious
feelings at arms length for only so long; then like the relentless tide, our
awareness of time, death and eternity pours in, leaving our strategy of
avoidance in a shambles. Behind the artificial barriers erected against
reality, we hear the truth of the words "Each man's life is but a breath."
(Psalm 39:5)

We could despair over the fact that "My days are swifter than a weaver's
shuttle…" (Job 7:6), but we could also respond with courage and faith,
for behind the reality of the temporal is the promise of the eternal.

To those who have placed their life in God's hands there is a quiet
confidence that is echoed by Paul: "…we do not lose heart. Though
outwardly we are wasting away, yet inwardly we are being renewed day by
day." (2 Corinthians 4:16)

The fear of the LORD is the beginning of wisdom; all who follow his precepts have good understanding. To him belongs eternal praise.

—*Psalm 111:10*

THE TRUTH IS A PERSON

To the psalmist, "fear" means that we acknowledge and submit to the reality of God as the author of all that exists. If we live a life built on the firm belief in God, then we open our eyes to the reality that all truth can only come from God.

We also diminish our own propensity for pride by seeing the reality of our own existence in relationship to the utter immensity of God. The very nature of God cannot be circumscribed by time or space. God's nature is eternal and genuine human wisdom perceives, if only dimly, that truth.

John begins his Gospel by saying the Word was before all time and has now come to earth in the person of Jesus Christ: "In the beginning was the Word, and the Word was with God, and the Word was God. He was with God in the beginning." (John 1:1) This passage builds on the Genesis account of the creation: "In the beginning God created the heavens and the earth." (Genesis 1:1) God pre-existed the heavens and the earth, as did the Word as did His Son, Jesus Christ, who says, "And now, Father, glorify me in your presence with the glory I had with you before the world began." (John 17:5)

When we are called to fear God, we are asked to acknowledge His Son, for all the wisdom of God is made known to us in the person of Jesus Christ.

What is truth? Truth is a person, and the name of that person is Jesus Christ.

Your name, O LORD, endures forever, your renown, O LORD, through all generations. For the LORD will vindicate his people and have compassion on his servants. The idols of the nations are silver and gold, made by the hands of men. They have mouths, but cannot speak, eyes, but they cannot see; they have ears, but cannot hear, nor is there breath in their mouths. Those who make them will be like them, and so will all who trust in them.

—Psalm 135:13–18

MADE TO WORSHIP

In his book, *The Purpose Driven Life*, Rick Warren tells us that man is made for worship. Even if we were isolated on a desert island, cut off from all humanity, we would still feel an ache in our hearts to worship something.

But who or what do we choose to worship? For it can be just as dangerous to worship something false as it is not to worship at all. This Psalm warns against the worship of man-made idols.

Idols are merely "gods" built by human hands. They satisfy our need to worship, but only on the most superficial level. God wants us to worship Him and nothing else. He warns us away from the inclination to worship something just because we find comfort in it. God gave Moses Ten Commandments, but the first four deal exclusively with our relationship with Him: *You shall have no other gods but me; you shall not make idols to worship; you shall not misuse my name; and you shall set aside one day to rest and to worship me.*

Jesus summed up the commandments this way: "Love the Lord your God with all your heart and with all your soul and with all your mind. This is the first and greatest commandment." (Matthew 22:37-38)

Though my father and mother forsake me, the LORD will receive me. Teach me your way, O LORD; lead me in a straight path because of my oppressors. Do not turn me over to the desire of my foes, for false witnesses rise up against me, breathing out violence. I am still confident of this: I will see the goodness of the LORD in the land of the living. Wait for the LORD; be strong and take heart and wait for the LORD.

—Psalm 27:10–14

BE STRONG, BE PATIENT

Why do you need to be strong in order to wait for the Lord? Here is one reason: God is not the God of instant gratification. In another context, He says through Isaiah, "...neither are your ways my ways." (Isaiah 55:8) He will use us and deliver us when it is His will to do so and not before.

Thus, Joseph languishes in prison accused of a crime he never committed until the time was right for his release. Moses escapes into the desert for forty years before being called by God to return to deliver His people from bondage. And even though, at the age of twelve, Jesus showed great understanding and amazed the teachers and scribes in the temple, he was not ready for another eighteen years to accomplish God's intention. In fact, even during his short three-year ministry, his true purpose kept being delayed for "his time had not yet come." (John 7:30)

So we should take heart: The Bible says that God will work His purpose in our lives. We need to call upon Him in prayer while exercising patience, even if our circumstances are difficult and no clear path is seen.

This is why, in waiting for the Lord, we need to be strong and steadfast. *It is not good to have zeal without knowledge, nor to be hasty and miss the way.*

—Proverbs 19:2

THE FRUIT OF THEIR ZEAL

The last century was the century of the political zealot; it was a time of enormous upheaval, terrible wars, and fanatical beliefs. The political leaders who brought civilization to a boil were zealous to establish a new political order and were willing to sacrifice millions of people to see their bloody vision to its logical end.

Whether it was Stalin, starving whole populations in Ukraine, or Hitler, massacring defenseless people in prison camps or Pol Pot, destroying nearly half of Cambodia, the fruit of their zeal was terror, torture and death. They were zealous, but they did not have knowledge. They substituted their own beliefs in political systems for God's eternal wisdom and they were bound to fail.

Zeal without the knowledge of God is a deadly weapon and we see it being used to this very day. The ministry of Jesus leads to liberty from sin, to love of God and to love of our neighbors. When they take possession of power, the schemes of the political zealot often lead to dislocation, devastation, and death. You can discern the difference by the outworking of the zeal: "by their fruits you will recognize them." (Matthew 7:16)

Who is like the wise man? Who knows the explanation of things?
Wisdom brightens a man's face and changes its hard appearance.

—Ecclesiastes 8:1

HE OPENED THE SCRIPTURES TO US

Wisdom and light are both essential attributes of God. John says, "God is light; in him there is no darkness at all." (1 John 1:5) The very first words of God in the creation story are, "Let there be light" (Genesis 1:3), and Jesus says, "This is the verdict: Light has come into the world, but men loved darkness instead of light because their deeds were evil." (John 3:19)

He who rejects wisdom can be said to live in darkness, but he who embraces God embraces wisdom and light. "The path of the righteous is like the first gleam of dawn, shining ever brighter till the full light of day." (Proverbs 4:18)

The association of wisdom, light and God is never more evident than when the two travelers, despondent over the terrible events in Jerusalem, suddenly discover that the Lord has been walking to Emmaus with them. Their reaction confirms that the wisdom of God indeed brightens a man's face through his awakened heart: "Were not our hearts burning within us while he talked with us on the road and opened the Scriptures to us?" (Luke 24:32)

Like a coating of glaze over earthenware are fervent lips with an evil heart. A malicious man disguises himself with his lips, but in his heart he harbors deceit. Though his speech is charming, do not believe him, for seven abominations fill his heart.

—Proverbs 26:23–25

SEVEN ABOMINATIONS

Malice is most effective when it wears a mask. The heart of the malicious man may be boiling with anger and hatred, but revealing the truth of his corruption would take the edge off the sweetness of his dark intention.

On the surface, he appears to be a close friend: "My companion attacks his friends; he violates his covenant. His speech is smooth as butter, yet war is in his heart; his words are more smooth than oil, yet they are drawn swords." (Psalm 55:20-21)

The man who gives his life over to serving God is especially susceptible to the malice of the wicked. David prays for deliverance from his enemies: "Those who seek my life set their traps, those who would harm me talk of my ruin; all day long they plot deception...Many are those who are my vigorous enemies; those who hate me without reason are numerous." (Psalm 38:11-12, 19)

From his earliest ministry, Jesus is under attack from Satan, from the religious leaders of Israel, from the Roman rulers and even from his own family. They reject him because his existence among them threatens the ground they stand on. In the end, Caiaphas, the high priest, reveals the reason why Jesus must be destroyed: "You do not realize that it is better for you that one man die for the people than the whole nation perish." (John 11:50)

While he maintains the outward appearance of a holy man, his heart is bitter with hatred and fear. He will accuse an innocent man and condemn him to death to preserve his corrupt seat of power. "For seven abominations fill his heart." (v25)

A man who loves wisdom brings joy to his father, but a companion of prostitutes squanders his wealth.

—Proverbs 29:3

ONCE LOST, NOW FOUND

It is hard to read this verse and not imagine that Jesus had it in mind when he told the parable of the lost son. On one level, the parable is about a young man who receives an inheritance from his father, but lacks wisdom and goes far away from home to "squander his wealth in wild living." (Luke 15:13)

You might think that the story would end here with the good son inheriting the father's estate, while the bad son receives the severe punishment he deserves. But Jesus turns the tables on our expectations. Instead of the bad son receiving punishment and the good son reward, the disobedient son repents of his profligate ways and returns home, ashamed and humiliated and expecting nothing: "The son said to him, 'Father, I have sinned against heaven and against you. I am no longer worthy to be called your son.'" (v21)

With that, the father immediately accepts him back into the household, just as God the Father accepts His own lost children back when they genuinely turn back and say, "I have sinned against you."

The father expresses emphatic joy at having his son back: "For this son of mine was dead and is alive again; he was lost and is found." (v24)

The Father wants all of His lost children back. And He is ready to celebrate when He sees us coming.

A wife of noble character who can find? She is worth far more than rubies. She makes linen garments and sells them, and supplies the merchants with sashes. She is clothed with strength and dignity; she can laugh at the days to come. She speaks with wisdom, and faithful instruction is on her tongue. She watches over the affairs of her household and does not eat the bread of idleness. Her children arise and call her blessed; her husband also, and he praises her: "Many women do noble things, but you surpass them all." Charm is deceptive, and beauty is fleeting; but a woman who fears the LORD is to be praised. Give her the reward she has earned, and let her works bring her praise at the city gate.

—*Proverbs 31:10, 24–31*

BEAUTY THAT TRANSCENDS YOUTH

"Charm is deceptive, and beauty is fleeting; but a woman who fears the Lord is to be praised." (v10)

So much is asked of women and so much is given by them. Women of noble character provide strength, dignity and wisdom. They are teachers and they manage their households with expert and strong hands. They are generous providers and exemplary citizens, upholding the family and supporting their husbands in everything. On almost every level, they are the link between the generation passing with the generation to come. Beauty may be fleeting, but the woman of noble character has a beauty that transcends youth, mirroring a soul right with God.

Wisdom will save you from the ways of wicked men, from men whose words are perverse, who leave the straight paths to walk in dark ways, who delight in doing wrong and rejoice in the perverseness of evil, whose paths are crooked and who are devious in their ways. It will save you also from the adulteress, from the wayward wife with her seductive words, who has left the partner of her youth and ignored the covenant she made before God. For her house leads down to death and her paths to the spirits of the dead. None who go to her return or attain the paths of life. Thus you will walk in the ways of good men and keep to the paths of the righteous. For the upright will live in the land, and the blameless will remain in it; but the wicked will be cut off from the land, and the unfaithful will be torn from it.

—Proverbs 2:12–22

A READJUSTMENT OF THE HEART

Recently, about nine people met at my office in New York City to launch an informal Bible discussion group. During the discussion, one young man expressed his frustration with the book of Proverbs.

"I read it," he said, "but all I came across was 'righteousness this' and 'righteousness that' without ever learning what righteousness is."

What is righteousness? Let's start with what it is *not*. The rich ruler (Luke 18:18) lived by many of the commandments given to Moses, but Jesus told him that he still lacked one thing: to sell all his worldly wealth and "then come and follow me." (v 22)The rich ruler refused because his wealth had a greater hold on him than God did.

But this is not the case with Abraham. At God's command, Abraham left everything, including his family and his home: "Abram believed the Lord, and he credited to him as righteousness." (Genesis 15:6)

Righteousness is not *self*-righteousness; it is not bragging rights about what a great person you are, even if you are a very good person. Rather it is a total readjustment of the heart so that you can move from doubt and detachment to a condition where you are willing not to be unwilling. Jesus summarizes it all: "The work of God is this: to believe in the one he has sent." (John 6:29)

Put your faith in God and Him only. Anything less is less than righteous.

May God be gracious to us and bless us and make his face shine upon us, that your ways may be known on earth, your salvation among all nations.

—*Psalm 67:1–2*

THE WORK OF AN EVANGELIST

Often we pray for our own well-being: "O, Lord, deliver me from this disease," or "Lord, save me from financial ruin."

Of course, it is perfectly right to pray for safety in a dangerous world or for financial or physical deliverance when our well-being is threatened. However, it is a far greater act to pray for what this sorrowful and lost world really needs by asking that God's "ways may be known on earth, (His) salvation among all nations."

The heart of God is love, and when we come to know this through God's grace, we are called out to share this love with the rest of the world, particularly with those who have not yet heard of God's goodness and graciousness.

Jesus calls his disciples to "go and make disciples of all nations…" (Matthew 28:19) He commands us to make his ways known to all nations near and far. As Paul tells Timothy: "…endure hardship, do the work of an evangelist, discharge all the duties of your ministry." (2 Timothy 4:5)

The righteous will flourish like a palm tree, they will grow like a cedar of Lebanon; planted in the house of the LORD, they will flourish in the courts of our God. They will still bear fruit in old age, they will stay fresh and green, proclaiming, "The LORD is upright; he is my Rock, and there is no wickedness in him."

—*Psalm 92:12–15*

SPIRITUAL WARFARE

The spiritual battle was finally won on the cross on Calvary, but at times it seems as though the wicked are in ascendance—for the enemy is a guerilla fighter, cunning and vicious and capable of appearing to be counted among the upright. He often adapts the guise of being among the holiest of men, though hidden from view is a heart full of malice and mayhem. And he has troops willingly working under his command: "These people come near to me with their mouth and honor me with their lips, but their hearts are far from me. Their worship of me is made up only of rules taught by men....Woe to those who go to great depths to hide their plans from the Lord, who do their work in darkness and think, 'Who sees us? who will know?'" (Isaiah 29:13-15)

On the other side are those who have been transformed through God's Grace and over whom darkness will not prevail. No matter what the circumstance, the righteous will flourish even when the situation may seem hopeless. "He is like a tree planted by streams of water, which yields its fruit in season and whose leaf does not wither." (Psalm 1:3)

While those who are righteous might prefer a peaceful and sequestered life, God is calling them to service. Are we ready? Are we willing? God has done His part. Will we do ours?

Good and upright is the LORD; therefore he instructs sinners in his ways. He guides the humble in what is right and teaches them his way. All the ways of the LORD are loving and faithful for those who keep the demands of his covenant.

—Psalm 25:8–10

AN OPEN INVITATION

Jesus is always commanding, but he never demands. He often prefaces an instruction with an all-important "if." He says, "if you believe in me…" or "if you will follow me…," then "All the ways of the Lord are loving and faithful…."(v10)

The commandments of God always imply that we have a choice. We can follow the way provided by God through His Son and His Word or like so many of Jesus' own disciples, we can turn aside to go our own way to follow the demands of our own mercurial hearts. Without God, all people are prone to "gratifying the cravings of our sinful nature and following its desires and thoughts." (Ephesians 2:3)

Jesus calls out to us to follow him, but the decision is ours. It is false to think of God as an enforcer of a series of impossibly complex laws. God *is* the lawmaker, but the most important law of God is love.

When we live within the orbit of God's love, then the choice to follow him will be easy and straightforward—and because of God's merciful nature, the invitation always remains wide open for every one of us.

But we must turn back as the Prodigal Son finally turned back. We must choose to accept the glorious gift being offered.

The mountains will bring prosperity to the people, the hills the fruit of righteousness. He will defend the afflicted among the people and save the children of the needy; he will crush the oppressor. He will endure as long as the sun, as long as the moon, through all generations. He will be like rain falling on a mown field, like showers watering the earth. In his days the righteous will flourish; prosperity will abound till the moon is no more.

—Psalm 72:3–7

FAITH IS OUR JOB

The author of Hebrews says, "Now faith is being sure of what we hope for and certain of what we do not see." (Hebrews 11:1) When faith is absent, despair and depression flood in, cutting us off from the future by incapacitating us with fear.

Read this passage from Psalms as a statement of truth and faith. The *truth* is God existed before time and "He will endure... through all generations." (v5) Faith is *our* job. We need to live with the belief that God will bring prosperity; He will defend the afflicted and crush the oppressor. Even if our backs are against the wall and the enemies are at the gate and the city has been given over to unrighteousness, we are to put all our trust in God, knowing, with Job, that our "Redeemer lives, and that in the end he will stand upon the earth." (Job 19:25)

The wicked man flees though no one pursues, but the righteous are as bold as a lion.

—*Proverbs 28:1*

BE BOLD

As the root is the source of nourishment to the tree, so fear is fed by the hidden tentacles of guilt.

To deal with fear and drive it out, we must first deal with the source that feeds it. Unfortunately, we often go after the symptom without touching the cause. Or we attempt to abolish the feeling of guilt by expanding the definition of what constitutes acceptable behavior.

If we buy into this strategy, then we are forced to abandon the fact that God is a God of justice as well as the God of love. If we say He is only a God of love and disregard justice, then we transform him into a God who approves of everything we might do. But have we really freed ourselves from God or have we chained ourselves into bitter bondage?

The problem is that this popular view runs counter to the character and nature of God. And this leads us into the trap of relative truth. But rationalization is not truth and denial is not reality. When we steal, we know it; when we cheat, we know it; when we commit sexual sins, we know it and we cannot successfully deny it away.

Instead, our transgressions give birth to pathological behaviors and soon we are fleeing when no one pursues. The righteous man is bold because he has nothing to fear. He has not betrayed God, but rather has embraced Him and now lives for Him.

Then I said, "Here I am, I have come—it is written about me in the scroll. I desire to do your will, O my God; your law is within my heart." I proclaim righteousness in the great assembly; I do not seal my lips, as you know, O LORD. I do not hide your righteousness in my heart; I speak of your faithfulness and salvation. I do not conceal your love and your truth from the great assembly.

—*Psalm 40:7–10*

YOUR LAW IS WITHIN MY HEART

Change is an iron law of the natural world, but it is a law that applies to spiritual reality as well. God calls us to change; He asks us to depart from the rutted path we tread and depart for places that might be new and unfamiliar. He calls us to service as He called Moses in the desert or David from the sheep pens or Paul from his zeal to persecute the followers of the Way.

We are called out of the passive into the dynamic life, but we must answer that call in the words of David: "Here I am, I have come...I desire to do your will, O my God; your law is written in my heart."(v7) When we acknowledge God with our lives, His way is no longer objectionable to us. And as we begin to walk in faith, His path becomes the better way and the way becomes clear.

By wisdom the LORD laid the earth's foundations, by understanding he set the heavens in place; by his knowledge the deeps were divided, and the clouds let drop the dew.

—Proverbs 3:19–20

THE FOUNDATION OF THE WORLD

The popular view is that the universe, and later the earth, just "happened." No God, no creator and no wisdom. Adapting this point of view has serious implications, including the idea that life itself is accidental and, therefore, meaningless. Few will overtly admit that they have chosen to adhere to the view that the universe is a random accident, but truthfully, it seems to have taken hold in many countries around the world, particularly in the West.

The Christian view is built on the Genesis story of creation, where God intentionally creates the heavens and the earth. Furthermore, it says that He found the act of creation to be good: "And God said, 'Let there be light,' and there was light. God saw the light was good, and he separated the light from the darkness." (Genesis 1:3-4)

The goodness of creation tells us that we exist first in God's own environment, and second, that the very foundation of the world has a moral basis. Wisdom, therefore, is recognizing who the creator is and seeing, at the same time, that all goodness flows from Him.

True wisdom for man is to order the world as God would have you order it. To be wise is not the same thing as being intelligent. Many intelligent people live apart from God and do not have access to God's wisdom. The wise man puts God first in every aspect of his life and subordinates everything else.

At the end of your life you will groan, when your flesh and body are spent. You will say, "How I hated discipline! How my heart spurned correction! I would not obey my teachers or listen to my instructors. I have come to the brink of utter ruin in the midst of the whole assembly."

—*Proverbs 5:11–14*

REGRETS

Is it possible to experience regret if we are right with the Lord? The short answer is yes, because even the greatest saint has fallen short and must seek God's forgiveness.

But what of those who would deny the Lord? If we knew such people well enough, we might be surprised at how often they bounce from crisis to crisis, feeling as the psalmist does that they have come to the brink of utter ruin. (v14) You might find that such a life is marked by a parade of regrets and lost opportunities.

There is a difference between the person who seeks forgiveness for offending the Lord and the person who regrets a mistake that has upset his own well being. If you place your life in the hands of the Lord, your only regret will be that you could not, in the course of your life, bear even more fruit in his name. If, on the other hand, your accumulated regrets focus on personal loss or missed opportunities for wealth or fame, then all you can do is stoically resign yourself to the dead end you find yourself in.

Let the redeemed of the LORD say this— those he redeemed from the hand of the foe, those he gathered from the lands, from east and west, from north and south. Some wandered in desert wastelands, finding no way to a city where they could settle. They were hungry and thirsty, and their lives ebbed away. Then they cried out to the LORD in their trouble, and he delivered them from their distress. He led them by a straight way to a city where they could settle. Let them give thanks to the LORD for his unfailing love and his wonderful deeds for men, for he satisfies the thirsty and fills the hungry with good things.

—Psalm 107:2–9

HE SATISFIES THE THIRSTY

It is possible to read this passage both as history and as allegory. As history, it is clear that the psalmist is referring to Moses and the exodus from Egypt. After the miraculous escape through the Red Sea, the Jewish people found themselves in a desert with little to sustain them. They wandered there for forty years before Joshua led them across the Jordan River into the land that Abraham had been promised generations before. On another level, this psalm applies to everyday experience because it reveals the universal pattern of human suffering and deliverance.

All men wander in a spiritual desert as long as they live apart from God. In this condition, men lack the spiritual provisions that would sustain them; it does not take long for deprivation to drain them of hope and bring them to a point where their lives begin to ebb away. (v5) It is when men face extreme circumstances that they turn to God for help.

Elsewhere it says, "Though I walk in the midst of trouble, you preserve my life" (Psalm 138:7) and "...call upon me in the day of trouble; I will deliver you and you will honor me." (Psalm 50:15)

The pattern is one of danger, of despair, of a call for help and of divine deliverance. It is when we are spared that we thank God for all He has done, even though we often soon forget: "Let them give thanks to the Lord for his unfailing love and his wonderful deeds for men, for he satisfies the thirsty and fills the hungry with good things."(v9)

For the LORD gives wisdom, and from his mouth come knowledge and understanding. He holds victory in store for the upright, he is a shield to those whose walk is blameless, for he guards the course of the just and protects the way of his faithful ones. Then you will understand what is right and just and fair—every good path. For wisdom will enter your heart, and knowledge will be pleasant to your soul. Discretion will protect you, and understanding will guard you.

—*Proverbs 2:6–11*

BE ALERT AND ARMED

If Satan were to revise this passage for his own purposes, he would only need to make small changes of emphasis in order to shift the focus away from God. He would offer the benefits while obscuring the source of those benefits. For example, he would imply that knowledge and understanding could be won through our own efforts and abilities. He would entice us into believing that it is just a matter of putting in the time and hard work to become "Masters of the Universe."

Wisdom, then, becomes nothing more than practical knowledge of everyday things and self-reliance becomes the altar where we worship. Satan encourages us to take credit for the good things that actually come from God. He would have us live as if wisdom, knowledge and understanding originated within us. Once we buy into this deception, the Evil One gains a foothold, which is enough to divert us from the path God intended for us from the beginning. Therefore, we must be alert and ready; otherwise, we can easily fall prey to the one who would devour us. (1 Peter 5:8).

Your word is a lamp to my feet and a light for my path. I have taken an oath and confirmed it, that I will follow your righteous laws. I have suffered much; preserve my life, O LORD, according to your word. Accept, O LORD, the willing praise of my mouth, and teach me your laws. Though I constantly take my life in my hands, I will not forget your law. The wicked have set a snare for me, but I have not strayed from your precepts. Your statutes are my heritage forever; they are the joy of my heart. My heart is set on keeping your decrees to the very end.

—Psalm 119:105–112

RESISTING THE LIGHT

How do we reach a point in our life when we can offer a "willing" spirit to the Lord? Typically, we display the spirit of a stubborn mule, unwilling to move forward or back. Sometimes we describe a child as "willful," but rarely do we perceive this rebellious spirit in our own hearts and minds.

But the more brittle we become as we ossify into monuments of willfulness, the greater the crisis when we hear the call of the Lord. This is what happened to Paul as he approached Damascus to stamp out the Church. Though he was highly regarded by the chief priests and Pharisees, he had become a religious monster. Then, unexpectedly, as he approached the city "a light from heaven flashed around him. He fell to the ground and heard a voice say to him, 'Saul, Saul why do you persecute me?" (Acts 9:3-4)

Paul is blinded by the heavenly light; he faces the crisis of conflicting purposes. He must either disregard the light from heaven or submit to the voice that tells him, "Now get up and go into the city, and you will be told what you must do." (Acts 9:6) From that moment on, Paul chooses to follow the commands of the Lord. This is what is meant by conversion. Paul is Paul, but he changed at that moment from an opponent of God to an Apostle of Christ. Paul experienced an extraordinary change of heart; and hence, a complete change in the direction of his life.

If you have played the fool and exalted yourself, or if you have planned evil, clap your hand over your mouth! For as churning the milk produces butter, and as twisting the nose produces blood, so stirring up anger produces strife.

—Proverbs 30:32–33

BE QUICK TO LISTEN, SLOW TO SPEAK

Behind the eruption of anger is a real or imagined feeling of injustice. Sometimes anger can be truly righteous, but we must be careful not to confuse our own sense of justice with God's.

If there is impurity within our own hearts, then there is a high probability that our holy righteousness will be undermined by our own *un*righteousness. Rather we need to remember that God Himself is "gracious and compassionate…slow to anger and abounding in love." (Jonah 4:2)

As children of God, we "should be quick to listen, slow to speak and slow to become angry, for a man's anger does not bring about the righteous life that God desires." (James 1:20)

For all can see that wise men die; the foolish and the senseless alike perish and leave their wealth to others. Their tombs will remain their houses forever, their dwellings for endless generations, though they had named lands after themselves. But man, despite his riches, does not endure; he is like the beasts that perish.

—Psalm 49:10–12

THE GIFT OF GOD IS ETERNAL LIFE

David repeatedly reminds us that life is short even when we have lived a great many years: "Man is but a breath; his days are like a fleeting shadow." (Psalm 144:4) Thus he says, "Teach us to number our days aright, that we may gain a heart of wisdom." (Psalm 90:12)

Elsewhere, Paul tells us that what we experience in this life is temporary (2 Corinthians 4:18) and Jesus tells us: "Do not store up for yourselves treasure on earth, where moth and rust destroys, and where thieves break in and steal." (Matthew 6:19)

The common denominator to all of these passages is the transitory nature of life on earth. But behind the appearance of the finality of death is the promise of eternal life for those who believe. "For our light and momentary troubles are achieving for us an eternal glory that far outweighs them all. So we fix our eyes not on what is seen, but on what is unseen. For what is seen is temporary, but what is unseen is eternal." (2 Corinthians 4:17-18)

Sow your seed in the morning, and at evening let not your hands be idle, for you do not know which will succeed, whether this or that, or whether both will do equally well.

—*Ecclesiastes 11:6*

BE WILLING TO RISK

The modern paradigm for the reasonable life is based on an obsessive need to predict results. This need to know the outcome before an event has occurred has become a substitute for faith.

In business and politics, market research and polling have become the way people try to eliminate all uncertainties from everyday existence. But does this work at the ground level?

When Jesus is confronted by a rich young ruler who wants to know how to gain eternal life, he does not tell the young man to acquire more things or even do good deeds. He says, *Risk everything*. (Luke 18:18-25) Step out of your predictable existence; leave that life behind you because, in reality, it is worthless. Instead, come and follow me.

If we are unwilling to risk, then we will never know what it means to walk in faith.

The LORD reigns, he is robed in majesty; the LORD is robed in majesty and is armed with strength. The world is firmly established; it cannot be moved. Your throne was established long ago; you are from all eternity. The seas have lifted up, O LORD, the seas have lifted up their voice; the seas have lifted up their pounding waves. Mightier than the thunder of the great waters, mightier than the breakers of the sea— the LORD on high is mighty. Your statutes stand firm; holiness adorns your house for endless days, O LORD.

—Psalm 93:1–5

WONDROUS GOD OF THE UNIVERSE

While we stand on the edge of the sea, contemplating its awesome power and mystery, David wants to remind us that the one who created the seas also created the entire universe. This is the God who created man and woman and while we may seem insignificant in comparison to oceans and planets and galaxies; this is a God who watches over our every thought and our every move.

In another Psalm, David says, "Your works are wonderful, I know that full well. My frame was not hidden from you when I was made in the secret place. When I was woven together in the depths of the earth, your eyes saw my unformed body...How precious to me are your thoughts, O God! How vast is the sum of them." (Psalm 139:14-17)

This is truly a wondrous God who created the stars in the heavens, the earth and the seas and all the creatures in it, and yet He is so close to us that He can know our every thought.

Even in darkness light dawns for the upright, for the gracious and compassionate and righteous man. Good will come to him who is generous and lends freely, who conducts his affairs with justice. Surely he will never be shaken; a righteous man will be remembered forever. He will have no fear of bad news; his heart is steadfast, trusting in the LORD. His heart is secure, he will have no fear; in the end he will look in triumph on his foes. He has scattered abroad his gifts to the poor, his righteousness endures forever; his horn will be lifted high in honor.

—Psalm 112:4–9

GOD ARMS ME WITH STRENGTH

David was once a mere shepherd from a little known town miles from Jerusalem. He was the youngest of many brothers and showed little promise of what he would become until God called him from the sheep pens to be the future king of Israel. He was chosen because God could see what others could not see.

David had all the qualities of righteousness that a good king must have. He was gracious, compassionate, generous and just. He had a brave and steadfast heart. But most of all, he was "a man after (God's) own heart." (1 Samuel 13:14) David had an opportunity to demonstrate these qualities even before he became king when he faced the Philistine giant Goliath, a warrior so powerful that no Israelite would dare battle him. When David stepped forward, he was told, "You are not able to go out against this Philistine and fight him; you are only a boy...." (1 Samuel 17:33)

David defied the common sense of those around him and said, "The Lord who delivered me from the paw of the lion and the paw of the bear will deliver me from the hand of this Philistine." (v37) David had the confidence that flows from a heart that trusts in God. He knew "that it is not by sword or spear that the Lord saves, for the battle is the Lord's...." (v47) His courage came from the sure knowledge that "It is God who arms me with strength and makes my way perfect." (Psalm 18:32)

When I consider your heavens, the work of your fingers, the moon and the stars, which you have set in place, what is man that you are mindful of him, the son of man that you care for him? You made him a little lower than the heavenly beings and crowned him with glory and honor.

—Psalm 8:3–5

THE HOPELESSNESS OF MAN WITHOUT GOD

What is man apart from God? If we look at recent history, we see a creature that, through his behavior, more accurately reflects the monsters of horror films than the being described here as "made a little lower than the heavenly beings and crowned...with glory and honor."(v5)

The long, sorry history of mankind wandering in the wilderness of godlessness is perfectly summarized in the first chapter of Paul's letter to the Romans. It is a brutal picture, but we deny the truth of it at our own peril: "...since they did not think it worthwhile to retain the knowledge of God, he gave them over to a depraved mind, to do what ought not to be done. They have become filled with every kind of wickedness, evil, greed and depravity. They are full of envy, murder, strife, deceit and malice. They are gossips, slanderers, God-haters, insolent, arrogant and boastful; they invent ways of doing evil; they disobey their parents; they are senseless, faithless, heartless, ruthless. Although they know God's righteous decree that those who do such things deserve death, they not only continue to do these very things but also approve of those who practice them." (Romans 1:28-32)

Man apart from God is a profoundly lost creature. It is dangerously naive to believe otherwise.

My son, give me your heart and let your eyes keep to my ways, for a prostitute is a deep pit and a wayward wife is a narrow well. Like a bandit she lies in wait, and multiplies the unfaithful among men.

—Proverbs 23:26–28

A PATTERN OF UNFAITHFULNESS

The cost of falling into this pit of sexually loose living often is terrible, causing the break up of marriages, dislocated children, guilt and grief, but the unwary youth rarely sees it this way.

When we live a faithless life, we betray those we love on many levels and before we fully see what is happening, a pattern of infection and conflict has taken over. No aspect of our life is exempt, but especially our relationship with God.

Hosea, a later prophet, pronounces God's condemnation of a favored land gone astray: "There is no faithfulness, no love, no acknowledgment of God in the land. There is only cursing, lying and murder, stealing and adultery; they break all bounds and bloodshed follows bloodshed...A spirit of prostitution leads them astray; they are unfaithful to their God." (Hosea 4:1-2, 12)

How we live, both publicly and privately, counts not only for today, but for all time. Everything we do really does matter.

An unfriendly man pursues selfish ends; he defies all sound judgment. A fool finds no pleasure in understanding but delights in airing his own opinions. When wickedness comes, so does contempt, and with shame comes disgrace. The words of a man's mouth are deep waters, but the fountain of wisdom is a bubbling brook. It is not good to be partial to the wicked or to deprive the innocent of justice. A fool's lips bring him strife, and his mouth invites a beating. A fool's mouth is his undoing, and his lips are a snare to his soul. The words of a gossip are like choice morsels; they go down to a man's inmost parts.

—Proverbs 18:1–8

WHOM DO YOU SAY I AM?

When Pontus Pilate questioned Jesus in the hours before the crucifixion, he asked, "What is truth?" (John 18:38)

Down through the centuries, those who have followed in the footsteps of Jesus Christ have based everything on the truth of his life, crucifixion and resurrection. Foolishly today, many professed Christians have transformed the truth of Jesus Christ into their "opinion" about Jesus Christ.

Truth is universal, timeless and *always* applicable. Opinions are individual, time-constricted and *sometimes* applicable. Opinions can be informed or ignorant, tested or invented, but they do not rise to the level of truth. Opinions save us from a crisis of confusion, but they do not save us.

We need to face Jesus and decide if he is the one who embodies the full truth of God. Pilate's political position blinded him to the truth, but we are without excuse. We need to answer in our own time and place the question Jesus asked his own disciples: "But whom do you say I am?" (Mark 8:29)

So Elihu son of Barakel the Buzite said: "I am young in years, and you are old; that is why I was fearful, not daring to tell you what I know." I thought, "Age should speak; advanced years should teach wisdom." But it is the spirit in a man, the breath of the Almighty, that gives him understanding. It is not only the old who are wise, not only the aged who understand what is right.

—*Job 32:6–9*

GOD IS SPIRIT

By speaking of "the spirit in a man, the breath of the Almighty," (v8) Elihu, the fourth questioner of Job, places himself at the very center of biblical orthodoxy.

In the second verse of Genesis, we are told that the "spirit of God was hovering over the waters." (Genesis 1:2) David, in his Psalm of contrition, pleads with God to not "cast me from your presence or take your Holy Spirit from me." (Psalm 51:11) Jesus tells the Samaritan woman that "God is spirit, and His worshipers must worship in spirit and in truth," (John 4:24) and Paul reveals that God is within those who love Him: "…your body is a temple of the Holy Spirit, who is in you, whom you have received from God." (1 Corinthians 6:19-20)

The spirit of God is everywhere, but if we have not asked Him into our hearts with humility and contrition, we will find that the world seems devoid of that very same spirit.

Why do the nations say, "Where is their God?" Our God is in heaven; he does whatever pleases him. But their idols are silver and gold, made by the hands of men. They have mouths, but cannot speak, eyes, but they cannot see; they have ears, but cannot hear, noses, but they cannot smell; they have hands, but cannot feel, feet, but they cannot walk; nor can they utter a sound with their throats. Those who make them will be like them, and so will all who trust in them.

—Psalm 115:2–8

IN THE IMAGE OF GOD OR IN THE IMAGE OF MAN?

Even when people deny the existence of God, they seem to show a need to substitute something godlike for the One they have denied. There is plenty of evidence that man has a hard time explaining existence without some reference to a creator or creative force. And many non-believers speak enthusiastically about spirits and spiritual reality. They just don't accept the God of the Bible.

Their denial of the God of Holy Scripture is little more than an unconscious reenactment of the original sin of Adam and Eve in the Garden. Remember, their act of rebellion was based on the false promise of becoming like God by coming to know what God knows.

It was the sin of pride and it remains just as dangerous today as it was then. Adam and Eve chose to overreach God's design for them and so they paid a dear price for their choice. Today, by denying the God of the Bible, men and women have fallen into a pattern of trying to reverse the design of creation. Creating idols or substitute gods is the natural result of denying God. It is merely an attempt at reversing the biblical account by creating a creator in the image of man.

How deserted lies the city, once so full of people! How like a widow is she, who once was great among the nations! She who was queen among the provinces has now become a slave. Bitterly she weeps at night, tears are upon her cheeks. Among all her lovers there is none to comfort her. All her friends have betrayed her; they have become her enemies.

—*Lamentations 1:1–2*

THE DOOMED CITY

It was inconceivable that Jerusalem would fall. *This* was the city founded on the mountain where Abraham took his son Isaac to be sacrificed to the Lord. *This* was the city of David. *This* was the site of the Holy Temple built by Solomon. God would surely protect it.

But history tells another story. Invaders came and broke down its walls; they destroyed the Temple; they ransacked its treasures and exiled the surviving population.

This disaster should not have been a surprise to the leaders in Jerusalem because God had sent messengers to warn of what would come if the leaders and the people refused to turn away from their wickedness. Both Isaiah and Jeremiah prophesized of the impending doom if the priests and people did not turn back to God: "Disaster will come upon you, and you will not know how to conjure it away. A calamity will fall upon you that you cannot ward off with a ransom; a catastrophe you cannot foresee will suddenly come upon you." (Isaiah 47:11)

God sent his prophets, but the people would not listen.

I waited patiently for the LORD; he turned to me and heard my cry. He lifted me out of the slimy pit, out of the mud and mire; he set my feet on a rock and gave me a firm place to stand. He put a new song in my mouth, a hymn of praise to our God. Many will see and fear and put their trust in the LORD.

—*Psalm 40:1–3*

GOD'S GRACIOUS PROTECTION

How does David do it? How can he be patient in the face of danger and death? How can any of us be courageous when we are surrounded on every side?

When it comes to unwavering faith in God's power to protect and lift up, David is one of the great biblical pillars we look to for inspiration. But David is not the source of his own strength. In his confessional psalm he attributes all joy, all goodness, all power to God himself through the gift of the Holy Spirit. (Psalm 51:11)

David knows that without God he would be defenseless against wicked men who "rise up against me, breathing out violence."(Psalm 27:12) Elsewhere, he describes what life feels like without the presence of God: "My heart is blighted and withered like grass; I forget to eat my food. Because of my loud groaning I am reduced to skin and bones."(Psalm 102:4-5) With the presence of the Holy Spirit, David has the confidence and courage to transform the impossible into the possible.

The good news is that God has made His Holy Spirit available to each one of us through the work of his son for all who accept this extraordinary gift of grace. "For it is by grace you have been saved, through faith-and this is not from yourselves, it is the gift of God-not by works, so that no one can boast. For we are God's workmanship, created in Christ Jesus to do good works, which God prepared in advance for us to do." (Ephesians 2:8-10) It is the Holy Spirit dwelling within that makes all the difference:

Thomas à Kempis says that God's "grace is the mistress of truth, the teacher of discipline, the enlightener of hearts, the comforter of the afflicted, and the refuge of the sorrowing. (God's) grace banishes sadness, expels fear, nurtures devotion, and breeds tears. Without (God's) grace, I am but a piece of dry wood—a useless log—fit only to be set aside."[11]

No man has power over the wind to contain it; so no one has power over the day of his death. As no one is discharged in time of war, so wickedness will not release those who practice it.

—Ecclesiastes 8:8

MY LORD AND MY GOD!

Solomon makes two statements about man that are contradicted in the gospel accounts of the life of Jesus.

First, he says that "No man has the power over the wind to contain it"; (v8) but we find Jesus doing just that when the boat he is in almost capsizes in a furious squall. "He got up, rebuked the wind and said to the waves, 'Quiet! Be still!' Then the wind died down and it was completely calm.... (His disciples) were terrified and asked each other, 'Who is this? Even the wind and the waves obey him.'" (Mark 4:39-41)

Second, Solomon says "...no one has power over the day of his death." (v8) By this he means that all men die, whatever the day might be, and even Jesus suffers death on a cross, but he is not contained by the grave. He rises on the third day and even the great doubter Thomas comes to believe in the risen Christ. "Thomas said to him, 'My Lord and my God!' Then Jesus said to him, 'Because you have seen me, you have believed; blessed are those who have not seen and yet have believed.'" (John 20:28-29)

Even the wisdom of Solomon cannot conceive of so great a person as Jesus who could control the forces of nature, including the power of death. But what was inconceivable to him should not be so to us. Rather with Thomas, we should bow before Jesus and say, "My Lord and My God!" (John 20:28)

But you, O Sovereign LORD, deal well with me for your name's sake; out of the goodness of your love, deliver me. For I am poor and needy, and my heart is wounded within me. I fade away like an evening shadow; I am shaken off like a locust. My knees give way from fasting; my body is thin and gaunt. I am an object of scorn to my accusers; when they see me, they shake their heads.

—Psalm 109:21–25

NOT MY WILL BE DONE

In this passage, we hear echoes of Isaiah: "He was despised and rejected by men, a man of sorrows, and familiar with suffering. Like one from whom men hide their faces he was despised and we esteemed him not." (Isaiah 53:3)

We also might think of the suffering experienced in another Psalm that describes the punishment of crucifixion: "I am poured out like water, and all my bones are out of joint. My heart has turned to wax; it has melted within me." (Psalm 22:14)

Then we might fix our gaze on Gethsemane on the Mount of Olives where a lone figure is praying while his friends sleep nearby. We hear his voice as he prepares for the agony to come: "'Father, if you are willing, take this cup from me, yet not my will but yours be done.'... And being in anguish, he prayed more earnestly, and his sweat was like drops of blood falling to the ground." (Luke 22:42-44)

Then we think of the implications of this scene. Jesus is preparing to go to the cross as a perfect sacrifice for all men so that we might not have to pay the terrible penalty ourselves. This may be difficult to fathom for those who are blind to their own separation from God through sin and rebellion.

If we believe that we are "really good people," then the message of the cross will have no traction. But if we know deep down in our hearts that we are in desperate need of a savior, then the suffering of the cross represents the work of a merciful, loving and just God who loved us so much that He gave His one and only Son that we might live.

Do you have eyes of flesh? Do you see as a mortal sees? Are your days like those of a mortal or your years like those of a man, that you must search out my faults and probe after my sin— though you know that I am not guilty and that no one can rescue me from your hand?

—Job 10:4–7

ARE WE PREPARED FOR THE TEMPEST?

Job is a good man; he has not turned against God by blaming God for the terrible suffering he has endured. Job's pain is all the greater because he knows that he is not guilty of any offense against God; he is not guilty of a crime or willful sin. This only heightens his perplexity, because he has lost everything without apparent reason. This is why he asks God, "Do you see as a mortal sees?" (v4)

The temptation for Job, and for all of us, is to follow the admonition of Job's wife when she sees the depth of his suffering. When we experience personal loss, do we turn against God and accuse him of betraying us? The book of Job tells us that we should remain faithful through all circumstances because there are times when God's purposes cannot be understood by reason alone. Faith is hard duty, for we will surely be tested in this life. Faith requires resolve, endurance, patience and humility so that we will stand firm, like a rock, when the tempest strikes.

God is our refuge and strength, an ever-present help in trouble. Therefore we will not fear, though the earth give way and the mountains fall into the heart of the sea, though its waters roar and foam and the mountains quake with their surging.

—Psalm 46:1–3

TRUST NOT IN THE STRENGTH OF MEN

Turmoil and tumult, wars and rumors of wars: this is the unexpected context of our times and of all times. "Nations are in an uproar, kingdoms fall; he lifts his voice, the earth melts." (Psalm 46:6)

We seek security through accumulated wealth and power but none of it avails. Our hope and our strength must come through the source of all strength, for "It is better to take refuge in the Lord than to trust in man. It is better to take refuge in the Lord than to trust in princes." (Psalm 118:8-9)

Do not say, "Why were the old days better than these?" For it is not wise to ask such questions.

—Ecclesiastes 7:10

THE PRESENT MOMENT

Memories can be sweet as well as bitter. "I thought about the former days, the years of long ago; I remember my songs in the night." (Psalm 77:5-6) It is hard to pass through a day without a smell or an image or a conversation summoning up memories of a far away time that we would long to recapture or obliterate.

But it is wrong to magnify the importance of the past because then we diminish the importance of the present. The past was never better or worse—only different—with different possibilities that can no longer be grasped. New opportunities present themselves every minute of every day.

We need to be aware that the present is the most important moment of our life. Jesus never tired of calling his followers to the present moment. His first words reported in the Gospel of Mark are "The time has come... The kingdom of God is near. Repent and believe the good news!" (Mark 1:15)

We are called to engage the present moment *now*. To dwell in another time, glorious or not, is to burden the present with the unnecessary weight of the past.

Do not be quick with your mouth, do not be hasty in your heart to utter anything before God. God is in heaven and you are on earth, so let your words be few. As a dream comes when there are many cares, so the speech of a fool when there are many words.

—Ecclesiastes 5:2–3

KEEPING GOD OUT

In my first year in college, I recall taking an anthropology class that attempted to provide a comprehensive definition of man as distinct from all the other species of the earth. I remember hearing of several definitions such as "tool maker," but the one that seemed to work the best was the concept that man was a "word maker."

Since this was a science class, no one pointed out that the Bible supported this idea—except for causation. For in the Bible, the word first comes from God: "In the beginning was the Word, and the Word was with God, and the Word was God." (John 1:1) So when God created man in his own image, He gave man the gift of the word as well as the responsibility to name the creatures of the earth. (Genesis 2: 19-22)

My science class arrived at the right definition of man; they just left out the reason why the *word* is central to the human experience. The mystery of the origin of the word was beyond the scope of this science class because it was assumed that all causation could only occur in nature. It would be considered scientific heresy to suggest that the word originated before nature.

C.S. Lewis: "Does the whole vast structure of modern naturalism depend not on positive evidence but simply on an a priori metaphysical prejudice? Was it devised not to get in facts but to keep out God?"[12]

The path of the righteous is like the first gleam of dawn, shining ever brighter till the full light of day. But the way of the wicked is like deep darkness; they do not know what makes them stumble.

—Proverbs 4:18–19

THE SUMMIT AND THE VALLEY

Many years ago, two friends and I decided to climb Haystack in the High Peak region of the Adirondacks. It is a wild and beautiful place with rocky peaks rising above lakes and ponds that reflect the silhouettes of the surrounding mountains.

In the waning hours of a late autumn afternoon, we brashly decided to cross the lake to climb to the summit before night closed in on us. Confidently, we ascended quickly and in a few hours we made the summit as the sun was falling towards the horizon.

Though we knew that we would have only a short time on top before starting down, the view of the surrounding high peaks overcame our better judgment and we stayed to enjoy the astonishing beauty and majesty of the world spread out before us on every side. The air was so clear it felt as if we could reach across the divide and touch the rounded summit of Mt. Marcy.

But now the declining sun began to paint the far away horizon shades of red and we realized that if we did not abandon the summit, the oncoming darkness would leave us stranded. While we yearned to stay in the light that lit God's glorious universe, we hurried down the trail rather than become enveloped in the blackness of night.

Eventually we made it back to camp. We had reluctantly returned to the valley where we were meant to be. Like the three disciples on the Mount of Transfiguration, we wanted to make permanent the glory of our moments in the light. But like those disciples, we were called off the mountain to return to the valley where the work of God is most desperately needed.

As children of God, we are to "shine like stars in the universe" (Philippians 2:15) even as we are called to descend the mountain to labor in the valley where the light often does not penetrate.

Better is one day in your courts than a thousand elsewhere; I would rather be a doorkeeper in the house of my God than dwell in the tents of the wicked. For the LORD God is a sun and shield; the LORD bestows favor and honor; no good thing does he withhold from those whose walk is blameless. O LORD Almighty, blessed is the man who trusts in you.

—Psalm 84:10–12

BLESSED IS HE WHO TRUSTS

Faith is the staff we hold in our hands when our "walk is blameless." (v11) For, unlike the fence-sitter, the faithful sojourner has the perseverance that comes from commitment, courage and self-sacrifice.

As Christians, we place our faith in the person of Jesus Christ by acknowledging his claims and the truthfulness of his witnesses. As we travel through this world, we need to be strong and courageous, because the world resists his followers as it resisted Jesus himself. And we embrace sacrifice because Jesus calls us out of our self-indulgent, sinful nature into service in his name on behalf of others. "O Lord Almighty, blessed is the man who trusts in you." (v12)

Then Job replied to the LORD: "I know that you can do all things; no plan of yours can be thwarted." You asked, "Who is this that obscures my counsel without knowledge?" Surely I spoke of things I did not understand, things too wonderful for me to know. You said, "Listen now, and I will speak; I will question you, and you shall answer me." My ears had heard of you but now my eyes have seen you. Therefore I despise myself and repent in dust and ashes.

—Job 42:1–6

IN AN INSTANT EVERYTHING CHANGED

Try to imagine what it would be like to suddenly find yourself standing before God. You did not expect to be there at all; until a mere moment ago, you were content with your small successes, and you expected, in your heart, to live long past your retirement. You were looking forward to moving south to the house you bought near the ocean. Everything was going as planned, but now, in a split second, you are standing before the throne of God.

What would you say? Would you try to justify your unspent life? Would you be defiant? Would you plead for mercy? After suffering mightily, Job faces God and his reaction should tell us a lot about how we should live in relationship to the holiness of God before we actually must stand before the throne of judgment.

When Job recognizes the majesty of God, he can only say, "I despise myself and repent in dust and ashes." (v6) Paul, in his letter to the Romans, gently guides us toward the right attitude: "Do not think of yourself more highly than you ought..." (Romans 12:3)

When we think highly of ourselves, we then turn the natural order of things upside down. We crowd God out with the smaller concerns of everyday life, losing sight of the time when we will stand before the creator of heaven and earth.

My son, pay attention to my wisdom, listen well to my words of insight, that you may maintain discretion and your lips may preserve knowledge. For the lips of an adulteress drip honey, and her speech is smoother than oil; but in the end she is bitter as gall, sharp as a double-edged sword. Her feet go down to death; her steps lead straight to the grave. She gives no thought to the way of life; her paths are crooked, but she knows it not.

—Proverbs 5:1-6

GENUINE FREEDOM

The Bible never claims that we do not have the freedom to engage in all kinds of liberties, including adultery and other forms of sexual license. But the Bible is a realistic book that helps us keep our eyes on the eternal consequences flowing out of our freely chosen actions.

The true path of freedom is the freedom from sinful inclinations and appetites. Paul: "You, my brothers, were called to be free. But do not use your freedom to indulge the sinful nature; rather serve one another in love." (Galatians 5:13) And Peter: "Live as free men, but do not use your freedom as a coverup for evil; live as servants of God." (1 Peter 2:16)

We are free, but freedom to commit adultery and any other sin is no freedom at all; it leads us away from God, not toward Him.

The rod of correction imparts wisdom, but a child left to himself disgraces his mother. Discipline your son, and he will give you peace; he will bring delight to your soul.

—Proverbs 29:15, 17

SOFT FOCUS PARENTING

The Bible tells us that we are not born as a blank slate; rather each baby has an inherent moral sense designed into the fabric of its DNA. If this is, in fact, true, then as parents, we are enabling bad behavior in the child when we withhold judgment and discipline in the name of compassion or sensitivity.

Today, too many parents seem to engage in soft focus parenting, thinking that punishment harms when discipline is really an act of love. "He who spares the rod hates his son, but he who loves him is careful to discipline him." (Proverbs 13:24) The battleground for all of us, from the earliest age, is to avoid the grip of sin as we seek the wisdom of God. The struggle with sin begins in early childhood; where there is no struggle, there is also no relationship with a righteous God.

Do not be overawed when a man grows rich, when the splendor of his house increases; for he will take nothing with him when he dies, his splendor will not descend with him. Though while he lived he counted himself blessed—and men praise you when you prosper—he will join the generation of his fathers, who will never see the light of life. A man who has riches without understanding is like the beasts that perish.

—Psalm 49:16–20

ARE THE RICH EXCLUDED?

It is hard to overcome the awe we often feel when we are in the presence of the rich and powerful, for it seems as if such people have special virtues. Even those blessed with wealth often believe in their own invulnerability: "The wealth of the rich is their fortified city; they imagine it an unscalable wall." (Proverbs 18:11)

This is one reason why his disciples are so shocked when Jesus says, "How hard it is for the rich to enter the kingdom God!" (Mark 10:23) It was assumed that the rich had a fast track to heaven while the poor would be left to wallow in the dust.

More recently, this common assumption has been turned on its head; now the poor have the inside track while the rich remain outside, condemned to eternal perdition. But when it comes to the final judgment, both assumptions are wrong. "Is (God) not the one…who shows no partiality to princes and does not favor the rich over the poor for they are all the work of his hands?" (Job 34:17-19)

The central question for rich and poor alike is the one posed by the rich young man: "'Good teacher,' he asked, 'what must I do to inherit eternal life?'" (Mark 10:17) While Jesus gives the reasons why the rich become lost, he never says that their being rich is the reason for their exclusion from eternal life.

God doesn't pick favorites by class, gender, wealth or even appearance. His desire is that all men and women would turn away from "the worries of this life, the deceitfulness of wealth and the desires for other things…," (Mark 4:19) and come and follow him.

For God does speak—now one way, now another—though man may not perceive it. In a dream, in a vision of the night, when deep sleep falls on men as they slumber in their beds, he may speak in their ears and terrify them with warnings, to turn man from wrongdoing and keep him from pride, to preserve his soul from the pit, his life from perishing by the sword.

—Job 33:14–18

THE SPIRIT OF TRUTH

God speaks to men through His Holy Spirit. He speaks through dreams and songs and answered and unanswered prayers. He shows signs and He has provided His authoritative Word through His Holy Scriptures.

It is a mistake to think that God can only communicate with men in a single way. God speaks through our gifts whether it is teaching, preaching, praying, singing, painting or any other blessed gift.

But in order to be used by God, we must relinquish our obsessive focus on self and open our hearts to the truth and power of the Holy Spirit. This is the promise that Jesus gave directly to his disciples and to all who believe. "If you love me, you will obey what I command. And I will ask the Father, and he will give you another Counselor-the Spirit of Truth." (John 14:15-17) "All this I have spoken while still with you. But the Counselor, the Holy Spirit, whom the Father will send in my name, will teach you all things and will remind you of everything I have said to you." (John 14:25-26) "When the Counselor comes, whom I will send to you from the Father, the Spirit of truth who goes out from the Father, he will testify about me. And you also must testify, for you have been with me from the beginning." (John 15:26-27)

To many this is a great mystery, but to those who believe, it is life itself.

Listen, my sons, to a father's instruction; pay attention and gain understanding. I give you sound learning, so do not forsake my teaching. When I was a boy in my father's house, still tender, and an only child of my mother, he taught me and said, "Lay hold of my words with all your heart; keep my commands and you will live. Get wisdom, get understanding; do not forget my words or swerve from them."

—Proverbs 4:1-5

BLESSED ARE THE PURE IN HEART

When the father says to his son, "Gain understanding by taking hold of my words with all your heart," he is making a distinction that is considered of little value in our information-soaked age. Today the experts generally think that learning is simply a matter of brain power, so they measure IQ with standardized tests to predetermine a child's promise of success in life.

But this approach places value on certain human gifts at the expense of others. Oswald Chambers says: "In the Bible, the heart, and not the brain, is revealed to be the center of thinking. The Bible puts in the heart all the active factors we have been apt to place in the brain. The head is the exact outward expression of the heart....as a tree is the outward expression of the root."[13]

Jesus doesn't say blessed are the scholars and intellectuals and all those with extraordinary IQs; He says," Blessed are the pure in heart for they will see God." (Matthew 5:8)

Confuse the wicked, O Lord, confound their speech, for I see violence and strife in the city. Day and night they prowl about on its walls; malice and abuse are within it. Destructive forces are at work in the city; threats and lies never leave its streets.

—Psalm 55:9–11

CITIZENS OF THE CITY

Long before Jerusalem fell to invaders, wickedness and corruption had undermined the strength of its foundations. Jerusalem had been built to honor and praise God; it was a citadel of peace; a place that protected the innocent and weak and promoted justice and godliness.

Yet when the leaders of the city forgot God and began to honor only themselves, then "malice and abuse" began to roam within it walls; then the destructive forces of "violence and strife" came out of hiding and "threats and lies" replaced truth and righteousness.

This persistent pattern of man betraying his creator can be traced back to the biblical account of the cities of the plains. "The outcry against Sodom and Gomorrah is so great and their sin so grievous that I will go down and see if what they have done is as bad as the outcry that has reached me." (Genesis 18:20-21)

What He found was worse, and even though He would have shown mercy if a few righteous men were found there, He found an utterly godless place where all "are corrupt and their ways are vile; there is no one who does good." (Psalm 53:1)

When men fall into full rebellion against God through sin, then the consequences are predictable; only the timing is not. As citizens of the city, we should always remember the pattern of drift and decline and turn back to God in all haste: "Put on sackcloth, O priests, and mourn; wail you who minister before the alter...For the day of the Lord is near; it will come like destruction from the Almighty." (Joel 1:13, 15)

When I applied my mind to know wisdom and to observe man's labor on earth— his eyes not seeing sleep day or night— then I saw all that God has done. No one can comprehend what goes on under the sun. Despite all his efforts to search it out, man cannot discover its meaning. Even if a wise man claims he knows, he cannot really comprehend it.

—Ecclesiastes 8:16–17

THE SECRET THINGS OF GOD

The intellectual and scientific enterprise of the past several centuries has been to disprove the idea that "No one can comprehend what goes on under the sun." (v17) When we liberate ourselves from God, the Creator, then we are free to begin to become substitute gods through the power of science and technology.

In Greek mythology, Prometheus stole fire from the gods of Olympus and gave it to the human race; in literature, Mary Shelley wrote a story about a Promethean doctor who used his science to create a new, perfect human being. Prometheus paid a terrible price for his crime, as did Victor Frankenstein, and we will, too, if we fail to acknowledge the limits of our own competence. The fire that lights the winter night could also become the flame of our ruin.

Believing we can know what the creator knows is foolish, and for the temporary good it might produce, science does not bring salvation. "The secret things belong to the Lord our God, but the things revealed belong to us and to our children forever, that we may follow all the words of this law." (Deuteronomy 29:29)

Using science to better understand the beauty and complexity of God's universe is a noble enterprise; when we forget God in our scientific pursuits, we are at risk of putting God to the test. (Luke 4:12)

Sacrifice thank offerings to God, fulfill your vows to the Most High, and call upon me in the day of trouble; I will deliver you, and you will honor me.

—Psalm 50:14–15

FIVE STEPS TO A GOD-CENTERED LIFE

Sometimes the words of the psalms are so concise that we pass over them and miss the deeper significance of what is being said. You might boil this passage down to the five key conditions that lead to a God–centered life.

The first word is **sacrifice**. Give away that which obstructs your relationship to the Lord.

The next word is **thanks**. Give praise to the Lord. Thank him for all the blessings and spiritual gifts he has showered upon you.

The third word is **call**. Do not rely on your own resources in times of trial. Call upon the Lord. Isaiah says, "Seek the Lord while he may be found; call on him while he is near." (Isaiah 55:6) And the Lord says to Jeremiah, "Call to me and I will answer you...." (Jeremiah 33:3)

The fourth word is **deliver**. The Lord makes a promise to David that he will deliver him. When we face trouble, we need to trust in the word of the Lord. He does deliver us from evil. Jesus says, "Do not let your hearts be troubled. Trust in God, trust also in me." (John 14:1)

Finally, the fifth word is **honor**. We should respond by knowing that God has blessed us; he has saved us and now it is our turn. We seek a way to give back to God our all. We will honor him in our hearts, our lives and our work. We will answer the call. When the Lord asks, "Whom shall I send? And who will go for us?" we will respond with Isaiah by saying, "Here am I. Send me!" (Isaiah 6:8)

All this I tested by wisdom and I said, "I am determined to be wise"— but this was beyond me. Whatever wisdom may be, it is far off and most profound— who can discover it? So I turned my mind to understand, to investigate and to search out wisdom and the scheme of things and to understand the stupidity of wickedness and the madness of folly.

—Ecclesiastes 7:23–25

A MERE PHANTOM

Wisdom cannot be gained without seeing the presence of God in the "scheme of things." Many modern thinkers do not look for the hand of God in the physical universe, but instead, pursue physical laws to explain the natural world. They would answer Solomon by saying, "We can understand, we can investigate and discover what is at the heart of everything!"

But in the end, all the theories of human progress through human knowledge come up short. The universe without God is devoid of meaning and purpose. It is a world of stone and dust with nothing but darkness lying ahead and with the conclusion always being this: "Each man's life is but a breath. Man is a mere phantom as he goes to and fro: He bustles about, but only in vain; he heaps up wealth, not knowing who will get it." (Psalm 39:5-6)

Yet you brought me out of the womb; you made me trust in you even at my mother's breast. From birth I was cast upon you; from my mother's womb you have been my God. Do not be far from me, for trouble is near and there is no one to help.

—Psalm 22:9–11

MY BURDEN IS LIGHT

It is easy to fall into the trap of believing that God can betray us. Look at what is being said: "…trouble is near and there is no one to help." (v11) When you contrast this statement with "…you brought me out of the womb; you made me trust in you…," (v9) you see the dilemma that suffering mankind faces.

If God created us, then why does He allow us to suffer? This is the problem that confronts Job. Suffering showers down on him out of nowhere and he is asked both to defend himself and justify God.

Like nothing else, though, suffering defines character. Even the greatest saint can be certain that he will face a multitude of troubles even in his own house.

Jesus experienced conflict from the earliest days of his ministry and he warns us that, as followers, we can expect nothing less. "In this world you will have trouble," but he adds, "…take heart! I have overcome the world." (John 16:33)

In the end, the experiences of the everyday cannot be equated with the eternal. Jesus sees beyond the horizon of this life and he asks us to do the same, but he also offers us comfort in our labors and in our suffering: "Come to me, all you who are weary and burdened, and I will give you rest. Take my yoke upon you and learn from me, for I am gentle and humble in heart, and you will find rest for your souls. For my yoke is easy and my burden is light." (Matthew 11:28-30)

If I sinned, you would be watching me and would not let my offense go unpunished. If I am guilty—woe to me! Even if I am innocent, I cannot lift my head, for I am full of shame and drowned in my affliction. If I hold my head high, you stalk me like a lion and again display your awesome power against me.

—Job 10:14–16

DESCENT INTO DARKNESS

Paul, in his letter to the Romans, expresses the deepest anguish over the conflicting desires within his heart, demonstrating that no one is exempt from the passions competing with the desire to love and follow the Lord. "When I want to do good, evil is right there with me…waging war against the law of my mind and making me a prisoner of the law of sin at work in my members." (Romans 7:21-23)

Think about what Paul is saying: When we turn our backs on God, the battle within our heart is over; standing alone and disarmed, we are defenseless against the power of the desire to sin. Without God's armor, we are stripped of all protection, including the will to resist. Our sinful nature takes full charge and the course of our life begins to descend into darkness: "They have become filled with every kind wickedness, evil, greed and depravity. They are full of envy, murder, strife, deceit and malice…Although they know God's righteous decree that those who do such things deserve death, they not only continue to do these very things but also approve of those who practice them." (Romans 1:29, 32)

I will instruct you and teach you in the way you should go; I will counsel you and watch over you. Do not be like the horse or the mule, which have no understanding but must be controlled by bit and bridle or they will not come to you. Many are the woes of the wicked, but the LORD'S unfailing love surrounds the man who trusts in him. Rejoice in the LORD and be glad, you righteous; sing, all you who are upright in heart!

—*Psalm 32:8–11*

STUBBORN LIKE A MULE

A mule is a sterile hybrid between a male donkey and a female horse—a strange and stubborn creature.

It would be safe to say that most people would consider it an insult if someone were to compare them to such an animal. The trouble is that many people act like mules when it comes to being obedient to the call of God. Instead, as willful sinners, (Psalm 19:13) they kick back in stubborn fury rather than acknowledge God's place in their lives. For them, it is nearly impossible to say with a sincere and contrite heart "your will be done...." (Matthew 6:10)

All of us face the same stark choice at some point in our lives. Either we can choose to be like the mule or we can become children of God. God wants us to return, but He will never force us to come back. If we want to be fully human, fully children of God, then we have to say with Jesus: "My Father... not as I will, but as you will." (Matthew 26:39)

For a man's ways are in full view of the LORD, and he examines all his paths. The evil deeds of a wicked man ensnare him; the cords of his sin hold him fast. He will die for lack of discipline, led astray by his own great folly.

—Proverbs 5:21–23

EVERYTHING WILL BE REVEALED

In the end, everything will be revealed. *Everything.*

For those who prefer to lurk in the shadows; to those who carry secrets safely tucked away; and to those who lead a double life, this is very bad news. For the promise is that every deed will be exposed for what it is: "For a man's ways are in full view of the Lord, and he examines all his paths." (v21) "Nothing in all creation is hidden from God's sight. Everything is uncovered and laid bare before the eyes of him whom we must give account." (Hebrews 4:13)

For he remembered his holy promise given to his servant Abraham. He brought out his people with rejoicing, his chosen ones with shouts of joy; he gave them the lands of the nations, and they fell heir to what others had toiled for— that they might keep his precepts and observe his laws.

—Psalm 105:42–45

ABRAHAM

Abraham's father, Terah, had set out for Canaan long before Abraham responded to God's call. We do not know whether God called Terah first, but we do know that he never got there. Instead, he stopped at Haran, settled, and never left. He began a journey that he never finished, but his son was different.

The Lord appeared to Abram (as he was then called) and said: "Leave your country, your people and your father's household and go to the land I will show you…So Abram left. (Genesis 12:1, 4)

Then God made a promise that must have seemed incredible because both Abram and his wife Sarai were very old and without children: "To your offspring I will give this land." (Genesis 12:7) And later God appears to Abram again and says "…a son coming from your own body will be your heir…Look up to the heavens and count the stars—if indeed you can count them…So shall your offspring be." (Genesis 15:4-5) Finally comes one of the great moments in the Bible: "Abram believed the Lord, and he credited to him as righteousness." (Genesis 15:6)

At the core of Judaism and Christianity is belief in the truthfulness and trustworthiness of God's word. Abram cast doubt aside and followed the Lord. He believed and by believing, he fulfilled God's purpose for his life and he began the journey that would find its culmination in an empty tomb outside the walls of Jerusalem.

At this, Job got up and tore his robe and shaved his head. Then he fell to the ground in worship and said: "Naked I came from my mother's womb, and naked I will depart. The LORD gave and the LORD has taken away; may the name of the LORD be praised." In all this, Job did not sin by charging God with wrongdoing.

—Job 1:20–22

BLESSINGS AND CURSES

Almost every catastrophe known to man came upon Job. His herds were stolen; his servants were slain and his own sons and daughters were suddenly killed.

How would you react upon experiencing such horrific events? It is inconceivably tragic, yet Job does not raise his fist toward heaven to accuse God of wrongdoing. He simply states a universal truth about the nature of life: "Naked I came from my mother's womb, and naked I will depart." (v21)

Praising the Lord is more than an utterance from the mouth; it is complete devotion to the creator of all things who "has brought down rulers from their thrones but lifted up the humble." (Luke 1:52)

Job rightly says to his wife, "Shall we accept good from God, and not trouble?" (Job 2:10) Job's integrity is based on his absolute faith in God.

This world heaps blessings and curses upon each one of us, but in the end, no matter what our circumstance, our full allegiance must be to the Lord

Say among the nations, "The LORD reigns." The world is firmly established, it cannot be moved; he will judge the peoples with equity. Let the heavens rejoice, let the earth be glad; let the sea resound, and all that is in it; let the fields be jubilant, and everything in them. Then all the trees of the forest will sing for joy; they will sing before the LORD, for he comes, he comes to judge the earth. He will judge the world in righteousness and the peoples in his truth.

—*Psalm 96:10–13*

HE CANNOT BE MOVED

To understand the claims of the psalmist, we have to read beyond the literal words to appreciate what we are being told. He says "The world is firmly established, it cannot be moved..." (v10), but we know the world-the earth and the stars and the moon are moving constantly and at great speed. And every living creature is moving, even if that movement is only blood flowing through the heart.

Movement and continual change represent a universal and observable fact, so we must infer that the psalmist is speaking of a spiritual truth that underpins the natural fact. For this moving universe is knitted together by *laws* that cannot be moved. A tiny change in the laws propelling the earth around the sun would end all life on earth instantly.

The question comes down to this: Who created the laws that allowed life to flourish? The psalmist says that everything in nature, the seas and the forests, the fields and the sky, all shout for joy to the one Lord who reigns over everything. The maker of heaven and earth and everything in it cannot be moved. He is the God who reigns. "Your statutes stand firm; holiness adorns your house for endless days, O Lord." (Psalm 93:5)

My son, if sinners entice you, do not give in to them. If they say, "Come along with us; let's lie in wait for someone's blood, let's waylay some harmless soul; let's swallow them alive, like the grave, and whole, like those who go down to the pit; we will get all sorts of valuable things and fill our houses with plunder; throw in your lot with us, and we will share a common purse"— my son, do not go along with them, do not set foot on their paths; for their feet rush into sin, they are swift to shed blood.

—Proverbs 1:10–16

THE DEPTH OF HIS LOVE

It is popular to believe that we have no power over self-destructive impulses and behaviors. According to this view, all men are slaves to their chemical and biological makeup. If this is true, it follows that we are excused from any need to change our ways.

No wonder this quasi-scientific understanding of human behavior is accepted by so many people. It opens a wide path for self-indulgent and adolescent behavior and exempts everyone from judgment, discipline and shame. It further permits us to disregard the idea that life is deeply moral, that "sin is lawlessness," (1 John 3:4) and that God is a God of judgment as well as mercy. In the passage from Proverbs, the father warns the son that there is great danger in embracing the sinful life: "...do not set foot on their paths, for their feet rush into sin, they are swift to shed blood." (v16)

Even though the son stands warned, he may choose to indulge his natural inclination to sin. But what seems natural to him is unnatural in the eyes of God. When we are permissive to our sinful nature, we pay the price of further alienation from God. Paul says, "'Everything is permissible for me'—but not everything is beneficial." (1 Corinthians 6:12)

God is always calling us to walk with him. Can we hear? Will we listen? Will we choose well?

My son, preserve sound judgment and discernment, do not let them out of your sight; they will be life for you, an ornament to grace your neck. Then you will go on your way in safety, and your foot will not stumble; when you lie down, you will not be afraid; when you lie down, your sleep will be sweet. Have no fear of sudden disaster or of the ruin that overtakes the wicked, for the LORD will be your confidence and will keep your foot from being snared.

—Proverbs 3:21–26

WHAT CAN MAN DO TO ME?

Your sleep will never be sweet when you negotiate with the devil. Fear destroys sleep and the author of fear is Satan. In your waking and sleeping hours, he accuses you, berates you and spreads doubts where there should be none.

This is what the father means when he says to his son, "preserve sound judgment and discernment, do not let them out of your sight." (v21)

When Jesus is tempted by Satan in the wilderness, he uses the word of God to combat the adversary and so prevails. "Then the devil left him, and angels came and attended him." (Matthew 4:11)

When we place our confidence in the Lord, then we have nothing to fear and we can say with David: "The Lord is with me; I will not be afraid. What can man do to me? The Lord is with me, he is my helper. I will look in triumph on my enemies." (Psalm 118:6-7)

Blessed are they whose ways are blameless, who walk according to the law of the LORD. Blessed are they who keep his statutes and seek him with all their heart. They do nothing wrong; they walk in his ways.

—Psalm 119:1–3

PUT ON LOVE

Christianity is more about relationships than about rules and regulations. While it asks the highest standards of each one of us, it does not force us to live up to those standards if we choose not to. We give back to Christ, not out of obligation to some abstract rule, but simply out of love. We love and give back because of the one who gave himself for each of us. And when we have accepted the offered gift of love, we expand the circle by lavishly spending that love on those who are in need of it, both within the Church and beyond.

"Therefore, as God's chosen people, holy and dearly loved, clothe yourselves with compassion, kindness, humility, gentleness and patience. Bear with each other and forgive whatever grievances you may have against one another. Forgive as the Lord forgave you. And over all these virtues put on love, which binds them together in perfect unity." (Colossians 3:12-14)

The kings of the earth did not believe, nor did any of the world's people, that enemies and foes could enter the gates of Jerusalem. But it happened because of the sins of her prophets and the iniquities of her priests, who shed within her the blood of the righteous.

—Lamentations 4:12–13

THE ENEMY WITHIN

The long and painful decline of Jerusalem began with the sin of its greatest king: David. God spared David, but conflict and rebellion would erupt and would infect the generations that followed.

By the time of the great prophets, Jerusalem had turned against God, and even her high priests had fallen into corrupt and venal practices: "The idols speak deceit, diviners see visions that lie; they tell dreams that are false, they give comfort in vain. Therefore the peoples wander like sheep oppressed for lack of a shepherd." (Zechariah 10:2)

A city that forsakes God and embraces sin is a city that will decay and die long before the enemy arrives to tear down its walls.

When you make a vow to God, do not delay in fulfilling it. He has no pleasure in fools; fulfill your vow. It is better not to vow than to make a vow and not fulfill it. Do not let your mouth lead you into sin. And do not protest to the temple messenger, "My vow was a mistake." Why should God be angry at what you say and destroy the work of your hands? Much dreaming and many words are meaningless. Therefore stand in awe of God.

—Ecclesiastes 5:4–7

DO YOU BELIEVE THIS?

Making a vow is serious business. We should never commit to something when we have no intention of keeping our word. Vows are promises that may be hard to keep, but when we make a promise, we pledge our word and stake our reputation on fulfilling our part of the bargain. Our word must be our bond.

Jesus' entire ministry is a promise made and a promise kept. God's Word rests on the shoulders of His Son. This promise means that the Son must die on a cross to pay for our sins. It also means that a way has been opened for mankind to be cleansed of all sin so that we can enter into an everlasting relationship with God, the Father through the work of the Son.

Here's the promise from the mouth of Jesus: "I am the resurrection and the life. He who believes in me will live, even though he dies, and whoever lives and believes in me will never die." (John 11:25-26) Then he turns to Martha, the sister of Lazarus, and asks: "Do you believe this?"(v26) Do you believe that I am the Son of God? Do you believe in this glorious promise? Or do you believe something else? Do you believe I am going to keep this promise?

Then he says to you and to me, What about you? Will you stake your life on the truth of my claim and my promise? Will you say with Peter that you are the "the Christ, the Son of the living God"? (Matthew 16:16) Or will you turn away?

Who has woe? Who has sorrow? Who has strife? Who has complaints? Who has needless bruises? Who has bloodshot eyes? Those who linger over wine, who go to sample bowls of mixed wine. Do not gaze at wine when it is red, when it sparkles in the cup, when it goes down smoothly! In the end it bites like a snake and poisons like a viper. Your eyes will see strange sights and your mind imagine confusing things. You will be like one sleeping on the high seas, lying on top of the rigging. "They hit me," you will say, "but I'm not hurt! They beat me, but I don't feel it! When will I wake up so I can find another drink?"

—Proverbs 23:29–35

BE HOLY IN ALL YOU DO

The drunkard drinks from the cup of despair; he drowns his sorrows and adversities in the false comfort of the bottle, but this is not a path that leads to God. Drunkenness opens the floodgates of darkness, driving out the Holy Spirit rather than enabling it.

This is why Peter warns us not to do what the pagans do, "living in debauchery, lust, drunkenness, orgies, carousing and detestable idolatry." (1 Peter 4:3) Instead, we are to taste the wine of the Holy Spirit, which is the desire of God for each one of us: "...just as he who called you is holy, so be holy in all you do; for it is written: 'Be holy because I am holy.'" (1 Peter 1:15-16)

Rise up, O LORD, confront them, bring them down; rescue me from the wicked by your sword. O LORD, by your hand save me from such men, from men of this world whose reward is in this life. You still the hunger of those you cherish; their sons have plenty, and they store up wealth for their children. And I—in righteousness I will see your face; when I awake, I will be satisfied with seeing your likeness.

—Psalm 17:13–15

WE HAVE AN INHERITANCE

The "lost son" of the parable takes his inheritance and heads off for a distant country to enjoy his riches. Instead, he squanders everything. In another story, a rich young ruler wants to inherit eternal life but won't give up his riches to take possession of what he most desired. In another parable, a rich man "lived in luxury every day," but neglected the poor man begging at his gate. When the rich man dies, he finds himself ensnared in the horror of hell and calls out to the poor man who has gone to heaven. Then he learns why there will be no help: "Son, remember that in your lifetime you received your good things, while Lazarus received bad things, but now he is comforted here and you are in agony." (Luke 16:25)

The splendors of wealth and power are seductive and serve to separate us from the Lord. We are admonished not to become slaves to wealth; rather, "Since, then, you have been raised with Christ, set your hearts on things above, where Christ is seated at the right hand of God. Set your minds on things above, not on earthly things." (Colossians 3:1-2)

Rulers persecute me without cause, but my heart trembles at your word. I rejoice in your promise like one who finds great spoil. I hate and abhor falsehood but I love your law. Seven times a day I praise you for your righteous laws. Great peace have they who love your law, and nothing can make them stumble. I wait for your salvation, O LORD, and I follow your commands. I obey your statutes, for I love them greatly. I obey your precepts and your statutes, for all my ways are known to you.

—Psalm 119:161–168

DANIEL

Daniel was exceptional in every respect. King Nebuchadnezzar found Daniel and his three companions to be "ten times better than all the magicians and enchanters in his whole kingdom." (Daniel 1:20)

If Daniel had only been a man of outstanding achievement, we would never have heard of him. Though he started out as a slave in exile, and though he rose to the highest ranks of power in Babylon, he never forgot the God who guided and loved him. His enemies thought they could destroy him by issuing a decree that forced all to worship the king only.

But Daniel never wavered: "Now when Daniel learned that the decree had been published, he went home to his upstairs room where the window opened toward Jerusalem. Three times a day he got down on his knees and prayed, giving thanks to his God, just as he done before." (Daniel 6:10) He prayed to the living God who saves, knowing the danger he faced.

His enemies seem to prevail—and Daniel is cast into a den of lions. It is at this moment that God intervenes miraculously.

Daniel's prayer in his time of great peril could easily have been the words of this Psalm: "Rulers persecute me without cause, but my heart trembles at your word...Seven times a day I praise you for your righteous laws. Great peace have they who love your law, and nothing can make them stumble." (v161, 164-5)

O LORD God Almighty, how long will your anger smolder against the prayers of your people? You have fed them with the bread of tears; you have made them drink tears by the bowlful. You have made us a source of contention to our neighbors, and our enemies mock us. Restore us, O God Almighty; make your face shine upon us, that we may be saved. You brought a vine out of Egypt; you drove out the nations and planted it.

—Psalm 80:4–8

THE TRUE VINE

Lineage is important in the Bible. We begin with Abram who believed the command of the Lord and it was credited to him as righteousness. God promised that Abram would be the father of many nations: "I will make you very fruitful." (Genesis 17:6)

His descendant Joseph, son of Jacob, son of Isaac, is sold into slavery in Egypt where his own descendants became slaves. Moses brings the vine out of Egypt and Joshua plants that vine in the land promised. And David, anointed by God to be King of Israel, receives a new promise: "I will establish his line forever, his throne as long as the heavens endure." (Psalm 89:29)

But the fruit of the promise does not become manifest for 1000 years: "In the sixth month, God sent the angel Gabriel to Nazareth, a town in Galilee, to a virgin pledged to be married to a man named Joseph, a descendant of David." (Luke 1:26-27)

So when Jesus says to his disciples on the eve of his crucifixion that he is the "true vine," he is reaching all the way back to Abraham, as well as all the way forward to us. He is the very embodiment of the promise. He is the promise. "I am the true vine; you are the branches. If a man remains in me and I in him, he will bear much fruit." (John 15:5)

Create in me a pure heart, O God, and renew a steadfast spirit within me. Do not cast me from your presence or take your Holy Spirit from me. Restore to me the joy of your salvation and grant me a willing spirit, to sustain me. Then I will teach transgressors your ways, and sinners will turn back to you.

—Psalm 51:10-13

WE MUST CALL OUT

David identifies the seriousness of the human dilemma when he says, "Surely I was sinful from birth, sinful from the time my mother conceived me." (Psalm 51:5)

Sin separates us from God. Therefore, sin must be washed out of the human heart, which is why Jesus tells us that we must be born again: "...no one can see the kingdom of God unless he is born again." (John 3:3) Consequently, David confesses his sin to God and prays for mercy that his iniquity might be blotted out and his heart made clean. David yearns to praise God once again and "teach transgressors your ways..." (v13)

Without confession, contrition and prayer we shut out the possibility of the Holy Spirit dwelling within; we remain in our sinful state alienated from God and from His purpose for us.

God wants to recover us; He is merciful and gracious and He can purify a sinful nature, transforming a sinner into a saint. But we need to call out, "Create in me a pure heart, O God, and renew a steadfast spirit within me." (v10)

Show me, O LORD, my life's end and the number of my days; let me know how fleeting is my life. You have made my days a mere handbreadth; the span of my years is as nothing before you. Each man's life is but a breath. Man is a mere phantom as he goes to and fro: He bustles about, but only in vain; he heaps up wealth, not knowing who will get it.

—Psalm 39:4–6

GOD'S WORD STANDS FOREVER

Isaiah tells us that "All men are like grass, and all their glory is like the flowers of the field. The grass withers and the flowers fall, because the breath of the Lord blows on them. Surely the people are grass. The grass withers and the flowers fall, but the word of our God stands forever." (Isaiah 40:6-8)

This is a reality check for all of us who might be tempted to get puffed up by our own accomplishments. Have you noticed how people like to build all kinds of monuments to their own grandeur, forgetting all the while that even the most substantial accomplishments will rust and rot with time? The idea of "memento mori" has fallen on disfavor in our generation because we have become consumed by the appeal of worshipping the here and now. Rather than giving our life over to God, we strive to heap up wealth even though wealth cannot save.

The eyes of the LORD are everywhere, keeping watch on the wicked and the good. The tongue that brings healing is a tree of life, but a deceitful tongue crushes the spirit. The house of the righteous contains great treasure, but the income of the wicked brings them trouble. A hot-tempered man stirs up dissension, but a patient man calms a quarrel. The way of the sluggard is blocked with thorns, but the path of the upright is a highway.

—Proverbs 15:3, 4, 6, 18, 19

HIGH TECH PROPHETS

In the early days of the Internet Revolution, many of the high-tech prophets sold the world on the transformative power of this new form of communication. Dot.Com wizards, hardly out of their teens, became instant paper millionaires and the world gazed in wonder on this new phenomenon. There was only one problem—the internet was created by people.

Soon a common medical term became an ominous threat to all users of the internet. *Viruses* started invading computers and computer networks. New businesses had to be built to fortify systems against alien invasions, and so the battle began.

We should not be surprised. The computer virus is really no different than a person becoming infected by sin. Everything is working according to plan when suddenly the system begins to demonstrate strange and uncharacteristic behaviors. A virus slips through the defenses and we become disabled. We begin to lie, or stir up dissension or stop working and start squandering our wealth and our gifts.

As Paul explains it, "I do not understand what I do. For what I want to do I do not do, but what I hate, I do." (Romans 7:15)

Once again, technology becomes the instrument of our human nature—including the sinful part of it.

Hear my words, you wise men; listen to me, you men of learning. For the ear tests words as the tongue tastes food. Let us discern for ourselves what is right; let us learn together what is good.

—Job 34:2–4

THE RIGHT RULE

If Christians were asked only to follow and memorize a set of rules, then Christianity could be properly categorized as a legalistic and moralistic religion. Many Christians do define Christian living as a moral "to do" checklist, but the Bible tells us that wisdom grows from a "discerning heart" that will guide us "to distinguish between right and wrong." (1 Kings 3:9)

To make right judgments requires all our faculties of knowledge, including the knowledge of the heart as well as the head. The best guide is the most obvious—follow the words and life of Jesus in everything we do.

For example, Jesus does not say we should *know* one another; He says, "*Love* each other as I have loved you." (John 15:12) From Paul: "And this is my prayer: that your love may abound more and more in knowledge and depth of insight, so that you may be able to discern what is best and may be pure and blameless until the day of Christ, filled with the fruit of righteousness that comes through Jesus Christ—to the glory and praise of God." (Philippians 1:9-11)

When I am afraid, I will trust in you. In God, whose word I praise, in God I trust; I will not be afraid. What can mortal man do to me? All day long they twist my words; they are always plotting to harm me. They conspire, they lurk, they watch my steps, eager to take my life.

—*Psalm 56:3–6*

AUTHENTIC TRUST

Have you recently checked your internal "trust meter"? We all have one, but we usually don't pay much attention to it because we operate on trust auto-pilot.

Remove us from our familiar environments, however, and watch our "trust meters" go haywire. Suddenly, suspicious characters lurk around every corner; business transactions that once were done on a handshake now must be reviewed by a battery of lawyers; tomorrow becomes an impending crisis; every stable aspect of life becomes a storm of trouble. When trust evaporates, fear and doubt flood into the breach.

Jesus shows us what the authentic life of trust looks like. During much of his ministry, Jesus was beset with threats and trouble on every side, but he kept his composure in every circumstance. For he placed his trust in the one place where it should repose—God the Father.

While Jesus came to save sinful men, He never put his trust in them. "...for he knew all men." (John 2:24) He did not need man's testimony about man, for he knew what was in a man. "In God I trust; I will not be afraid" (v3) should be the very rock we stand on. Then in times of confusion and change, we can remain confident and secure: "Do not let your hearts be troubled. Trust in God, trust also in me." (John 14:1)

Who can speak and have it happen if the Lord has not decreed it? Is it not from the mouth of the Most High that both calamities and good things come? Why should any living man complain when punished for his sins?

—*Lamentations 3:37–39*

EXCUSES DO NOT SAVE

If we truly believed in divine justice, we would neither complain about our calamities, nor brag about our successes. But most of us, when caught in wrongdoing, immediately rummage around in our vast bag of excuses to find the perfect get-free card.

When we hear, for example, "It wasn't my fault, she made me do it," we should recognize that these are the same words that Adam used when confronted by God in the garden: "The man said, 'The woman you put here with me—she gave me some fruit from the tree, and I ate it.'" (Genesis 3:12)

We marvel at Adam's ingenuity because he blames both God and Eve in the same breath. If it is God's fault for creating Eve to be Adam's companion, then God should let him off the hook. And if it is Eve's fault, then she should be punished.

Clever, but God makes the rules and the rule was "you will not eat of the tree of knowledge of good and evil." By eating the fruit, Adam rebelled against God's word. No excuse would change that, nor will any excuse help us if we turn against God.

Praise the LORD. Praise the LORD from the heavens, praise him in the heights above. Praise him, all his angels, praise him, all his heavenly hosts. Praise him, sun and moon, praise him, all you shining stars. Praise him, you highest heavens and you waters above the skies. Let them praise the name of the LORD, for he commanded and they were created. He set them in place for ever and ever; he gave a decree that will never pass away.

—Psalm 148:1–6

THE VAST CANVAS

Have you ever ventured outside on a clear, cold winter night and gazed into the heavens? Millions of tiny stars speckle the vast expanse, lighting up the world so that all can see the evidence of the glory, beauty and majesty of the creator of all things.

When rightly seen, all the world unifies in wonder at the vast canvas of the universe that displays the handprint of God in everything: "Therefore, I wish to offer and present to You the jubilant joy found in all devout hearts, their burning love, their ecstasies, their supernatural illuminations and heavenly visions, together with all the virtues and praises that have been or shall ever be given You by the creatures of heaven and earth, for myself and for all who have been recommended to my prayers and that You may receive fitting praise from men and be glorified without end."[14]

Be happy, young man, while you are young, and let your heart give you joy in the days of your youth. Follow the ways of your heart and whatever your eyes see, but know that for all these things God will bring you to judgment.

—Ecclesiastes 11:9

LIVE LIFE TO THE FULL

Solomon seems to contradict himself here. First, he says, "follow the ways of your heart and whatever your eyes see…" (v9) which would suggest that he is saying, "Let us eat and drink …for tomorrow we die!" (Isaiah 22:13) But then he issues a warning that God will bring everything to judgment.

Which is it? According to Paul, the answer hinges on whether or not we believe in the resurrection. "For if the dead are not raised, then Christ has not been raised either. And if Christ has not been raised, your faith is futile; you are still in your sins…If only for this life we have hope in Christ, we are to be pitied more than all men." (1 Corinthians 15:16-19)

Elsewhere in Ecclesiastes, Solomon seems to agree with Paul: "God will bring to judgment both the righteous and the wicked…." (Ecclesiastes 3:17)

It boils down to this: If you believe there is no God, then the logical conclusion would be that this is the only life you will ever have; therefore, you should enjoy it while you still have time. If, though, you believe in God and you believe He is a just God who will bring both the good and wicked to judgment, then the purpose of your youth and your old age shifts to enjoying fellowship with God for the time allotted to you here.

Live life to the full, but live it to the full for God.

How can a young man keep his way pure? By living according to your word. I seek you with all my heart; do not let me stray from your commands. I have hidden your word in my heart that I might not sin against you.

—Psalm 119:9–11

HIS OUTSTRETCHED HAND

"LORD, who may dwell in your sanctuary? Who may live on your holy hill?" (Psalm 15:1)

Who, indeed? For many, the assumption is that all children are born innocent. With this in mind, the parent believes metaphorically that the child is born on the hill of human goodness and that their job, as parents, is simply to help the child stay there.

The Bible reverses this assumption. It tells us that life's journey is an ascent because we are born with an active disposition to sin. Left alone, we will not even bother to make the attempt to draw closer to God. There has been only one born without sin and he came into this world to deal with the fact of sin, once and for all. When we call upon his name to guide us, we recognize that, without his outstretched hand, our condition is hopeless, and on our own, we cannot even begin the long climb that will bring us into the presence of the Lord.

The fear of the LORD is the beginning of knowledge, but fools despise wisdom and discipline. Listen, my son, to your father's instruction and do not forsake your mother's teaching.

—Proverbs 1:7–8

THE BEGINNING OF WISDOM

"Many are the plans in a man's heart, but it is the Lord's purpose that prevails." (Proverbs 19:21)

The beginning of wisdom is to know in your heart that God is the foundation behind and through all things. With the right foundation, many good things can be built. Without that foundation, our "plans fail for lack of counsel." (Proverbs 15:22)

Do good to your servant according to your word, O LORD. Teach me knowledge and good judgment, for I believe in your commands. Before I was afflicted I went astray, but now I obey your word. You are good, and what you do is good; teach me your decrees. Though the arrogant have smeared me with lies, I keep your precepts with all my heart. Their hearts are callous and unfeeling, but I delight in your law. It was good for me to be afflicted so that I might learn your decrees. The law from your mouth is more precious to me than thousands of pieces of silver and gold.

—Psalm 119:65–72

WHY DO WE SUFFER?

The psalmist says he "went astray" before he was afflicted and that it was through suffering that he turned away from his folly, realizing that only God is good and what He does is good. He now "delights in [God's] law." (v70) And by expressing joy in suffering, he pinpoints one of the central paradoxes for those who follow Christ.

Paul was not a stranger to suffering. At one point in his second letter to the Corinthians, he catalogues the sufferings he endured for the greater glory of Christ: "in great endurance; in troubles, hardships and distresses; in beatings, imprisonments and riots; in hard work, sleepless nights and hunger...." (2 Corinthians 6:4, 5)

But rather than lament his bad fortune, he speaks triumphantly about the good fortune of being able to suffer for so great a purpose. "Rather as servants of God, we commend ourselves in every way;...in truthful speech and in the power of God; with weapons of righteousness in the right hand and in the left; through glory and dishonor, bad report and good report; genuine, yet regarded as impostors; known, yet regarded as unknown; dying, and yet we live on; beaten, and yet not killed; sorrowful, yet always rejoicing; poor, yet making many rich, having nothing, and yet possessing everything." (2 Corinthians 6:4-10)

In his first letter, Peter explains why we accept suffering with a joyful and abundant heart: "To this you were called, because Christ suffered for you, leaving you an example, that you should follow in his steps." (1 Peter 2:21)

As a father has compassion on his children, so the LORD has compassion on those who fear him; for he knows how we are formed, he remembers that we are dust. As for man, his days are like grass, he flourishes like a flower of the field; the wind blows over it and it is gone, and its place remembers it no more. But from everlasting to everlasting the LORD'S love is with those who fear him, and his righteousness with their children's children— with those who keep his covenant and remember to obey his precepts.

—Psalm 103:13–18

IN HIS OWN IMAGE

When the psalmist says that God remembers that we are dust, he is echoing the second of two creation stories in the book of Genesis: "The Lord God formed the man from the dust of the ground and breathed into his nostrils the breath of life, and the man became a living being." (Genesis 2:7)

If dust represented all we ever were, then the story of mankind would be a sad tale indeed. But elsewhere it says, "You made him a little lower than the heavenly beings and crowned him with glory and honor." (Psalm 8:5)

This dust, this clay, has a divine shape to it as the first creation story confirms: "So God created man in his own image, in the image of God he created him: male and female he created them." (Genesis 1:27) The composition may be made up of the elements of the earth, but the heart is the heart crafted by the eternal love of God. The dust can sully the image, but the heart yearns for the holiness of God.

But as for me, I will always have hope; I will praise you more and more. My mouth will tell of your righteousness, of your salvation all day long, though I know not its measure. I will come and proclaim your mighty acts, O Sovereign LORD; I will proclaim your righteousness, yours alone. Since my youth, O God, you have taught me, and to this day I declare your marvelous deeds. Even when I am old and gray, do not forsake me, O God, till I declare your power to the next generation, your might to all who are to come.

—Psalm 71:14–18

HE WILL ANSWER OUR PRAYER

Faith often is born out of the darkest moments of a crisis, for a time of crisis will often shake us loose from the preoccupations of more ordinary times. When trouble comes, it strips us of all the usual armaments because we feel the threat of "…terror on every side." (Psalm 31:13)

It is then that we awake to the reality of the need for God, "…for I am in distress; my eyes grow weak with sorrow, my soul and my body with grief." (Psalm 31:9)

When God answers us, and He will, it is not always in the way we desire, but behind His answer is His infinite love and mercy. And when we respond, hope opens before us like a landscape of infinite beauty and we say in gratitude and joy, "I will praise you more and more. My mouth will tell of your righteousness, of your salvation all day long, though I know not its measure." (v14, 15)

It is better to take refuge in the LORD than to trust in man. It is better to take refuge in the LORD than to trust in princes.

—Psalm 118:8–9

ACCEPT NO SUBSTITUTES

It seems almost inevitable that our spiritual eyes are in danger of being seduced by the physical reality of this world. After all, so much of the world is a thing of great beauty, inspiring awe and wonder.

But if we choose to worship nature rather than the creator of the heavens and the earth, then we are substituting the shadow for the reality. For what we have here is only "a copy and shadow of what is in heaven." (Hebrews 8:5)

This also applies to the temptation to idolize and even worship men rather than the one true man. It is tempting to put our faith in the rich and powerful, but, except for Jesus Christ, no man is worthy of such trust. They are mere counterfeits of the original, for when it comes to natural man, "There is no one righteous, not even one; there is no one who understands, no one who seeks God. All have turned away, they have together become worthless; there is no one who does good, not even one." (Romans 3:10-12)

To believe the truth of the psalmist's words is far more fruitful than to seek gods amongst mere mortals.

I am the most ignorant of men; I do not have a man's understanding. I have not learned wisdom, nor have I knowledge of the Holy One. Who has gone up to heaven and come down? Who has gathered up the wind in the hollow of his hands?

—Proverbs 30:2–4

THE FACE OF GOD

Job asks, "Who then can understand the thunder of his power?" (Job 26:14) Solomon asks, "Who has gathered up the wind in the hollow of his hands?" (v4) And Jesus, speaking to Nicodemus, says "I tell you the truth, no one can see the kingdom of God, unless he is born again…I have spoken to you of earthly things and you do not believe; how then will you believe if I speak of heavenly things?" (John 3:3, 12)

Nicodemus represents the state of the darkened human mind before the advent of the Son. Men could marvel at the vast dimensions of the universe and praise the splendor and beauty of the seas and mountains and the earth itself, but the face of God remained remote. Even the wisest and holiest of men could confess to being ignorant when standing before God.

Then God sent His Son into the world to bring the truth of His light to all men who wished to see. Jesus was not just a healer and teacher and prophet; He was and is the Son of the Living God and he made it known to all who would hear and who could see: "Don't you know me, Philip, even after I have been among you such a long time? Anyone who has seen me has seen the Father. How can you say, 'Show us the Father?' Don't you believe that I am in the Father, and that the Father is in me? The words I say to you are not just my own. Rather, it is the Father, living in me, who is doing his work." (John 14:9-10)

I will sing of the LORD'S great love forever; with my mouth I will make your faithfulness known through all generations. I will declare that your love stands firm forever, that you established your faithfulness in heaven itself. You said, "I have made a covenant with my chosen one, I have sworn to David my servant, I will establish your line forever and make your throne firm through all generations."

—*Psalm 89:1–4*

A LIGHT FOR REVELATION

God spoke to Nathan, the trusted prophet of King David: "The Lord declares to you that the Lord himself will establish a house for you…I will raise up your offspring to succeed you…I will establish his kingdom. He is the one who will build a house for my Name and I will establish the throne of his kingdom forever. I will be his father and he will be my son…Your house [referring to David] and your kingdom will endure forever before me, your throne will be established forever." (2 Samuel 7:11-14, 16)

The Gospel of Matthew records many of the prophecies fulfilled with the birth of Christ, but many people miss the prophecy of the Davidic branch because it is recorded in a long genealogy at the very beginning of the gospel story. But Matthew knew the significance of identifying who Jesus was from the very beginning through the prophecies of Isaiah, Micah, Nathan and others.

The advent of the birth of Christ was an expected event; it was the fulfillment of the promise of God to the prophets and passed down through the Hebrew Scriptures. Simeon, a righteous and devout man, says, on seeing the Christ child, "For my eyes have seen your salvation, which you have prepared in the sight of all people, a light for revelation to the Gentiles and for glory to your people Israel." (Luke 2:30-32)

A wise king winnows out the wicked; he drives the threshing wheel over them. The lamp of the LORD searches the spirit of a man; it searches out his inmost being. Love and faithfulness keep a king safe; through love his throne is made secure. The glory of young men is their strength, gray hair the splendor of the old.

—*Proverbs 20:26–29*

THE WISE KING AS SERVANT

History is littered with failed rulers who surrounded themselves with foolish and wicked advisors.

When Solomon died after a forty-year reign, his son, Rehoboam, succeeded him as king. The people of Israel had been heavily burdened with taxes during Solomon's time and so they came before the new king and implored him for relief.

He sent the people away while he conferred with his advisors. First, he consulted with the elders who said, "If today you will be a servant to these people and serve them and give them a favorable answer, they will always be your servants." (1 Kings 12:7) Then Rehoboam turned to his youthful companions who told him to assert his power over the people by saying, "My father laid on you a heavy yoke; I will make it even heavier. My father scourged you with whips; I will scourge you with scorpions." (1 Kings 12:11)

The king rejected wise counsel and followed the misguided advice of the foolish and inexperienced companions and so peace in the land was fractured. The people rose up and civil war broke out.

The wise ruler will always think of himself as the servant of the people. The foolish king always thinks that the people are there to serve him.

Help, LORD, for the godly are no more; the faithful have vanished from among men. Everyone lies to his neighbor; their flattering lips speak with deception.

—Psalm 12:1–2

ENGINES OF WAR

In *The Lord of the Rings*, Lord Sauron seeks the ring that will give him complete power over Middle Earth. He is a dark presence who destroys in order to construct vast engines of evil.

Sauron is a character in a novel, but we don't need to travel far into our own modern times to find the same lust for mayhem spreading its shadow of death throughout an unsuspecting world. Thunderous cannons shake the earth because determined rulers have banished God from the earth. When men attempt to live without God, "there is no one who does good, not even one." (Psalm 14:3)

According to Paul, a godless world looks very much like the world Sauron envisions: "Their throats are open graves; their tongues practice deceit. The poison of vipers is on their lips. Their mouths are full of cursing and bitterness. Their feet are swift to shed blood: ruin and misery mark their ways and the way of peace they do not know." (Romans 3:13-16)

Do not revile the king even in your thoughts, or curse the rich in your bedroom, because a bird of the air may carry your words, and a bird on the wing may report what you say.

—Ecclesiastes 10:20

CAN ANYONE HIDE FROM THE LORD?

This image of a bird, any bird, carrying an unflattering thought straight to the king is, on the surface, ridiculous.

To read this literally would be to miss the point. However, there is a spiritual truth planted within the picture of the bird flying straight to the palace of the king. If the king is the "King of Kings and the Lord of Lords" (Revelation 19:16), then nothing near or far, high or low, escapes his searching eye. "For the eyes of the Lord range throughout the earth to strengthen those whose hearts are fully committed to him." (2 Chronicles 16:9) No word, uttered in the most desolate place, will not be heard. No thought, however fleeting, will go unnoticed. "'Am I only a God nearby,' declares the Lord, 'and not a God far away? Can anyone hide in secret places so that I cannot see him?' declares the Lord. Do not I fill heaven and earth?' declares the Lord." (Jeremiah 23:23-24)

What do you say? Do you side with those who act in the dark, thinking "God has forgotten, he covers his face and never sees"? (Psalm 10:11) Or do you say with David, "O Lord, you have searched me and you know me. You know when I sit and when I rise, you perceive my thoughts from afar"? (Psalm 139:1-2)

Love and faithfulness meet together; righteousness and peace kiss each other. Faithfulness springs forth from the earth, and righteousness looks down from heaven. The LORD will indeed give what is good, and our land will yield its harvest. Righteousness goes before him and prepares the way for his steps.

—*Psalm 85:10–13*

GOD IS LOVE

Here is a startling fact: All righteousness comes from God.

We are surprised by this because we often assume men are naturally good. When we hear of a neighbor who has done a terrible thing, our first reaction is one of complete surprise. Or when a mother hears that her son has been arrested for some crime, we usually hear her say that her boy is really a good kid. Not so. Jesus tells us that "there is only One who is good." (Matthew 19:17)

Despite what men and women may claim for themselves or what others might claim for them, there is no goodness, no righteousness and no holiness that can be obtained without redemption. We need to drink from the nurturing spring of the source of all life.

Without Christ, the spring will dry up and we will begin to die through sin because we do not have the source within us to protect and guide us. "…if anyone is in Christ, he is a new creation; the old has gone, the new has come! All this is from God, who reconciled us to himself through Christ and gave us the ministry of reconciliation…And he has committed to us the message of reconciliation…Be reconciled to God. God made him who had no sin to be sin for us, so that in him we might become the righteousness of God. (2 Corinthians 5:17-21)

Your statutes are wonderful; therefore I obey them. The unfolding of your words gives light; it gives understanding to the simple. I open my mouth and pant, longing for your commands. Turn to me and have mercy on me, as you always do to those who love your name. Direct my footsteps according to your word; let no sin rule over me. Redeem me from the oppression of men, that I may obey your precepts. Make your face shine upon your servant and teach me your decrees. Streams of tears flow from my eyes, for your law is not obeyed.

—Psalm 119:129–136

THE WORK OF THE DISCIPLE

The prologue to John's Gospel (John 1:1-18) serves as an overture to the revelation that Jesus Christ is the Son of God and as the Son, he is the light that God has sent into a dark world.

John, like all of the disciples, was an unlikely witness to the ministry of Jesus, but he is crucial to God's plan because Jesus would need witnesses who believed in the resurrected Christ so that the power of God's holy work could be shared with those who followed. The way had been prepared for the coming of the Christ through the word of the prophets, but then, hundreds of years of silence passed until a new prophet emerged to announce the coming of God's holy one.

And just as John the Baptist said, "He who comes after me has surpassed me because he was before me," (John 1:15) so, too, the witnesses who would come after would be called to come forward to share the revelation that Jesus is the Christ.

The Gospel of John is the truth of Jesus told to a generation that did not walk with him. The words of John are filled with light, love, and life because they are saturated by the power of the Holy Spirit.

To be filled with the Holy Spirit is to know beyond knowing what the psalmist means when he says, "The unfolding of your words gives light; it gives understanding to the simple." (v129)

Giving understanding of God's revelation to a new generation is the work of all disciples. Proclaiming the truth of the word through the power of the Holy Spirit is a work always in progress. "Because you have seen me, you have believed; blessed are those who have not seen and yet have believed." (John 20:29)

The angel of the LORD encamps around those who fear him, and he delivers them. Taste and see that the LORD is good; blessed is the man who takes refuge in him. Fear the LORD, you his saints, for those who fear him lack nothing. The lions may grow weak and hungry, but those who seek the LORD lack no good thing. Come, my children, listen to me; I will teach you the fear of the LORD. Whoever of you loves life and desires to see many good days, keep your tongue from evil and your lips from speaking lies. Turn from evil and do good; seek peace and pursue it.

—Psalm 34:7–14

REAL FOOD

When we take refuge in the Lord, our appetite for the food of this world begins to diminish. Speaking in the language of the Holy Spirit, Jesus tells his disciples, "I have food to eat that you know nothing about." (John 4:32) Later he says, "I am the bread of life. He who comes to me will never go hungry, and he who believes in me will never be thirsty." (John 6:35)

At the last supper, Jesus established the sacrament of the Eucharist identifying his body and blood as the real food that opens the way to eternal life: "…Jesus took bread, gave thanks and broke it, and gave it to his disciples, saying, 'Take and eat; this is my body.' Then he took the cup, gave thanks and offered it to them, saying, 'Drink from it, all of you. This is my blood of the covenant, which is poured out for many for the forgiveness of sins." (Matthew 26:26-28)

Taste and see the Lord; taste and believe he is the son of God; taste and receive the gift of eternal life freely given to all who believe.

Relent, O LORD! How long will it be? Have compassion on your servants. Satisfy us in the morning with your unfailing love, that we may sing for joy and be glad all our days. Make us glad for as many days as you have afflicted us, for as many years as we have seen trouble. May your deeds be shown to your servants, your splendor to their children. May the favor of the Lord our God rest upon us; establish the work of our hands for us— yes, establish the work of our hands.

—*Psalm 90:13–17*

THE ANSWER

The answer to David's question, "How long will it be?" (v13) came one thousand years later with the incredible collision of the miraculous and the natural.

The answer came to a young woman in Nazareth who was engaged to be married to a man who was a descendant of David. She was visited by an angel who told her that she was highly favored by the Lord, and though she was a virgin, she would give birth to a child through the power of the Holy Spirit and that she would give her baby child the name Jesus.

The angel Gabriel tells her, "He will be great and will be called the Son of the Most High. The Lord will give him the throne of his father David, and he will reign over the house of Jacob forever; his kingdom will never end." (Luke 1:32-33) When Mary asks, "How will this be...since I am a virgin?" the angel answers in a way that should encourage all of us: "…nothing is impossible with God." (Luke 1:37)

Just as Mary submitted to the impossible, so we are called to do the same, saying with her, "My soul glorifies the Lord and my spirit rejoices in God my savior, for he has been mindful of the humble state of his servant." (Luke 1:46-48)

"Because he loves me," says the LORD, "I will rescue him; I will protect him, for he acknowledges my name. He will call upon me, and I will answer him; I will be with him in trouble, I will deliver him and honor him. With long life will I satisfy him and show him my salvation."

—*Psalm 91:14–16*

THE GOD OF LIGHT, LIFE AND LOVE

We have heard it said that the God of the Old Testament is an angry and distant God. People who say this might point to the destruction of Sodom and Gomorrah or the Great Flood that nearly destroyed everything living on the earth or they might even show God's cruel behavior to Israel's enemies, such as the destruction of the inhabitants of Jericho.

But all of this is a point of view seeking a justification. God is never cruel, but humans are; God hates sin, but we are steeped in it; He loves righteousness, but we flee from it.

God's purpose for us began to be worked out when He chose Abram to become the father of many nations. Even so, God's purpose would not be fully revealed for two thousand years. And that purpose was built on love. "'Because he loves me,' says the Lord, 'I will rescue him; I will protect him, for he acknowledges my name.'" (v14)

This clearly is the God of Abraham, Isaac and Jacob, and it is the God of Jesus. This is the God who will answer my prayers, who will protect me from trouble and will point the way to eternal life. This is the God who troubled to reopen the door to a loving relationship with each one of His children through His son, Jesus Christ. This is the same God who will pluck me out of disaster and place me on firm ground. This is the God of life, the God of light and, most of all, the God of love.

Sons are a heritage from the LORD, children a reward from him. Like arrows in the hands of a warrior are sons born in one's youth. Blessed is the man whose quiver is full of them. They will not be put to shame when they contend with their enemies in the gate.

—Psalm 127:3–5

A CALL TO DUTY

Every child is a miracle from God. How else should we view it? So small, so beautiful, so dependent! If we see the child as a blessed gift from God, then we are going to take our duty seriously and will instruct our children in the way of the Lord.

But here is where we often go wrong. When we fail in this vital role, we either spoil or discourage the child and everyone suffers as a result.

Eli was a great priest of Israel and he had two sons, Hophni and Phinehas, but they were wicked men in the eyes of the Lord, for their father would not control them. They stole from the offerings of sacrifice and, by their foolish behavior, they showed contempt for the God of Israel. Finally, Eli confronted his sons, but it was too late. The Lord declared, "Those who honor me I will honor, but those who despise me will be disdained. The time is coming when I will cut short your strength and the strength of your father's house, so that there will not be an old man in your family line and you will see distress in my dwelling." (1 Samuel 2:30-32)

And it happened as God said. As parents, we are called to duty so that the wonderful blessing of having children does not grow into a curse and a regret.

Those who are far from you will perish; you destroy all who are unfaithful to you. But as for me, it is good to be near God. I have made the Sovereign LORD my refuge; I will tell of all your deeds.

—Psalm 73:27–28

THE GIFT

The world on the eve of the birth of Jesus Christ was a world sick with sin. Violence crackled in the cold air as Jerusalem cringed under the iron yoke of Rome. Herod, who ruled as a surrogate, was so corrupt that he sent his soldiers to search out and destroy the defenseless child spoken of by the Magi. The world was threatening and heartless, but there was also an air of expectation that something momentous was happening.

Wise men from the east had traveled long distances to come to Jerusalem to find the child destined to be a king. They asked, "Where is the one who has been born king of the Jews? We saw his star in the east and have come to worship him." (Matthew 2:2)

Now, as we prepare to celebrate the feast of the birth of the Christ child, we should remember that he entered a resistant and unwelcoming world overcome with sin. He came at a particular time to a particular place so that he could seek out and call back sinners for all time and from any place.

When we think of Christmas, we think of gifts, little realizing that the gifts we give are mere symbols of the greatest gift of all. Jesus was born into a heartless world to reveal the true heart of God. Jesus came into our world on that cold winter night not as a conqueror, but as a savior. He came to set the prisoners of sin free once and for all.

The LORD swore an oath to David, a sure oath that he will not revoke:
"One of your own descendants I will place on your throne— if your
sons keep my covenant and the statutes I teach them, then their sons
will sit on your throne for ever and ever."

—Psalm 132:11–12

THE PROMISE FULFILLED

God's promise to King David would find its fulfillment a thousand years later in a small town on the outskirts of Jerusalem. Prophets who lived after David's time told of signs that would confirm the advent of the Messiah. One sign was told by Isaiah: "The virgin will be with child and will give birth to a son, and will call him Immanuel."(Isaiah 7:14)

Another prophet, Micah, said that the Messiah would be born in the city of David: "But you, Bethlehem, in the land of Judah, are by no means least among the rulers of Judah, for out of you will come a ruler who will be a shepherd of my people Israel." (Micah 5:2)

Other prophecies include the flight into Egypt (Hosea 11:1) and the slaughter of the innocents. (Jeremiah 31:15)

Christmas Day has been celebrated for almost two thousand years, but the advent of the child named Jesus was anticipated for a full thousand years before it actually occurred. All the scriptures point to this child as the one Israel had been waiting for. Later, during Christ's three year public ministry, John the Baptist asked, "Are you the one who was to come or should we expect someone else?" (Luke 7:20)

Jesus answered John, but the question still stands for each one of us: Do I believe the weight of all the evidence—the prophets, the scriptures, the Apostles, the words of Christ himself, or do I believe something else?

Your love, O LORD, reaches to the heavens, your faithfulness to the skies. Your righteousness is like the mighty mountains, your justice like the great deep. O LORD, you preserve both man and beast. How priceless is your unfailing love! Both high and low among men find refuge in the shadow of your wings. They feast on the abundance of your house; you give them drink from your river of delights. For with you is the fountain of life; in your light we see light.

—Psalm 36:5–9

WALKING IN THE LIGHT

"If we claim to have fellowship with him yet walk in the darkness, we lie and do not live by the truth." (1 John 1:6)

By walking in the light, we turn away the works of darkness that, among other things, serve as a barrier to a life-giving relationship to God the Father through the work of His Son. When we claim to walk in the light of fellowship with God, we put the very honor of God on the line with our actions and our lives. Thus, when we claim the gift of God's love, we are also proclaiming, not just in words, but in action, that we are children of God, staking everything on that fact.

So how are we to live if we claim to be children of God? If we live by the first great commandment (Mark 12:28-31) to give our all to God, then we are also called to live by the second commandment as well. The two commandments cannot be separated from one another; otherwise, we will proclaim our love of God with our lips, but deny it in our lives.

The God-given purpose of our time here is to be beacons of light in a darkened and dangerous world by spreading the truth of God's love, faithfulness, and righteousness for anyone to see in small things and large things as we are gifted to do.

"Because of the oppression of the weak and the groaning of the needy, I will now arise," says the LORD. "I will protect them from those who malign them." And the words of the LORD are flawless, like silver refined in a furnace of clay, purified seven times.

—*Psalm 12:5–6*

BLESSED ARE THE POOR

God looks after the most insignificant among us. It does not matter to Him that we may be poor or powerless in worldly terms; He only asks that we trust in His flawless Word.

This is exactly what Christ taught in his Sermon on the Mount: "Blessed are the poor in spirit for theirs is the kingdom of heaven. Blessed are those who mourn, for they will be comforted. Blessed are the meek, for they will inherit the earth." (Matthew 5:3-5)

God's Word is flawless for He never shows the kind of favoritism that men habitually show to those who have political power or great wealth. He demonstrated this in the very life and circumstances of His own son who was not born in a palace built for kings. And when it came time for the son to die, he was sentenced along with common criminals and was mocked by his tormentors who put a crown of thorns on his head. "He was despised and rejected by men, a man of sorrows, and familiar with suffering." (Isaiah 53:3).

Yet this is the one who is called "King of Kings and Lord of Lords." (Revelation 19:16) God's ways are surely wondrous and His Word is surely flawless. For His love caused Him to become one of us so that we could become more like Him.

A foolish son is his father's ruin, and a quarrelsome wife is like a constant dripping. Houses and wealth are inherited from parents, but a prudent wife is from the LORD.

—Proverbs 19:13–14

THE GOOD WIFE

Nothing will separate a man from happiness faster than a quarrelsome and resentful wife. When it comes to choosing a wife as a lifelong companion to share all of life's blessings and woes, men have become fools because their focus is so singular and shallow. For in the end, a wife's character counts above everything else; she will become a partner in every important decision. She will be a mother, an educator, a provider of the good things in life and she will be steadfast, strong and wise in times of stress and trouble.

A good wife will never divide a man from home and wealth, but will help to build both. "She is worth more than rubies. Her husband has full confidence in her and lacks nothing of value. She brings him good, not harm, all the days of her life." (Proverbs 31:10-11)

The LORD blessed the latter part of Job's life more than the first. He had fourteen thousand sheep, six thousand camels, a thousand yoke of oxen and a thousand donkeys. And he also had seven sons and three daughters. The first daughter he named Jemimah, the second Keziah and the third Keren-Happuch. Nowhere in all the land were there found women as beautiful as Job's daughters, and their father granted them an inheritance along with their brothers. After this, Job lived a hundred and forty years; he saw his children and their children to the fourth generation.

—Job 42:12–16

TO KNOW GOD

The story of Job ends as it began. We first meet him as a man who is rich in every way—rich in family, rich in property and rich in God's love. This is a man we would certainly count as blessed.

But between the beginning and end, Job experiences what it is like to live without God's full protection. Job's afflictions were terrible and it seemed to him that God had completely abandoned him to Satan.

Through it all, Job remains faithful, refusing to compromise his integrity just to relieve his terrible suffering. While Job understands that God is not punishing him for a particular transgression, reconciliation can only come when he completely submits himself to God's will. Job comes to understand that every blessing comes from God: "Surely I spoke of things I did not understand, things too wonderful for me to know." (Job 42:3)

Then he acknowledges what it means to actually experience God: "My ears had heard of you but now my eyes have seen you. Therefore I despise myself and repent in dust and ashes." (Job 42:5-6)

To know *about* God is not to *know* God. Knowing God takes our whole being: our heart, soul, strength and mind. For to know God is to love God and to love God is the source of all joy, all abundance and all goodness.

Sing to the LORD, you saints of his; praise his holy name. For his anger lasts only a moment, but his favor lasts a lifetime; weeping may remain for a night, but rejoicing comes in the morning.

—*Psalm 30:4–5*

THE COLOR OF LOVE

Revelers of the night seek to escape the light of the emerging dawn. They need to find shelter in the shadows, for they are naturally prowlers of the night.

For the man of God, however, the new light of day represents all the spiritual blessings of God in all their natural glory. The rising sun extinguishes the gloom of the fading darkness and paints the world with the same brush that God used to create it in the first place. The primary color is the color of love, for "The heavens declare the glory of God, the skies proclaim the work of his hands." (Psalm 19:1) And that color reveals the splendor and the majesty of creation everywhere: "The streams of God are filled with water to provide the people with grain, for so you have ordained it. You drench its furrows and level its ridges; you soften it with showers and bless its crops. You crown the year with your bounty, and your carts overflow with abundance." (Psalm 65:9-11)

Truly, "where morning dawns and evening fades, you call forth songs of joy." (Psalm 65:8)

Now all has been heard; here is the conclusion of the matter: Fear God and keep his commandments, for this is the whole duty of man. For God will bring every deed into judgment, including every hidden thing, whether it is good or evil.

—Ecclesiastes 12:13–14

THE BRIGHT MORNING STAR

Solomon says it comes down to this: "Fear God and keep his commandments." (v13)

Jesus says the same thing, but makes it personal.

In Revelation, Jesus says to John, "Behold I am coming soon! My reward is with me and I will give to everyone according to what he has done. I am the Alpha and the Omega, the First and the Last, the Beginning and the End. Blessed are those who wash their robes, that they may have the right to the tree of life and may go through the gates into the city…I, Jesus, have sent my angel to give you this testimony for the churches. I am the Root and the Offspring of David, and the bright Morning Star." (Revelation 22:12-14, 16)

NEW BEGINNINGS

Then I heard the voice of the Lord saying, "Whom shall I send? And who will go for us?" And I said, "Here am I. Send me!"

Isaiah 6:8

ENDNOTES

[1] "Dover Beach"

[2] *Biblical Psychology*, p.110

[3] *Mere Christianity*, bk. 3, chap. 4, par. 8

[4] *On the Passion of Christ* pp. 63-64

[5] *Biblical Psychology*, p.104

[6] *Biblical Psychology*, p.220

[7] *Biblical Psychology*, p.129

[8] *Biblical Psychology*, p.170

[9] *Merchant of Venice*, Act 5: Sc. 1, lines 71-79

[10] *Imitation of Christ*, bk. 3, chap. 14, p.96

[11] *Imitation of Christ*, 55:6, p.167

[12] *Is Theology Poetry?*, p.136

[13] *Biblical Psychology*, pp. 91-92

[14] *The Imitation of Christ*, bk. 4, chap. 17, p.212

BIBLIOGRAPHY

Aquinas, Thomas. *Mediations for Everyday*. Ft. Collins,
Colorado: Roman Catholic Books, 1945

Augustine, Saint. *Confessions*. Trans. by Henry Chadwick.
New York and Oxford: Oxford University Press, 1991

Chambers, Oswald. *Biblical Psychology: Christ-Centered
Solutions for Daily Problems*. Grand Rapids, Michigan:
Discovery House, 1995, pp. 91-92

Chambers, Oswald. *Devotions for a Deeper Life*. Grand
Rapids, Michigan: Zondervan, 1970

Chambers, Oswald. *My Utmost for His Highest: An Updated
Edition in Today's Language*. Edited by James Reimann.
Grand Rapids, Michigan: Discovery House, 1992

Chambers, Oswald. *Still Higher for His Highest*. Grand
Rapids, Michigan: Zondervan, 1970

Cranmer, Thomas. *The First English Prayer Book*. Edited by
Robert Van De Meyer. Harrisburg, Pennsylvania: Morehouse
Publishing, 1999

Eldredge, John. *Epic: The Story God Is Telling and the Role That
Is Yours to Play*. Nashville, Tennessee: Nelson Books, 2004

Gardner, Helen, editor. *The New Oxford Book of English Verse,
1250-1950*. Oxford University Press, 1972, p. 703

Gilder, George. *Men and Marriage*. Gretna, Louisiana:
Pelican Publishing Co., 1986

Kampmann, Eric. *Tree of Life: A Book of Wisdom for Men:
Biblical Wisdom For Everyday Living*. New York, New York:
Beaufort Books, 2003

Kempis, Thomas à. *The Imitation of Christ*. Trans. by Joseph N. Tylenda. New York, New York: Vintage Books, a division of Random House, 1998

Kempis, Thomas à. *On the Passion of Christ: According to the Four Evangelists: Prayers and Meditations*. Trans. by Joseph N. Tylenda. San Francisco, California: Ignatius Press, 2004

Lewis, C.S. *Mere Christianity*. New York, New York: Harper San Francisco, a division of HarperCollins, 2001, p.92

Lewis, C.S. *The Weight of Glory*. New York, New York: Harper San Francisco, a division of HarperCollins, 2001, p.136

Lewis, C.S. *A Year with C.S. Lewis: Daily Readings from His Classic Works*. New York, New York: Harper San Francisco, a division of HarperCollins, 2003

New International Version Holy Bible, Scofield Study System, New York, New York: Oxford University Press, 2004

Shakespeare, William. *Merchant of Venice*. New York, New York: Everyman Library, Knopf, a division of Random House, 1996

Storm, Howard. *My Descent Into Death: A Second Chance at Life*. New York, New York: Doubleday Publishers, a division of Random House, 2005

Stott, John. *Basic Christianity*. Downers Grove, Illinois: InterVarsity Press, 1971

Warren, Rick. *The Purpose Driven Life: What On Earth Am I Here For?* Grand Rapids, Michigan: Zondervan, 2002

INDEXES

OLD TESTAMENT SCRIPTURE REFERENCES

GENESIS:

1:1	*Sep-24*
1:2	*Oct-22*
1:3	*Sep-28*
1:27	*Jan-2*
1:27; 2:7	*Dec-10*
1:3-4	*Oct-9*
2:8	*Jun-21*
2:19-22	*Oct-31*
2:21-25	*Jul-30*
2:8,15	*Jan-24*
2:9,15; 3:23-24	*Jun-18*
3:5	*May-28*
3:5	*Aug-19*
3:12	*Dec-4*
3:19	*Aug-25*
3:12-13	*Jun-30*
4:12,14	*Sep-13*
8:21	*Jul-18*
12:1,4,7; 15:4-6	*Nov-17*
15:6	*Oct-2*
17:6	*Nov-28*
18:20-21	*Nov-9*

EXODUS:

19:6	*Mar-22*

NUMBERS:

14:18	*Jul-7*

DEUTERONOMY:

4:2	*Jan-14*
6:4-5	*Apr-12*
6:4-7	*Jun-27*
6:4,8	*Mar-24*
6:5	*Jun-8*
8:3	*Apr-17*
29:29	*Nov-10*
30:15,19-20	*Jan-16*
30:15-16,19-20	*Sep-6*
30:19-20	*May-31*
32:10-11	*May-16*

JOSHUA:

1:6	*Sep-16*
1:9	*Jul-21*

JUDGES:

13:5	*Mar-13*

RUTH:

Ruth 2	*Jan-15*

1 SAMUEL:

2:12, 8:3	*Jul-8*
2:30-32	*Dec-23*
8:11-17	*Jul-17*
8:5,7,9	*Jul-4*
13:14	*Oct-18*

2 SAMUEL:

23:3-4	*Jan-8*
7:12-13	*Mar-22*
18:33	*Jul-8*
7:11-16	*Jul-23*
22:33	*Sep-7*
7:11-14,16	*Dec-14*

OLD TESTAMENT SCRIPTURE REFERENCES

1 KINGS:

3:9,11-12	*Jan-31*
12:7,11	*Dec-15*
18:17,19:2	*Sep-19*
19:12	*Apr-7*

2 CHRONICLES:

15:2	*Jan-18*
16:9	*Dec-17*

JOB:

1:6-8	*Jan-3*
1:20-22	*Nov-18*
2:3	*Jan-11*
2:9-10	*Feb-9*
3:23-25	*Mar-18*
4:12-17	*Apr-14*
6:14-17	*Aug-12*
7:1-5	*May-24*
7:6-10	*Jun-13*
7:17-18	*Mar-1*
7:17-21	*Jul-14*
9:25-26	*Sep-23*
9:33	*Aug-24*
10:4-7	*Oct-28*
10:14-16	*Nov-14*
13:13-19	*Apr-29*
14:1-6	*Jan-13*
15:14-16	*Feb-6*
19:23-27	*Apr-10*
19:25	*Oct-6*
19:25-56	*Feb-19*
21:22-26	*Feb-4*
24:15	*Sep-4*

26:14	*Dec-13*
26:27-33	*Mar-11*
27:2-6	*Apr-6*
28:20-28	*May-8*
29:1-6	*Jun-18*
30:20-23	*Jul-9*
30:24-31	*Aug-30*
31:13-15	*Sep-17*
32:6-9	*Oct-22*
33:14-18	*Nov-7*
34:2-4	*Dec-2*
34:17-19	*Nov-6*
35:9-11	*Jan-9*
36:22-26	*Feb-1*
36:27-33	*May-9*
37:14,19-24	*Mar-25*
38:1-7	*Apr-3*
38:16-18	*May-10*
38:34-38	*Feb-11*
39:13-18	*Jul-5*
39:26-30	*Aug-8*
41:1-11	*Jun-9*
42:1-6	*Nov-3*
42:3; 38:2-4	*Sep-21*
42:12-16	*Dec-29*

PSALMS:

1:1-3	*Jan-4*
2:3	*Jul-12*
2:1-4	*Jan-23*
4:2-3	*Feb-3*
5:1-3	*Aug-27*
5:4-6	*Jun-17*
7:7-9	*Mar-29*

OLD TESTAMENT SCRIPTURE REFERENCES

7:14-16	*Apr-18*	28:6-9	*May-18*
8:5	*Aug-7*	30:1-3	*Mar-9*
8:3-5	*Oct-19*	30:4-5	*Dec-30*
10:2-5	*Jul-4*	30:8-12	*Feb-14*
10:2-5	*Jul-6*	30:10-12	*Aug-30*
10:11; 139:1-2	*Dec-17*	31:9-10	*Aug-9*
12:8	*May-31*	32:1-5	*Mar-6*
12:1-2	*Dec-16*	32:8-11	*Nov-15*
12:5-6	*Dec-27*	33:1-5	*Jul-15*
12:7-8	*May-3*	33:6-11	*Aug-19*
14:3	*Mar-11*	33:13-15	*Sep-17*
14:1; 111:10	*Jul-16*	33:16-19	*Sep-7*
15:1-5	*Jan-10*	34:8	*Jan-20*
17:1-3	*Feb-26*	34:7-14	*Dec-20*
17:13-15	*Nov-26*	36:1-2	*Mar-17*
18:3-6	*Apr-16*	36:5-9	*Dec-26*
18:16-19	*Mar-8*	37:1-4	*Mar-2*
18:25-26	*May-2*	37:5-7	*Apr-7*
18:30-36	*Aug-6*	37:32-33	*Jun-12*
19:1-4	*Aug-22*	38:1-4	*Jan-12*
19:7-11	*Sep-1*	38:11-12,19; 55:20-21	*Sep-29*
20:7-9	*Jun-26*	38:17-20	*May-15*
22:1	*Jul-9*	39:5	*Sep-23*
22:6-8	*Mar-26*	39:4-6	*Nov-30*
22:9-11	*Nov-13*	39:5-6	*Nov-12*
23:1-6	*Sep-11*	40:1-3	*Oct-25*
24:3-6	*Aug-3*	40:7-10	*Oct-8*
25:4-7	*Jan-29*	41:4	*Aug-10*
25:8-10	*Oct-5*	41:1-3	*Mar-16*
25:16-21	*May-19*	42:1-4	*Jan-30*
26:2-5	*Jul-25*	42:5-7	*Jan-18*
27:4	*Jul-2*	42:8-11	*Feb-16*
27:10-14	*Sep-26*	43:2-5	*Mar-23*
28:1-2	*Feb-22*	44:1-3	*Jan-5*

OLD TESTAMENT SCRIPTURE REFERENCES

OLD TESTAMENT SCRIPTURE REFERENCES

93:1-5	*Oct-17*	119:9-11	*Dec-7*
94:8-11	*Jun-23*	119:9-19	*Feb-2*
94:16-19	*Aug-13*	119:105-112	*Oct-13*
94:20-23	*Jul-17*	119:129-136	*Dec-19*
95:1-7	*Jun-2*	119:161-168	*Nov-27*
96:10-13	*Nov-19*	119:49-56	*Aug-29*
97:10-12	*Apr-21*	119:65-72	*Dec-9*
98:7-9	*Jun-19*	119:97-104	*Aug-26*
100:1-5	*May-4*	121:1-8	*Jul-13*
101:1-4	*Aug-21*	123:1-4	*May-22*
101:6-7	*Sep-9*	127:1-2	*Sep-5*
102:1-7	*Feb-10*	127:3-5	*Dec-23*
102:23-28	*Mar-5*	128:1-4	*Mar-12*
103:2-5	*Jul-10*	130:1-6	*May-25*
103:13-18	*Dec-10*	131:1-3	*May-13*
104:10-13	*Mar-7*	132:11-12	*Dec-25*
104:24-26	*Sep-21*	135:13-18	*Sep-25*
105:1-5	*Jun-15*	137:1-5	*Feb-8*
105:42-45	*Nov-17*	138:6-8	*Jun-29*
107:2-9	*Oct-11*	139:15	*Jan-7*
107:23-31	*Apr-2*	139:1-4	*Jul-1*
108:1-5	*Aug-11*	139:7-10	*Aug-4*
109:21-25	*Oct-27*	139:13-16	*Jan-2*
110:2-3	*Jun-7*	140:1-5	*Jun-11*
111:10	*Sep-24*	141:4	*Feb-24*
112:4-9	*Oct-18*	141:3-4	*Apr-11*
114:3-8	*May-27*	144:4; 102:3; 62:10	*Jul-26*
115:2-8	*Oct-23*	146:3-4	*Feb-5*
115:16-18	*Jan-24*	147:4-5	*Apr-13*
116:15-16	*Sep-16*	147:7-8	*May-1*
118:6-7	*Nov-21*	147:15-18	*Jun-22*
118:8-9	*Dec-12*	148:1-6	*Dec-5*
118:22-24	*Apr-9*	148:7-13	*Jan-19*
119:1-3	*Nov-22*		

OLD TESTAMENT SCRIPTURE REFERENCES

OLD TESTAMENT SCRIPTURE REFERENCES

23:13-14	*May-17*	30:32-33	*Oct-14*
23:19-21	*Jun-16*	31:1-7	*Mar-13*
23:22-25	*Sep-15*	31:8-9	*Sep-10*
23:26-28	*Oct-20*	31:10-23	*Jun-21*
23:29-35	*Nov-25*	31:10, 24-31	*Oct-1*
24:12	*Mar-30*		
24:3-4	*Apr-22*	**ECCLESIASTES:**	
24:13-14	*Jan-20*	1:3-11	*Feb-1*
24:15-20	*Feb-21*	2:10-11	*Mar-15*
24:30-34	*Apr-20*	2:10-11	*Apr-25*
25:2	*Sep-21*	2:24-26	*Apr-17*
25:26	*Jun-4*	3:11	*Feb-23*
26:1-4	*Jun-6*	3:1-8	*May-11*
26:6-8	*Jul-24*	3:9-11	*Jun-1*
26:9-12	*Aug-16*	3:14-15	*Jul-11*
26:13-16	*Jul-21*	3:16-17	*Aug-5*
26:23-25	*Sep-29*	4:9-10	*Jun-21*
27:1	*Aug-20*	4:9-12	*Sep-8*
27:4	*Apr-4*	5:2-3	*Oct-31*
28:1	*Oct-7*	5:4-7	*Nov-24*
28:12, 15-16	*Jul-4*	5:10-12	*Sep-14*
28:13, 17-18	*Apr-24*	5:13-15	*Jan-17*
29:3	*Sep-30*	5:18-20	*Feb-13*
29:15, 17	*Nov-5*	7:2	*Jan-26*
30:20	*Jun-30*	7:10	*Oct-30*
30:2-4	*Dec-13*	7:20	*Aug-14*
30:5-6	*Jan-14*	7:20	*Sep-22*
30:7-9	*Feb-15*	7:11-12	*Apr-15*
30:11-14	*Mar-14*	7:13-14	*May-14*
30:15-16	*Apr-25*	7:23-25	*Nov-12*
30:18-19	*May-16*	8:1	*Sep-28*
30:21-23	*Jul-30*	8:8	*Oct-26*
30:24-28	*Aug-2*	8:16-17	*Nov-10*
30:29-31	*Sep-20*	10:20	*Dec-17*

OLD TESTAMENT SCRIPTURE REFERENCES

11:5	*Jun-8*	53:2-3	*Jun-25*
11:6	*Oct-16*	53:2-3	*Sep-20*
11:9	*Dec-6*	53:4-6	*Jul-14*
11:3-4	*Jan-15*	55:6	*Jan-4*
12:13	*Jun-13*	55:8	*Sep-26*
12:1-5	*May-5*	55:8-9	*Jun-9*
12:9-12	*Jun-10*	55:6; 6:8	*Nov-11*
12:13-14	*Dec-31*		

SONG OF SONGS:

JEREMIAH:

2:10-13	*Apr-1*	1:5	*Jan-7*
4:12-15	*Jun-20*	1:14,16	*Mar-4*
6:10	*Aug-1*	5:7-9	*Feb-25*
7:11-13	*May-1*	6:16	*Jan-10*
8:5-7	*Jun-14*	6:13-14	*Jan-22*
		9:23-24	*Feb-17*
		10:12	*Jan-21*

ISAIAH:

1:2	*Feb-18*	11:9-10,21	*Sep-12*
1:21-23	*Mar-31*	17:9	*Mar-30*
2:13	*Dec-6*	17:9	*Jul-25*
5:20	*Feb-6*	23:10-11	*Sep-2*
5:26-30	*Apr-16*	23:23-24	*Dec-17*
7:14	*Dec-25*	24:10-13	*Jun-25*
10:1-2,3	*Sep-6*	31:15	*Dec-25*
14:22	*Aug-13*	33:3	*Nov-11*
29:13-15	*Oct-4*		

LAMENTATIONS:

40:6-8	*Nov-30*	1:1	*Feb-8*
47:11	*Oct-24*	1:1-2	*Oct-24*
49:1	*Jan-7*	1:8-10	*Mar-31*
51:6	*Mar-5*	1:1,3; 2:14	*Apr-28*
53:3	*Oct-27*	1:18-19	*Jul-12*
53:3	*Dec-27*	2:11-13	*Sep-12*
53:5	*Mar-26*	2:14-16	*Sep-2*
53:6	*Apr-30*		

OLD TESTAMENT SCRIPTURE REFERENCES

NEW TESTAMENT SCRIPTURE REFERENCES

MATTHEW:

1:21	*Jan-6*
1:21	*May-25*
1:31-32	*Aug-2*
2:2	*Dec-24*
4:11	*Nov-21*
4:19	*Jun-9*
5:8	*Nov-8*
5:12	*Mar-16*
5:12	*Jun-11*
5:45	*Jun-12*
5:48	*Sep-1*
5:3-5	*Dec-27*
5:10-11	*Mar-12*
5:10-11	*Sep-19*
5:11-12	*May-24*
5:44-46	*Jul-31*
6:5	*Jun-5*
6:19	*Aug-23*
6:19	*Oct-15*
6:24	*May-6*
6:34	*May-14*
6:1-2	*Sep-10*
6:10; 26:39	*Nov-15*
6:18-33	*Mar-2*
6:19-21	*May-20*
6:31-33	*Aug-20*
7:14	*Jan-4*
7:15	*Sep-2*
7:16	*Sep-27*
7:24	*Apr-22*
7:15-16	*Jan-22*
7:24-25	*Jul-28*
8:17	*Feb-12*

10:9-10	*Jan-10*
10:24; 20:26-28	*May-22*
11:28-30	*Apr-24*
11:28-30	*Nov-13*
12:35-37	*Aug-5*
16:16	*Nov-24*
17:17	*Sep-20*
19:17	*Dec-18*
20:28	*Jan-23*
22:13	*Jul-12*
22:36	*Apr-12*
22:37-38	*Sep-25*
26:26-28	*Dec-20*
27:4	*Sep-13*
27:3-5	*Jun-4*
28:19	*Oct-3*

MARK:

1:10	*Feb-7*
1:15	*Oct-30*
1:11; 9:7	*Feb-18*
2:5	*Mar-6*
4:19	*Mar-15*
4:18-20	*Jun-1*
4:19; 10:17,23	*Nov-6*
4:39-41	*Oct-26*
7:21	*Mar-11*
7:20-23	*May-26*
8:29	*Jan-30*
8:29	*Aug-22*
8:29	*Oct-21*
8:31	*Feb-19*
9:35	*Sep-20*
10:17	*Feb-23*

NEW TESTAMENT SCRIPTURE REFERENCES

NEW TESTAMENT SCRIPTURE REFERENCES

NEW TESTAMENT SCRIPTURE REFERENCES

EPHESIANS:

1:4	*Jan-7*
1:18	*Aug-22*
2:3	*Oct-5*
2:3-5	*Jul-11*
2:8-10	*Oct-25*
4:4	*Feb-7*
4:14	*Jun-3*
4:26-27	*Jul-7*
5:25	*Jul-30*
5:18-20	*Feb-1*
5:18-20	*Jun-2*
5:28,31	*Jun-21*
6:4	*Jun-27*
6:10	*Feb-28*
6:12	*Jan-11*
6:12	*Mar-10*
6:14	*Sep-16*
6:20	*May-15*
6:10-20	*Aug-6*

PHILIPPIANS:

1:9-11	*Dec-2*
2:15	*Nov-1*
2:6-7	*Aug-3*
2:6-7	*Sep-9*
2:15-16	*Jan-10*
2:15-16	*Aug-17*
2:6,7	*Sep-20*
3:10,12-14	*Jun-24*
3:13-14	*Mar-7*
4:7	*Jan-23*
4:8	*May-3*

COLOSSIANS:

1:13-14	*Jun-16*
1:19-20	*Sep-3*
3:1-2	*Nov-26*
3:12-14	*Nov-22*

1 TIMOTHY:

6:8-10	*Feb-15*
6:11-12	*Aug-21*
6:11-12	*Sep-15*

2 TIMOTHY:

2:23-26	*Mar-19*
4:5	*Oct-3*

HEBREWS:

2:1	*Feb-3*
4:13	*Nov-16*
6:4-6	*Jan-20*
8:5	*Dec-12*
11:1	*Oct-6*

JAMES:

1:5	*Jan-29*
1:15	*Jul-16*
3:5-6	*Apr-11*
5:16	*Feb-26*

JAMES:

1:20	*Oct-14*
2:6-7	*Aug-3*
4:7-8	*Sep-14*

NEW TESTAMENT SCRIPTURE REFERENCES

1 PETER:

1:15-16; 4:3	*Nov-25*
2:16	*Apr-8*
2:16	*Nov-4*
2:21	*Dec-9*
2:4-5	*Apr-22*
5:8	*Mar-10*
5:8	*Oct-12*
5:9	*Sep-16*
5:5-6	*May-13*

2 PETER:

1:3	*Jul-24*
2:9-10	*Jun-17*

1 JOHN:

1:5	*Jan-27*
1:5	*Sep-28*
1:6	*Dec-26*
2:16	*Aug-14*
3:4	*Nov-20*
4:16	*Jul-20*
4:2-3	*Sep-2*
4:16,19	*Jun-14*
5:11-12	*Apr-21*

REVELATION:

19:16	*Mar-22*
19:16	*Sep-20*
19:16	*Dec-27*
21:1-2	*Apr-28*
22:16	*Aug-1*
22:12-14,16	*Dec-31*
22:13,14,16	*Aug-24*

SUBJECT INDEX

A

B

C

D

E

F

G

M

N

O

P

S

T

W

Y